Distance Writing and Computer-Assisted Interventions in Psychiatry and Mental Health

Recent Titles in
Developments in Clinical Psychology
Glenn R. Caddy, Series Editor

Distance Writing and Computer-Assisted Interventions in Psychiatry and Mental Health

Edited by
Luciano L'Abate

Foreword by Douglas K. Snyder

Developments in Clinical Psychology
Glenn R. Caddy, Series Editor

ABLEX PUBLISHING
Westport, Connecticut • London

Library of Congress Cataloging-in-Publication Data

Distance writing and computer-assisted interventions in psychiatry and mental health / edited by Luciano L'Abate ; foreword by Douglas K. Snyder.

    p.   cm.—(Developments in clinical psychology)
    Includes bibliographical references and index.
    ISBN 1–56750–524–4 (cloth)—ISBN 1–56750–525–2 (pbk.)
    1. Written communication—Therapeutic use. 2. Psychotherapy—Computer-assisted instruction. I. L'Abate, Luciano, 1928– II. Series.
    RC489.W75 D57 2001
    616.89—dc21   00–027546

British Library Cataloguing in Publication Data is available.

Library of Congress Catalog Card Number: 00–027546
ISBN: 1–56750–524–4
     1–56750–525–2 (pbk.)

First published in 2001

Ablex Publishing, 88 Post Road West, Westport, CT 06881
An imprint of Greenwood Publishing Group, Inc.
www.ablexbooks.com

Printed in the United States of America

The paper used in this book complies with the Permanent Paper Standard issued by the National Information Standards Organization (Z39.48–1984).

10 9 8 7 6 5 4 3 2 1

Copyright Acknowledgment

The editor and publisher gratefully acknowledge permission for the use of the following material:

A portion of Chapter 12 originally appeared in Luciano L'Abate's article, "Decisions We (Mental Health Professionals) Need to Make (Whether We Like Them or Not): A Reply to Cummings and Hoyt." THE FAMILY JOURNAL: COUNSELING AND THERAPY FOR COUPLES AND FAMILIES, Vol. 7 No. 3, July 1999 227–230 © 1999 Sage Publications, Inc. Used by permission of Sage Publications and Jon Carlson, editor of *The Family Journal*.

Contents

Foreword

Douglas K. Snyder

On any given day, as many as 50 million Americans suffer from an emotional, behavioral, or addictive disorder. Fewer than one-third of them will seek professional help. Among those seeking help, many will find their access limited by the availability of mental health professionals and restrictions imposed by managed care on whom they can see, for how long, and for what conditions. Given the shortage of mental health resources and a growing disparity between the need for versus availability of services, the mental health professions face a daunting challenge of developing new modalities of intervention and enhancing the efficiency of existing approaches to treatment and prevention.

The use of writing as a complement or alternative to verbal discourse has a long history in the treatment of emotional and behavioral disorders that crosses diagnostic categories and theoretical systems. Diverse applications emerge when one considers the various functions that writing might serve. At a rudimentary level, writing facilitates documentation and recollection. Thus, one might instruct a client to record dreams and associations to their content to promote retention and subsequent exploration in face-to-face therapy, or maintain a diary of angry feelings and their context to facilitate a functional analysis of precipitating and perpetuating factors linked to anger dyscontrol.

Second, writing promotes organization of thoughts and plans for action. For example, one might use writing assignments to help a distressed couple prioritize long-term goals for their relationship, identify related proximal and intermediate objectives, and articulate stepwise plans for accomplishing these.

Considerable research has emerged in the past 15 years documenting a third function of writing in promoting catharsis or emotional processing of hurtful or traumatic events. Evidence reviewed in this book and elsewhere indicates that merely writing about trauma in the absence of face-to-face therapeutic contact can produce significant psychological and physical benefits. The use of written expression to promote emotional processing can be extended to remote or recent past injuries as well as to future events—as for those with progressive disease confronting their own death and its impact on loved ones.

In addition to an expressive role, writing can serve an exploratory or discovery function. In the context of writing, persons sometimes uncover thoughts or feelings of which they had previously been unaware. A reflective or analytical approach to writing facilitates self-awareness and lends itself not only to therapeutic approaches emphasizing introspection and self-understanding, but also to interpersonal approaches in which knowledge of self is a prerequisite to clear expression of needs and satisfying relationships with others.

Finally, writing serves a communicative function. For individuals whose anxiety interferes with effective face-to-face dialogue, writing often provides a medium through which thoughts and feelings can be articulated in a more reflective and deliberate manner. Writing can also serve as a means for client and therapist to communicate with each other between sessions, promoting continuity of work and reducing disruption caused by geographic distance or lengthy intervals between sessions. A recent treatment developed for couples recovering from an extramarital affair assigns letters to be written by each partner to the other to promote expression of intense and hurtful feelings in a softened manner that can be accepted and understood more readily by the other (Gordon, Baucom, & Snyder, 2000).

This new and important text on the use of writing in interventions and training in mental health extends previous work by L'Abate and colleagues (e.g., L'Abate, 1992, 1999). In this volume, L'Abate and his collaborators describe the functions of writing in mental health as they vary across the structure of written assignments, their specificity and level of abstraction, and their specific application context. The work described here suggests endless purposes that guided writing might serve—whether in promoting contemplation of need and readiness for change prior to entering psychotherapy, enhancing established therapeutic modalities or serving as an alternative when circumstances preclude face-to-face interventions, or promoting maintenance of gains following successful treatment.

More intriguing still are new applications outside traditional delivery of mental health services. The addition of writing assignments to the training and supervision of therapists and other mental health providers, particularly as adapted to computer-based applications, opens a novel arena for extending empirically supported training techniques in a more efficient and researchable manner. Other applications not explored here but potentially around the corner might involve the use of writing in mentoring teachers and assisting them in attending to pedagogical process, or assisting executive managers in promoting systematic change in an organizational setting.

Despite the incorporation of writing into various treatment approaches for many decades, little is known about either the mediators or moderators of its effects. By what means does the process of writing about emotional and behavioral concerns produce positive effects? For whom, and under what circumstances, does writing promote positive therapeutic outcomes? These and similar questions will both challenge and anchor the systematic use of writing in mental health interventions and training in the years ahead.

One line of research must address the format of writing assignments themselves. How do the effects of writing compare across level of structure (e.g., open-ended, focused, guided, or programmed assignments)? For which treatments or for whom should writing assignments emphasize general or abstract constructs versus more specific or concrete content?

A second domain of research should address the impact of writing alone and in combination with alternative interventions. What are the long-term consequences of expressive writing on physiological functioning compared to insight-oriented face-to-face therapy or behavioral interventions targeting self-monitoring and modification of autonomic arousal? Which treatment modalities show an incremental positive impact when integrated with distance writing (DW)—and at which phases of the treatment, adopting which writing format, do these benefits accrue?

Finally, research on writing as a complement or alternative to more traditional intervention techniques needs to examine risk factors contributing to iatrogenic effects. Under what circumstances might written assignments provoke defensiveness or deterioration? For whom might such tasks detract from therapeutic processing of emotional material or interfere with translation of insight or understanding into behavior change? Such potential risks, although suggested previously in the literature, have generated little research examining the magnitude of their effect or conditions in which they are more likely to be observed.

The use of writing in psychotherapy has a long tradition. However, systematic examination of its processes, outcomes, and diverse applications has just begun. This text goes far in integrating the current status of DW and computer-assisted interventions (CAI) in the mental health disciplines. Hopefully, further examination of the information presented here will result in an additional text several years hence addressing unresolved issues and offering empirically supported applications across new domains.

REFERENCES

Gordon, K. C., Baucom, D. H., & Snyder, D. K. (2000). The use of forgiveness in marital therapy. In M. E. McCullough, K. I. Pargament, & C. E. Thoresen (Eds.), *Forgiveness: Theory, research, and practice* (pp. 203–227). New York: Guilford.

L'Abate, L. (1992). *Programmed writing: A self-administered approach for interventions with individuals, couples, and families.* Pacific Grove, CA: Brooks/Cole.
L'Abate, L. (1999). Taking the bull by the horns: Beyond talk in psychological interventions. *The Family Journal: Counseling and Therapy for Couples and Families, 7,* 206–220.

Preface

The purpose of this anthology is to bring to the attention of mental health professionals in their respective disciplines (counselors, family and marriage therapists, mental health nurses, psychologists, psychiatrists, social workers, and pastoral counselors) the possible advantages and some disadvantages of DW and CAI. DW is defined as writing by respondents away from the eyes and presence of a professional helper. This medium of intervention has a long history of ad hoc usage by a few mental health professionals, but it is still not a part of mainstream mental health practices. Most mental health professionals are not aware of its effectiveness as a systematic alternative or planned adjunct to traditional, face-to-face therapeutic practices based on talk. Consequently, we can safely assume that DW and CAI have been underutilized by mental health professionals in spite of their substantive empirical support and clinical advantages. Both DW and CAI can be used in tandem, before, after, or in conjunction with ongoing verbal therapy. In some cases, where no other help is available, these procedures can be used without professional face-to-face contact (through correspondence or computers) provided adequate controls are used, as in the case of incarcerated criminals, or missionary and military personnel.

The overall plan of this book goes from the general to the specific. An introductory chapter expands on clinical uses and implications of DW/CAI and especially programmed DW (PDW) consisting of workbooks. In Chapter 2, James W. Pennebaker gives a highly personal narrative about how he, as a social psychologist, entered the whole area of expressive writing. Even though what he writes in this chapter may be repeated in the next, the flavor of the two chapters is quite different and the editor begs the reader's forebearance for whatever repetition is found from one chapter to the next. The importance of this information made it worth repeating.

In Part II, Brian A. Esterling and Pennebaker report on results of research about the complex relationships among written emotional disclosure, immune functions, and physical illness in Chapter 3. Then, the general empirical foundations for DW/CAI are set by Daniel L. Segal and Edward J. Murray in Chapter 4. They summarize research about the relationship between focused expressive writing (FEW) and psychotherapy analogs. This chapter serves as a link between talk-based therapeutic practices and expressive writing. In Chapter 5, Joshua M. Smyth and Luciano L'Abate report on the results of their meta-analysis about the use of workbooks in physical and mental health.

In Part III, where clinical applications are considered, Roger L. Gould, in Chapter 6, a pioneer on the use of CAI with patients, reports how his feedback-driven, "mastering-stress" computer program for outpatient interventions works and is available on the Internet for any interested consumer. In Chapter 7, Piero De Giacomo and Sabina De Nigris introduce computer applications of three different CAI workbooks with psychiatric patients. In Chapter 8, Oliver McMahan and L'Abate report on paradoxical results from a study of PDW with seminarian couples. In Chapter 9, Rudy Reed, McMahan, and L'Abate present preliminary results from a pilot study with incarcerated offenders. In spite of its shortcomings (no control group as yet and no long-term follow-up), this study illustrates the possibilities of combining talk therapy with workbooks.

In Part IV, devoted to teaching psychotherapy through writing, Karin B. Jordan in Chapter 10 reports on her experiences with teaching psychotherapy through workbooks. In Chapter 11, Richard J. Riordan, Gary L. Arthur, and Jeffrey Ashby expand on some uses of writing in clinical supervision.

In Part V, about the status and future of DW and CAI, in the concluding Chapter 12, L'Abate considers the implications of DW and CAI for the delivery of mental health services. The future for the widespread usage of both DW and CAI in mental health practices and research is wide open.

PART 1

Introduction

CHAPTER 1

Distance Writing and Computer-Assisted Interventions in Psychiatry and Mental Health

Luciano L'Abate

The purpose of this chapter is to introduce and illustrate how writing, and especially distance writing (DW), away from a professional's presence, can be added to the ongoing practice of psychological interventions, including training, preventive, psychotherapeutic, and rehabilitative approaches. DW gives professional helpers and respondents (patients, clients, individuals, couples, and families) more choices than were available heretofore. It widens professional mental health repertoires by offering professionals as well as respondents options and possibilities not otherwise available through traditional professional relationships. DW can be used as an alternative medium when face-to-face, verbal therapy, that is talk, is not feasible for logistic (distance) or diagnostic reasons. It can be used as an alternative or additional medium of intervention to traditional verbal and nonverbal media. There are individuals who can express more in writing than they can verbally. The step from DW to computer-assisted interventions (CAI) is a short one. Computers must be "loaded" with programs based on the written word when such a structure is added to unstructured interventions. Computers with relevant software in clinics, hospitals, and public and university libraries may well become the third avenue of service delivery in outpatient mental health, above and beyond face-to-face talk psychotherapies and medication (Bloom, 1992; Bradley, Welch, & Skilbeck, 1993; L'Abate, 1986, 1991, 1992, 1997a, 1999a, 1999b, 1999c; Marks, Shaw, & Parkin, 1998; Nickelson, 1998; Schwartz, 1984; Stamm, 1998).

WORKING AT A DISTANCE FROM RESPONDENTS

We must be mindful that at their best psychological interventions help a great deal only one-third of those who start treatment, while one-third improves somewhat. However, the remaining one-third does not get better or even deteriorates. Could it be that, among those who do not improve, another medium of communication rather than talk may be more appropriate? Furthermore, among those who do improve, could improvement be sped up and length of treatment shortened by administering written homework assignments? Can DW/CAI make psychological interventions more cost-effective and shorter in duration? What options are available for those respondents who just improve somewhat and those who deteriorate? Would working at a distance from them allow for a more impersonal, and hence more objective, process? DW and CAI are options that probably could be used by almost everyone, mostly by those who need help the most, but who may not want it, especially if it implies a face-to-face, talk-based relationship, as illustrated in most chapters. DW/CAI can be used to increase the professional repertoire and help a greater number of respondents than would be possible solely on the basis of talk and face-to-face contact (L'Abate, 1986, 1991, 1992, 1997a, 1999c).

The term "therapeutic" in the use of DW/CAI deserves and needs qualification. Not all DW/CAI for supposedly "therapeutic" reasons is indeed therapeutic. In two studies reviewed in Chapter 7, at least at the beginning of this type of intervention, DW may seem countertherapeutic. After the beginning four assignments, programmed distance writing (PDW) does produce strong emotional reactions to the point of lowering rather than raising mean test scores at postevaluation. Before expanding on DW/CAI, however, we need to consider the larger context of psychological, mental health interventions.

THE LARGER CONTEXT OF PSYCHOLOGICAL INTERVENTIONS

Managed care is perhaps the most significant development that has impacted not only mental health practices but also the entire field of medicine. Cost-effectiveness and accountability have become the new buzzwords. The number of visits to psychotherapists are limited by fiat from an external, oftentimes unknown and questionably qualified, agent. It is clear that the days of prolonged or intensive psychotherapy are long gone, except for those few who can afford to pay out of their own pockets or hospitalized patients who need it. Torrey's (1997) controversial book about the disastrous effects of deinstitutionalizion and the need to deal with mental illness rather than mental health reminds us that new avenues of service delivery need to be explored. These avenues may involve, among others, delivery of mental health services and treatments at a distance from professionals. There are too many distressed people who do not receive any form of treatment to expect that face-to-face, talk-based interventions, no matter how effective, will reach the many who do need help. For a more balanced view of the issues confronted by Torrey one should, however, consult Albee's (1997) review of the same book.

The distressing results of a survey conducted by Clemens and Hales (1997) remind us about the profound distrust in which the mental health community is held by the population at large. In the United States, "16% have sought help from mental-health professionals, but 59% have no faith in them." In addition, the majority of those surveyed (1,792 above 18 years of age) preferred to change their diets to treat a health problem rather than to take medication. Depression was the third most common "disease," and 49% self-medicate "to avoid paying for a doctor's visit." This survey indicates that more cost-effective and mass-produced ways are needed that will allow mental health practitioners to reach more people per unit of professional time, as well as people who cannot be reached through face-to-face situations.

This distrust of mental health help is likely widespread elsewhere in the world. Rather than coming up with defensive rationalizations and facile externalizations for such distrust, it behooves us to find ways and means to help people whose distrust is even greater than that of the general population—those people affected by mental illness. They are the very ones who need help the most, but who deny or refuse it the most, because that is the very nature of their illness (L'Abate, 1994, 1997c). Apparently, face-to-face "verbal" confrontation may be too painful and possibly too shameful for some people, and certainly inefficient in the case of many (L'Abate, 1999a, 1999b, 1999c). Furthermore, these people may not be as comfortable using ear-mouth verbal processing to communicate if they are people whose eye-hand coordination makes them rely on writing more than talking. Can we find better ways to help them? We believe that DW and CAI, among other avenues, offer possible alternatives for help.

THE NARROWER CONTEXT OF DISTANCE WRITING

Writing is less public, more private, and less interactive than speaking and nonverbal communication. It is called "distance writing" when it is shared and becomes interactive with another person, professional or otherwise. Within this larger context, we can now look at the use of DW/CAI in psychological interventions. Elsewhere, L'Abate (1992, 1994, 1997b, 1999c) has argued that DW, in contrast to nonverbal and verbal media, which are learned spontaneously and automatically, is a medium that is developmentally acquired through deliberate teaching and deliberate learning. Normatively, at least in Western culture, it takes place after nonverbal and verbal skills have been somewhat mastered. One needs to develop either nonverbal or verbal skills or both to master writing. Hence, writing requires higher and more advanced cognitive functioning than the other two media.

In addition to development comparisons, we need to consider structural comparisons of how the three media—nonverbal, verbal, and writing—are used inside and outside a professional's office. For instance, some mental health professionals may be able to influence verbally a respondent's habits in diet, exercise, and the use of vitamins, impacting also the nonverbal medium outside the therapist's office (Hays, 1999; Wiener, 1999). However, it could be stated, without fear of contradiction, that traditional psychological interventions take place through the verbal medium (i.e., "talk"). Usually, these interventions take place without contracts involving diet, physical exercise, or written homework assignments (i.e., DW). Often, emphasis on talk, without any other requirements, takes place at the expense of the other two media, which are not, as yet, part of mainstream practice in mental health. While the nonverbal medium shares some of the problems with psychotherapy (in terms of being difficult to record, codify, and classify), writing, and especially DW, has a long, but mostly unknown history. It has been used, if not for therapeutic purposes, certainly for para-preventive and para-therapeutic ones (L'Abate, 1992). Writing is much easier to codify and classify than both verbal and nonverbal media. Talk is cheap and expensive at the same time. It is inefficient and uncontrollable in comparison to writing. We cannot control what professionals and respondents alike will say in the *sancto-sanctorum* of the therapy office. It can be distorted, forgotten, or misinterpreted. It is infinite in that there is no evidence to back it up (L'Abate, 1999c). DW, on the other hand, becomes finite once it is determined beforehand what topic or theme respondents should write about.

Furthermore, little attention has been paid in the literature about issues of control and regulation in psychological interventions (L'Abate, 1984; Shapiro & Astin, 1998). These issues are crucial if we want to help people who are either out-of-control, use control in inappropriate ways, or have too much of it. To help them, it is important to convince them (and to be convinced ourselves) about the necessity to approach and expose themselves to what they have avoided for a long time. We tend to avoid (repress, suppress, displace) painful, dysphoric feelings, often produced from past traumas (L'Abate, 1997c; Pennebaker, 1997, Chapters 2 and 3). We need to teach people how to regulate their lives by keeping pre-set appointments, not just in the professional's office, but especially in their homes, to help them approach what they have avoided for a long time. They are encouraged to approach these feelings, as indicated in Chapters 2, 3, and 4, according to a prearranged plan of written homework assignments (i.e., every other day, every day, once a week, at 8 A.M., 6 P.M., 9 P.M., etc.). Without these controls, as well as pre- and post-intervention evaluations and signed informed consent forms, it is going to be difficult to assign homework, especially if professional helpers have not experienced such assignments themselves or are ambivalent or even negative about using them.

Another issue relates to how much responsibility we want our clients to have for the process and outcome of treatment. Should they take responsibility and become actively involved in the process and outcome of treatment, or should they remain passive and leave the ultimate responsibility in the hands and on the shoulders of professionals? The more active professionals are, the more likely that their respondents might become more passive. The more active respondents are allowed and encouraged to be, the greater will be the possibility of a more positive outcome. Activity without a goal and a process, however, is not enough. If talk remains the main if not the sole medium of communication between professionals and respondents, it will be difficult, if not impossible, to allow and encourage respondents to assume actively the ultimate responsibility for the process and outcome of any professional psychological intervention. The rather pessimistic results of Clemens and Hales' (1997) survey indicate the wide gap that exists between professionals and public opinion about mental health practices and professions. Could it be that this gap is due, at least in part, to the use of the spoken word, while, in other professions and institutions in the Western world, the written medium is the norm? This generality may need qualification.

Historical Highlights in the Use of Distance Writing/ Computer-Assisted Interventions

Even though one day there will be an entire book devoted to the history of DW for preventive and pre-therapeutic or para-therapeutic purposes, whatever has been written thus far will suffice for the time being (L'Abate, 1991, 1992). In searching for the historical antecedents of DW, a few highlights will be stressed. DW finds its roots in the autobiographical movement toward the latter part of the nineteenth century. In the early 1940s, Allport (1942) supported the use of "personal documents" to understand personality, including autobiography. Perhaps, Allport's position spawned a resurgence of the use of autobiography with college students in the early 1950s. In the mid-1960s, Pearson (1965) edited a symposium about the use of writing in psychotherapy with contributions of then well-known therapists. Some of them are still alive today. The first research study about "therapeutic writing" is contained in Phillips and Wiener's (1966) pioneering contribution about brief psychotherapy. In 1986 Pennebaker and Beal (Pennebaker, 1997) published a classic paper that found statistically significant differences in immune system and physiological measures among undergraduates who wrote about their hurts ("traumas") for 20 minutes a day for four consecutive days. A control group who wrote for the same amount of time about trivial topics failed to show any differences on post-test. This study has been replicated and amplified (using additional experimental groups that spoke into a microphone) many times with similar results (Esterling, L'Abate, Murray, & Pennebaker, 1999), as discussed in Chapters 2, 3, and 4.

In the same year (1986), L'Abate published three workbooks for couples on depression, negotiation, and intimacy. These workbooks were derived directly from isomorphic theoretical models, suggesting that workbooks could become an economical and more dynamic source of theory testing than talk. Birren and Hedlund (1987) used the autobiographical and "guided" approach with seniors. ("Guided" will be explained below.) More recently, Riordan (1996) published

Table 1-1
Toward a Classification of Writing Continua

Expressive (poetry)/Instructive (textbooks)

Creative-Spontaneous (contextual, constructive of stories)/Contrived (vocabulary, spelling, style, logic, sentence construction, and combination)

Unstructured/Structured
    Open-ended (journals, diaries): advantages versus disadvantages
    Focused (one topic, as in autobiographies and Pennebaker's expressive format): advantages versus disadvantages
    Guided (questions about written compositions): advantages versus disadvantages
    Programmed (as in workbooks): advantages versus disadvantages

Goal (prescriptive/cathartic)

Content (traumatic/trivial)

Abstraction (high/low)

Specificity (high/low)

Source: Adapted from L'Abate (1986), Table 1.2.

a clinical review of DW, which he called "scriptotherapy." Smyth (1998) published a meta-analysis of all of the studies documenting physical and mental health improvements as a result of DW, using Pennebaker's model, also referred to as "expressive writing," as explained in greater detail in Chapters 2, 3, and 4.

Computer applications as "psychotherapeutic analogs" were reviewed by Bloom (1992). He concluded that even disturbed individuals could benefit by using computer-assisted training. In the same year, *Programmed Writing* (L'Abate, 1992) was published, which was viewed as a precursor to structured CAI. In 1996, L'Abate developed pages on the World Wide Web, where more up-to-date workbooks for individuals, couples, and families are available to qualified mental health professionals (see Appendix C at the end of this chapter).

A Classification of Distance Writing

As shown in Table 1-1, writing can be classified according to at least three major continua defined by their extremes: (1) Expressive/Instructive, (2) Creative-Spontaneous/Contrived, and (3) Unstructured/Structured. Many contributions in this book fall within the instructive, contrived, and structured sides of the three continua, with the exception of Chapters 2, 3, 10, and 11.

Within these aspects of DW there are five, sometimes overlapping, dimensions that are relevant from a therapeutic viewpoint, because each dimension has different functions in regard to clinical interventions. The most important dimension, of course, is *structure per se*, which can vary from a little to a great deal.

It can be: (1) *open-ended* ("Write whatever comes into your mind") as in a diary or journal; (2) *focused* ("Write about your depression for 30 minutes every other day at 9 o'clock in the evening"), as in Pennebaker's expressive writing; (3) *guided* ("Please answer in writing the following questions that I have written down after I read your previous assignment on depression"); or (4) *programmed* ("You will need to complete the first of eight assignments in a workbook on depression"). Most of the workbooks developed thus far (see Appendix C) are examples of PDW (L'Abate, 1986, 1992). Workbooks can provide blueprints for a wider variety of clinical conditions that may not be clear or well-known to professionals, no matter how experienced and knowledgeable they may be, as discussed further below.

A second dimension of writing is *goal*, which can be *prescriptive* ("During the next week you need to practice the following behavior . . .") or *cathartic* ("During the next four days write down for 15 [20] minutes a day all of the traumas and hurts that you have received in your life and that you may have not shared with anybody"). The latter approach has been used by Pennebaker (1997), who is one of the pioneers in the use of DW for para-therapeutic purposes, as discussed in Chapters 2, 3, and 4. A third dimension is *content*, which can vary from *traumatic*, as in the example provided above, to *trivial* ("Write about your clothes, cars you have owned, places you have lived, etc."). In fact, a workbook about trivial topics has been written to serve as a control for other workbooks in research projects (see Appendix C). A fourth dimension is the *level of abstraction*, which can vary from very *concrete* ("List or log every time you use the 'You' pronoun with your spouse") to very *abstract* ("Write about the meaning of existence"). The fifth dimension deals with *specificity*, ranging from very *general* ("Write your autobiography") to very *specific*, as in the example given above about logging the frequency of the 'you' pronoun. An example of a beginning assignment for depression illustrating what is meant by PDW in general is given in Appendix A. A workbook consists of a series of assignments linked together by a common theme or topic.

Distance Writing and Cerebral Functioning

This section is highly speculative. Indeed, what follows should be considered as wildly hypothetical. This writer is aware of going out on a limb, proposing vistas that may be completely invalid but nevertheless tempting. A consideration that will receive more specific attention in Chapter 9, dealing with incarcerated felons, relates to writing and hemispheric functioning. One could argue, for instance, that talk and writing differ in the relative cerebral dominance. Possibly, talk about one's sad, and fearful feelings may rely predominantly on the right rather than on the left hemisphere, making psychotherapy a right hemisphere function. Apparently (Ornstein, 1997), talk about one's happy, joyous, or impersonal experiences may rely predominantly on the left rather than on the right hemisphere. Could thinking that requires writing rely predominantly on the left hemisphere? The reverse may be possible as far as plain talking is concerned. Immediate, spontaneous talk may rely predominantly on the right rather than on the left hemisphere. In dealing with criminals, a population extremely resistant to talk therapies, it is well known (see Chapter 9) that the left hemisphere is relatively less functional than the right one. Perhaps acting-out, violent, and "blue-collar" crime, requiring immediacy, may rely predominantly on the right rather than on the left hemisphere. "White-collar" crimes, like embezzlement, cheating, fraud, and the like, requiring cunning, deception, and planning, on the other hand, may rely predominantly on the left rather than on the right hemisphere. DW/CAI, therefore, may help especially criminals, possibly correcting defective thinking patterns that might not be changed through talk therapies. In addition, DW/CAI would do away with the subtle and not-so-subtle interpersonal tensions that are usually present in talk-based, face-to-face professional relationships.

Consequently, if language is more related to the right hemisphere, then writing may be more related to the left hemisphere (Ornstein, 1997). If this is the case, then writing might use or even stimulate parts of the brain that are not stimulated by talking. Hence, both talking and writing might derive from different parts of the brain and, in return, stimulate them as well. If this hypothesis is correct, then both talking and writing would be synergistic with each other. Consequently, both together could produce multiplicative results because they may stem from and focus on two different hemispheres. Consequently, we need to use them both and not rely solely on talk to obtain positive changes in distressed people or offenders. This simplistic and rather naive generalization (right hemisphere for therapeutic talk, left hemisphere for "therapeutic" writing) has been questioned by Schiffer (1998), who, suggested a different framework, differentiating between a more troubled and less mature hemisphere versus a less troubled and more mature hemisphere, regardless of dominance. Either hemisphere can be troubled while the other is relatively the more mature one. Of course, both hemispheres could be troubled in mentally ill patients and both could be mature in well-functioning individuals.

The issue is not as simple as presented thus far because one needs to ask: "What kind of writing?" For instance, if indeed it is true that different emotions are related to different hemispheres, then the issue of what kind of writing becomes crucial. Apparently, the left hemisphere could be more related to positive feelings and the right hemisphere could be more related to "negative" feelings, like hurt, traumas, and sadness (Ornstein, 1997). Again, if this conclusion is correct, then one would predict that writing about traumatic and painful events might relate predominantly to the right rather than to the left hemisphere functions. This would be the case in expressive writing that accesses the right more than the left hemisphere (Chapters 2, 3, and 4). By the same token, if writing focuses strictly on cognitive and rational issues, as in the case of workbooks (PDW), it may require more left hemisphere functions. Clearly, this is an intriguing area to explore using different kinds of writing. It remains an uncharted frontier for researchers to explore at will.

The literature on brain functioning is so vast that it is impossible for this writer to review it and to rely solely on primary sources. At least two secondary sources have summarized and integrated whatever evidence has been found thus far about cerebral dominance (Ornstein, 1997; Schiffer, 1998). It is necessary to cite Ornstein extensively to support some hypotheses about cerebral functioning and writing elucidated here.

In the first place, concerning the specialization of functions, Ornstein, quoting primary sources, concludes that hemispheric specialization began through evolution. The process derived first from the right hemisphere, needed by a person to move and to act to survive, while the left hemisphere, especially with the advent of reading, might have developed later. Learning to read and write may have even increased this specialization (1997: 40).

In the second place, one cannot make absolute statements about literality of cerebral functions. As Ornstein concluded, the right hemisphere is more related to spatial functions. If that is the case, then the left hemisphere may be more related to temporal functions. If the right hemisphere is related to hurt and sad feelings, then the left hemisphere may be more related to joyous and happy feelings (1997: 76). To reinforce this important point, Ornstein proposed that so-called negative feelings may relate, together with large muscle movements requiring action, to the right hemisphere. This conclusion would support a theoretical position (L'Abate, 1994, 1997c) that would make anger, externalizations, impulsivity, and violence predominantly a function of the right hemisphere, since such behaviors take place almost without thinking about possible consequences.

In the third place, Ornstein concluded that students who do not consider school relevant to their lives could be dominated more by the right than by the left hemisphere. He generalized this possibility to class distinctions, like middle-class people being more left hemisphere–oriented than lower-class ones (1997: 92). If this is the case, could one also speculate that therapists may be more right hemisphere–oriented, while researchers (and writing-oriented clinicians!) may be more left hemisphere–oriented? Could this possibility "explain" the chasm between the former and the latter? This conclusion was supported further by findings that in Singapore schools, where 284 students were separated into three achievement groups (normal, express, and special), high achievers were more left hemisphere-oriented than low achievers (1997: 94–95).

More relevant to the seemingly simplistic differentiation of "thinking = left hemisphere; speaking = right hemisphere," Ornstein concluded that "the right hemisphere is deeply involved in complex language" (1997: 101), but, apparently there is "activation of the left hemisphere in response to pleasure, activation of the right in response to disgust. . . . These negative emotions generally arise out of approach-avoidance situations" (1997: 155).

This latter point is theoretically relevant to the position that, if valid, approach-avoidance, that is, distance functions that are basic to the development of intimacy, would relate predominantly to the right rather than to the left hemisphere. By the same token, if the left hemisphere is predominantly related to thinking, then thinking would seem basic to the development of discharge-delay, that is control/regulatory functions necessary for negotiation and problem solving in intimate relationships. The theoretical position (L'Abate, 1994, 1997c) that personality socialization and interpersonal competence are composed of both love and negotiation may find its physiological bases in linking love and intimacy predominantly with right hemisphere functioning. Negotiation and problem solving, then, would be linked predominatly with left hemisphere functioning. How wild can one get? Not as wild as social psychologists who have stressed the existence of two different processes of social information (Chaiken & Trope, 1999). The various models presented by the latter distinguish between qualitatively and quantitatively different models of decision making and problem solving, like affective versus cognitive models. Hence, these models seem to support the possibility of different hemispheric functions that still need to be defined further.

The rest of this chapter will be devoted to functions, advantages, dangers, and disadvantages of PDW as exemplified by workbooks because they represent most of the contributions in this book, as found in Chapters 5, 6, 7, 8, and 9.

Functions and Benefits of Programmed Direct Writing

Some of the possible benefits of workbooks (PDW) are summarized in Appendix B. In addition to the benefits outlined in this appendix, PDW assignments have the potential to improve behavior by bringing groups, couples, and families together to focus and work on issues that are relevant to their functioning. For instance, DW and CAI serve as:

1. Coping strategies by teaching respondents how to solve problems together with others and on their own, without the direct presence of a professional, especially with well-functioning respondents.

2. Means of self-growth whereby homework assignments may enlarge the awareness of respondents without having to rely solely on the professional's time and energy.

3. A process synergistic and/or isomorphic with face-to-face talk sessions, as examples provided in some chapters will suggest.

4. A way of linking evaluation with treatment in a way that is either expensive or very difficult to achieve through talk.

5. Preparation for face-to-face, verbal interventions, whereby written homework assignments teach respondents how to answer questions that allow for individual, dyadic, and family feedback under controlled conditions.

6. A way of assessing motivation for change and assumption of personal responsibility, because it is difficult in writing to blame others, especially if the homework assignment is designed for the individual. We know no one, as yet, who has gotten mad at a piece of paper or a computer because of its impersonal nature, even though, at worst, many pieces of paper have ended up in the round file.

7. A tool to use after an intervention is terminated. Former psychotherapy patients, for instance, may profit by completing homework assignments in writing (L'Abate, 1997a).

In addition to the foregoing advantages, DW and CAI assignments may have additional advantages:

1. Giving respondents something concrete to do about their problems above and beyond the 50-minute face-to-face talk session.
2. Providing impetus for carrying face-to-face, talk-based therapy session themes further and deeper.
3. Providing structure and focus when problem(s) need to be broken down into more manageable parts.
4. Increasing the sense of direction (and generalization) in treatment from the professional's office to the home.
5. Increasing respondents' sense of responsibility for their own progress in treatment.
6. Increasing choices available to professionals as well as to respondents.
7. Increasing awareness and critical evaluation of set beliefs, cognitions, and behavioral patterns with a greater sense of choice about them.

Of course, unless a written contract about the use of DW homework assignments is presented from the very beginning (first session) of intervention through an informed consent form, resistance to change without such an initial contract will be great (Jensen, Josephson, & Frey, 1989). There might be resistance even after the contract is signed. However, not completing or answering prescribed assignments is often as lucrative "grist for the intervention mill" as completing them. Sources of resistance to change, like fear of change on one hand, and dependency on the therapist's magic, on the other hand, can be brought out and confronted on the basis of actual behavior rather than on the basis of just talk.

PDW may afford an alternative approach with single respondents, couples, and families. For instance, if depression is prominent from the outset, in addition to face-to-face therapy, the depressed partner can be given homework assignments from one of the many depression workbooks available (see Appendix A). The driven, supposedly nondepressed partner can be administered a workbook for driven, Type-A personalities (L'Abate, 1992). If relevant, both partners could be administered a depression workbook based on an interpersonal view of depression. Both spouses would complete each assignment individually, share their completed assignments as a couple at home, and then share their experiences in the whole process with the professional. PDW, therefore, might produce four feedback loops that may increase the process of positive change: (1) from the paper (or computer) containing systematic questioning for the individual; (2) from the individual to the partner, friend, or other family members; (3) from an individual, couple, or family to the professional; and (4) from the professional back to respondents.

Examples of Programmed Direct Writing: Links with Evaluation

While Pennebaker's focused approach is practically universal—it can be applied to most human beings—the advantage of workbooks is their specificity, explicitness, and versatility, that is, they can be tailored to the specific needs of a particular individual, couple, or family, as shown in Appendix C. For instance, if an individual is depressed, there is now a variety of workbooks available to deal with this condition. The diagnosis of depression can be made from history and symptoms alone or from high peaks on depression scales of various clinical, objective personality tests. Workbooks to match each of the content scales of the MMPI-2, or the clinical scales of the Personality Assessment Inventory (PAI), the Myers-Briggs Type Indicator, or NEO (Neuroticism Extraversion Openness) are available. Hence, the specific match between a clinical condition and a workbook can be achieved much more easily through PDW than through talk. For referral symptoms without a supporting objective test profile, there are workbooks for many other conditions. Thus, through PDW, it is possible to link intervention with either deviant scores on a personality test or with specific clinical or subclinical conditions as judged by a professional.

Through PDW, any test, originally constructed for *diagnostic* and at best *predictive* functions, can become *prescriptive*, once a workbook is developed from the test itself. In this regard, it was possible to develop workbooks from single-scale tests, like the Beck or the Hamilton Anxiety and Depression Inventories. This development can take place provided the number of items in the scale does not exceed 18 to 21. Too many items would make the workbook too unwieldy and complex for most respondents. By the same token, most multiscale tests, with items in the hundreds, like the MMPI-2, the PAI, or the NEO and many others, produced workbooks that matched each scale in the test, one workbook for each scale. In this fashion, it is possible to match evaluation with treatment in a way that would be practically impossible to achieve through talk.

Workbooks for Individuals: Children, Adolescents, and Adults

In children, adolescents, or adults, the two major dimensions of dysfunctionality, internalization and externalization, can be evaluated and confronted with matching workbooks, either through single- or multiple-scale tests or through a referral question or problem. Extremes of psychopathology, which include both dimensions of internalization and externalization, can be matched with appropriate workbooks. By the same token, there are five workbooks that allow relatively well-functioning respondents to work, perhaps after psychotherapy termination, on multiple abilities, normalizing experiences, and social skills (see Appendix C). Furthermore, if Ornstein's (1997) conclusions are valid, then externalizations may relate predominantly to right hemisphere functioning, while intellectualizations may relate predominantly to left hemisphere functioning.

Through PDW it is possible to link evaluation with treatment in ways that are difficult or expensive to obtain through talk. For instance, as already indicated, there are workbooks that are isomorphic with the content scales of the MMPI-2 (L'Abate, 1992) and the Five Factor Model of Personality (NEO), where assignments for both peaks and valleys of the five dimensions comprising this test are available. A similar workbook of lessons isomorphic with the clinical dimensions of the Personality Assessment Inventory (PAI) is available as also for the Myers-Briggs Type Indicator. For alcoholics there is the *AA 12-Steps in 4* workbook. For impulsive and acting-out individuals there is the Social Training workbook and its Addendum, not to count workbooks on anger, hostility, and aggression, among others. A social growth program, to deal with generalized anxiety and discomfort, is also available.

Workbooks for Couples

The first three workbooks to be written were also isomorphic with theoretical models of interpersonal depression, negotiation, and intimacy (L'Abate, 1986). For example, a couple comes in for marital therapy due to persistent and intense fighting. It is clear from the initial interview that the wife is depressed and that the husband, an admitted workaholic, is a driven, somewhat impulsive individual. In addition to face-to-face talk therapy, DW could help in many ways. First, after signing an informed consent form, both partners would be asked to write down, as homework assignments, a list of all their hurts, following Pennebaker's format (Chapters 2, 3, and 4). Some hurts might not have been disclosed to anyone. Second, a workbook to deal with excessive arguing and fighting is administered. It is to be answered by both partners at home at prearranged, preset times. This workbook consists of a first assignment asking partners to describe the content, frequency, intensity, and rate of arguing/fighting. The second assignment contains ten positive "explanations" of the fighting, which each partner needs to consider and rank in order of relevance to him or her.

The third assignment contains instructions on how to fight "dirty" following detailed guidelines on how to do it, that is "prescription of the symptom." The couple is also instructed to tape-record this fight. Often, couples refuse to complete this assignment because they have had a "discussion" instead. Couples who do complete this assignment, however, bring to the professional's office a tape of their fight. Then, they are given a score sheet to count the frequency of those "suicidal" (i.e., "they kill the self") characteristics that are individually prominent during the fight. Essentially, each partner has to content-analyze the tape to become aware of how "dirty" he or she has fought. Once the score sheet is brought back, each partner is given the assignment that is isomorphic with the characteristic that is most prominent in the content analysis. If one partner uses mostly the "you" pronoun, she or he receives an assignment on the destructive use of this pronoun. If the other partner "brings up the past" more frequently, he or she receives an assignment on the destructive aspects of bringing up the past, and so on (L'Abate, 1999a, 1999b, 1999c).

For couples, workbooks can be administered according to either a symptom or peak scores on marital inventories. An example of the former is found in the workbook about fighting and arguing, just cited. An example of the latter is found in workbooks derived from the Marital Satisfaction or Marital Conflict Inventories.

Another way to match evaluation with intervention is found in the Problems in Relationships Program, consisting of an evaluation instrument with matching homework assignments. The Problems in Relationships Scale (PIRS) instrument was found to be quite valid (see Chapter 8) in providing profiles on 20 dimensions of polarizations that are generally found in conflictful couples (expressive versus nonexpressive, dominant versus submissive, straight versus devious, etc.). Partners complete individually and then discuss together assignments that match relationship dimensions in which they show the greater extent of discrepancy. The PIRS illustrates how a nomothetic (for all couples) evaluation instrument can be applied in an idiographic manner (specific to one couple) to match homework assignments isomorphic with dimensions measured by the evaluation instrument (L'Abate, 1992).

Workbooks for Families

Most workbooks for families can be administered by either test profile or by referral question alone, as in lying, sibling rivalry, temper tantrums, verbal abuse, stealing, binge eating, negativity, shyness, and domestic violence. More recently, workbooks for adoptive or foster parents, family interviews, family feelings, revised temper tantrums, and time-out procedures are available.

Tangential or parallel practices after administration of DW assignments to respondents can take place. For instance, after each written assignment is completed and brought to the professional to receive feedback, one can ask the following questions: (1) What part of this writing assignment worked or didn't work for you?; (2) In what area of your experience might this practice be or not be helpful to you? and, with families resistant to the use of writing assignments, (3) Can you come up with another medium that would allow you to deal with your problems as effectively as this one, or better? As in any homework assignment, PDW permits assessing motivation for change in respondents ("If you want change, you will need to work for it").

DANGERS AND DISADVANTAGES IN THE USE OF DISTANCE WRITING COMPUTER-ASSISTED INTERVENTIONS

It is important to use safeguards in a practice that is still new and not part of the accepted and traditional therapeutic mainstream. The application of a new medium of psychological intervention, especially at a distance from a respondent, is fraught with a variety of ethical and professional issues. Some of these issues cannot as yet be considered here because there is no way of knowing what they will be.

For starters, it is important that both DW and CAI be considered as "training," "education," or even "prevention" or "intervention" rather than psychotherapy. The latter term is part of mainstream mental health practices that do not include DW or CAI. Psychotherapy denotes: (1) a face-to-face professional relationship (2) based on talk. Neither of these two aspects are present in either DW or CAI. Hence, neither type of intervention should be equated with psychotherapy. Furthermore, one cannot claim that either DW or CAI is therapeutic unless it is demonstrated that they are. To substantiate this claim, it behooves mental health professionals planning to use either medium to follow certain necessary guidelines. The first consists of the administration on a pre- and post-intervention basis of paper-and-pencil, self-report inventories measuring the condition that is being dealt with, either through DW or CAI. The second guideline consists of using an informed consent form that indicates which types of respondents would not benefit from either medium, as far as we know, and some of the potential dangers that may derive from either practice. These issues need further elaboration.

First, one must consult ethical and professional guidelines already published in one's professional discipline and in the state in which one is practicing. Second, one ought to be mindful of not doing any harm, and discontinuing any approach or workbook that may produce unexpected and unforeseeable reactions from respondents. Third, one ought to assure respondents of complete confidentiality in the use of either medium, making sure that professional actions go with words (i.e., disclosure to external parties will be provided only with written permission from respondents, or when severe abuse or criminal behavior is present, or when required by law). Fourth, especially in the practice of CAI, one must ensure that what was written and communicated through a computer is linked directly to the respondent who claims to have written it. How is the professional to know who wrote what? There are a variety of ways to ensure this link (secret passwords, written affidavits from third parties, written assurances from family members, etc.). Fifth, many of the foregoing problems can be dealt with (if not solved) through the consistent use of a necessarily lengthy and complex informed consent form (*http://www.mentalhealthhelp.com*). Some contents of this form can be reduced to a verbal format, provided that there are other witnesses to the initial therapeutic contract, in addition to the respondents and the professional. We are all aware of how talk can be distorted, forgotten, or misused. This informed consent form must be administered from the very first session with some discussion before being signed by respondents toward the end of the second or third session. It should not be sprung on respondents during the course of already ongoing verbal therapy, without a preliminary and full discussion and disclosure about PDW's benefits and potential dangers, all contained in the informed consent form.

The major danger of PDW is the mismatch between a condition and the workbook administered to deal with it. For instance, a paranoid individual may appear anxious and not disclose or make apparent at the outset the extent of the paranoia, especially if no screening test has been administered beforehand. He or she may be administered an anxiety workbook that eventually might elicit the more florid symptoms of paranoia or produce no positive outcome. A couple may hide the extent of physical abuse and be accepted for PDW while the abuse may be continuing. All of the potential dangers in PDW and CAI may be minimized (never eliminated) by a careful evaluation of the referral symptom as given not only by the respondent but also by family members or friends who are familiar with the condition. Unless careful, objective, and subjective screening is performed from the very outset, the danger of administering a mismatched workbook is real and potentially destructive, not only to the respondent but also to the professional. Clearly, this is uncharted territory that requires careful and responsible study on the part of anyone using either PDW or CAI.

There is no question that a great deal of professional resistance toward the use of DW/CAI will ensue once the use of either medium becomes competitive with talk in psychological interventions. One can and should expect that such resistance is part of any response to innovation and change in mental health practices. One ought to be prepared to deal with it as in any resistance to change found in human systems. One ought to be mindful also that such resistance cannot be dealt with through rational discussion, empirical research evidence, or mandated managed care dicta. No matter how convincing the discussion, how strong the evidence, or how mandatory the dicta may be, resistance to change is inevitable in systems under stress, and the mental health disciplines are not exempt. Like many issues of change, this is an emotional one. Like all emotional issues, it will take more than discussion, evidence, or dicta to overcome. In the long run, when personal and professional benefits override emotional considerations, perhaps both media will be added to the therapeutic armamentarium, not to supplant psychotherapy or medication, but to bolster and supplement both (L'Abate, 1997a, 1997b, 1999a, 1999b, 1999c).

Of course, the use of PDW in clinical practice is not unique to the contributors of this volume. There are many workbooks on the market dealing with a variety of clinical or pre-clinical conditions. An annotated bibliography of self-help workbooks is available (*http://www.mentalhhelp.com*). One must keep in mind that the rationale as well as the evidence for the usefulness of many workbooks is still inadequate, as indicated in Chapter 5. As discussed earlier, L'Abate (1994, 1997b) has presented a rationale for the clinical use of DW and PDW in terms of a developmental sequence that starts with the nonverbal medium, goes on to the verbal one, and then progresses to writing. The first two media are learned automatically. The third medium, writing, is the product of teaching and learning. Hence, DW and especially PDW represent the most cognitive of all the skills we learn. Why not use them for further, cost-effective, mass-oriented interventions?

CLINICAL IMPLICATIONS OF DISTANCE WRITING COMPUTER-ASSISTED INTERVENTIONS

In addition to the easier and more direct link between evaluation and intervention, there is the age-old issue of generalization. How are we going to transfer behavior from the professional's office to the home, school, or even the workplace? This generalization is not going to happen easily through talking. If the behavior is not practiced in situ, how do we hope to have it happen there? Hence, written homework assignments may make the transfer from the office to the home, school, or workplace quicker, easier, and, perhaps, more lasting.

There is no way that mental health professionals can learn all of the theoretical and therapeutic systems available on the mental health market. Through "canned" (i.e., already written workbooks) prearranged assignments, however, professional helpers can use other approaches that may not be present in their existent theoretical armamentarium. For instance, there are many depression workbooks that were derived from the work of other depression experts. It might be difficult for many professionals to know and to apply them without an already written workbook, a blueprint and a plan of how the treatment is going to take place, above and beyond just talk.

One might also argue that to compare results for different treatments, PDW is a medium where such a comparison can take place, since talk is very expensive to evaluate. Hence, it is much easier to perform research functions through PDW than through talk. For instance, using Beck's cognitive viewpoint L'Abate, Boyce, Fraizer, and Russ (1992) were able to compare it with two other depression workbooks in ways that would have been expensive using the spoken word. PDW allows professional helpers to tailor-make ad hoc assignments for specific patterns not covered elsewhere in their training and experience. Specific assignments and workbooks can be written on the basis of present clinical experience, existing evaluation instruments (Maruish, 1994, 1999), self-help books, and different theoretical viewpoints.

Another issue relates to the educational and intellectual level required by PDW. For instance, how could illiterate or blind persons be helped by the written medium? There are a variety of ways to answer this question. First of all, the programmed written medium can be reduced to audio- or videotapes, with illiterate respondents answering through a tape recorder. In the second place, in institutions, like jails, penitentiaries, or even schools, it is possible to enlist individuals who have successfully completed a workbook program, having them serve as volunteer instructors to more limited individuals. In the third place, workbooks can be down-written or simplified to a lower educational level. For instance, adults could be administered workbooks designed for children or adolescents. By the same token, how effective is verbal psychotherapy with the same kind of individuals? Shouldn't this question be answered before focusing on the possible limitations of PDW?

CONCLUSION

A lot of water has passed under the bridge of DW during the past few years. PDW and CAI have the potential to reach populations that heretofore have been neglected or have been underserved by the mental health community. Among these populations one can mention, among many others, military and missionary families, incarcerated felons, elementary, middle, high school, and college students, the handicapped, and shut-ins. Advances in DW/CAI, together with advances in virtual reality therapy, psychoeducational social skills training programs, computer-based neurobiofeedback, and manualized psychotherapies, have the potential to revolutionize the practices of prevention, psychotherapy, and rehabilitation as we know them. These relatively new approaches challenge current traditional psychotherapeutic practices but, on the other hand, raise more questions than can be answered at this time. The danger of the status quo is stasis. The dangers of trying out new interventions remain unknown unless we apply them. Nonetheless, we should be aware of possible benefits as well as shortcomings.

DW/CAI in clinical practice have the potential to widen the repertoire of therapists and to give more options to more respondents per unit of the professional's time. DW in its different forms, including CAI, may open doors that would otherwise would stay closed by the exclusive use of traditional talk therapies. DW/CAI could well become the most cost-effective, mass-oriented approaches to help troubled people, preventively, para-therapeutically, and rehabilitatively. It is difficult, if not impossible, for approaches based on talk and face-to-face contact with a professional to become as cost-effective and mass-oriented as DW/CAI. Hence, the sky is the limit for applications of DW/CAI in the delivery of mental health services. In the future, public libraries, hospitals, jails, and university libraries will have readily available computers that will administer unstructured and structured interventions at a distance from professionals, but always on-line with them.

NOTE

I am indebted to Rubin Battino and Robert Pressman for their helpful corrections and suggestions to improve previous drafts of this chapter.

APPENDIX A
EXAMPLE OF AN ASSIGNMENT FOR DEPRESSION

TERRIFIC TRIANGLES: THE FAMILY DRAMA

Name_____ Date_____

The purpose of this workbook is to teach couples and families how to deal with depression and depressive feelings. The purpose of this assignment is to learn more about destructive patterns that interfere with living together.

1. To keep the family together and to protect it from change, we often play a triangle in which we, in one way or another, play all three parts at different times. The three parts are Victim, Persecutor, and Rescuer. These basic parts have variations within themselves. For instance, we may play the judge of other family members, and, on the basis of this part, we may then become jury and executioners. Below you will find three lists that relate to the three basic parts. Read them.

Persecutor	Victim	Rescuer
Judge	Criminal	Therapist
Parent	Defendant	Know-it-all
Juror	Invalid (sick)	Expert (teacher, preacher, consultant)
Policeman	Child	Big Daddy
Patriot	Drug addict	Tycoon
Detective	Servant	Peacemaker
Hellfire & brimstone preacher	Martyr	Red Cross Nurse or Paramedic
Executioner	Sinner	Meddler
Inquisitor	Culprit	Saint
Oppressor	"Poor little me"	Superman/superwoman
Inspector general	Oppressed	Wholesaler
Interrogator	Innocent	Advice giver

2. Circle the part and the variations on the part that you recognize in yourself. Then choose which of these parts you play best (a), second best (b), and third best (c). Write in detail how you play each part:

a. _____

b. _____

c. _____

3. What happens to the rest of the family when you play these parts? Please explain in detail:

4. Do you need to play these parts and what do you get out of playing them? Please answer in detail:

5. Who is responsible for your playing these parts?

6. How do you get yourself set up to play these parts? Please explain in detail:

7. Unless you like playing these parts and you do get something positive out of playing them, how can you avoid setting yourself up to play them? Please explain:

Homework: During the coming week each family member must continue to play these three parts as well as they have been doing in the past. However, family members should jot down and log every time they find themselves playing one of these parts. In addition, since keeping logs is usually not enough, make an appointment with each other at specific, pre-stated, pre-arranged, and pre-determined times (8 o'clock P.M. on Tuesday, for instance) to play these parts and learn to control them, rather than these parts controlling the family. If you can start them, you can stop them. The purpose of these meetings is for family members to become painfully aware of how these parts are played within and outside the family. If necessary, members may need to have more than one family meeting to play these parts until these parts no longer affect the family (unless, of course, the family wants these parts to control them). Keep notes of these family meetings to bring (mail, e-mail, or fax) to your professional helper.

Source: L'Abate, 1986.

APPENDIX B
SOME POSSIBLE BENEFITS OF WORKBOOKS
IN CLINICAL PRACTICE

- Save time in clinical practice by maximizing effectiveness of interventions
- Conserve energy and effort by maximizing respondents' involvement in the treatment process
- Reach underserved populations (homebound, handicapped, military, missionary, Peace Corps volunteers, incarcerated felons, juveniles, etc.)
- Serve patients who cannot afford weekly face-to-face interventions
- Maintain the continuum of care between sessions
- Conform to managed care requirements
- Decrease the number of unproductive sessions
- Conduct controlled research inexpensively

Furthermore, workbooks may have the following functions:

- Help train beginning graduate students, as well as seasoned professionals, to deal with a variety of mental health issues in individuals, couples, and families by initially using workbooks as scripts for structured interviews and as guidelines for interventions
- Reduce guesswork in treatment planning, by serving as specific and explicit treatment plans
- Offer prepared scripts with clear feedback guidelines for written homework assignments as alternatives or additions to ongoing face-to-face interventions

- Follow diagnosis-specific treatment plans based on leading mental health assessment tools or referral questions
- Provide uniform treatment and convenient protocols for verbal face-to-face, tape-recorded, written, or electronic media (such as TV, fax, and computer) venues
- Serve as software for computer-mediated counseling, mental health training, prevention, psychotherapy, and rehabilitation
- Conduct inexpensive and easily controlled research, thus minimizing the need for elaborate record keeping, coding, and classification
- Reduce research time by reaching more respondents per unit of researcher's time
- Conduct clinically relevant research with a variety of workbooks for a number of specific clinical conditions or syndromes

APPENDIX C
MATERIALS AVAILABLE FROM WORKBOOKS
FOR BETTER LIVING

For more information about these workbooks, please access *http://www.mentalhealthhelp. com.*

I. WORKBOOKS FOR INDIVIDUALS

A. Youth: Children and Adolescents (ages 8 to 17)

1. Based on Psychological Test Profiles (General)

a. Externalizations (Anger, Acting-Out, Hostility, and Aggression)

Juvenile Psychopathy can be used either in conjunction with a self-report or paper-and-pencil test or simply on the basis of persistent acting-out behavior (3 assignments+)

School Conduct is drawn from different sources to cover socially maladjusted and conduct-disordered youngsters (3 assignments+)

School Social Skills (S³) developed from the test by the same name of Brown, Black, and Downs (1984) contains four different workbooks about Adult and Peer Relations, School Rules, and Classroom Behavior (7 assignments+)

Social Training consists of 20 terms that control behavior and teaches respondents to think before they act (20 assignments)

Unusual and Troublesome Behavior is drawn from the checklist by the same name developed by M. G. Aman and Nirbhay N. Singh for youth in residential and community settings (3 assignments+)

b. Internalizations (Anxiety, Depression, Fears)

Anxiety in Youth is drawn from the scale by the same name developed by P. L. Newcomer, E. Barenbaum, and B. R. Bryant (3 assignments+)

Emotional Problems is drawn from a differential test by the same name by E. J. Kelly and edited by G. J. Vitali to cover emotionally disturbed youngsters (3 assignments+)

Depression Anxiety in Youth is drawn from the scale by the same name developed by P. L. Newcomer, E. Barenbaum, and B. R. Bryant (3 assignments+)

2. Based on Referral Question (Specific)

a. Externalizations

Addendum to Social Training is written from the viewpoint of how many acting-out individuals think (10 assignments)

Anger in Children and Adolescents is based on the meta-analysis of destructive behaviors by B. Lahey and collaborators (3 assignments+)

Juvenile Psychopathy can be used either in conjunction with a self-report or paper-and-pencil test or simply on the basis of persistent acting-out behavior (3 assignments+)

Post-traumatic Stress Disorder Symptoms in children exposed to disaster based on the extensive confirmatory factor analyses by J. L. Anthony, C. J. Lonigan, and S. A. Hecht (3 assignments+)

Social Training consists of 20 terms that control behavior and force respondents to think before they act (20 assignments)

b. Internalizations

See workbooks for adults that can also be applied with few changes in wording to children and adolescents.

c. Both Internalizations and Externalizations

1. By Test Profile. Self-Others Profile Charts are two theory-derived workbooks that allow a quick and focused determination of disturbances in self, in intimate others, and in both self and others (elementary, middle school, and high school versions of the chart available) (6 assignments+)

2. By Referral Question. See workbooks for adults that could also be applied with few changes in wording to children and adolescents.

B. Adults

Evaluation

Social Information Form is an 85-item quantified, either self-report or structured interview about developmental history

1. Based on Psychological Test Profiles (General)

Big Five Markers consists of L. Goldberg's factor analysis of the Five Factors Model (FFM) of personality (12 assignments+)

Butcher Treatment Planning Inventory was written in conjunction with the first instrument to specifically assess treatment resistance (3 assignments+)

Five Factors Model of Personality (NEO) is one of the most popular, research-based, trait-oriented personality inventories (12 assignments+)

Myers-Briggs Type Indicator is based on the theories of Carl Jung concerning personality types (10 assignments+)

Minnesota Multiphasic Personality Inventory-2 consists of 15 separate workbooks matching the 15 content scales (15 assignments+)

Personality Assessment Inventory (PAI) covers most common psychiatric conditions or syndromes, including phobias, anxiety, and traumas, among others (23 assignments+)

Self-Others Profile Charts are two theory-derived workbooks that allow a quick and focused determination of disturbances in the self, in intimate others, and in both self and others (6 assignments+)

2. Based on Referral Question (Specific)

a. For Externalization and Acting-Out Disorders

AA 12 Steps in 4 is a condensation of the well-known approach for alcoholics or addicts who want to work on forgiving themselves (4 assignments)

Adult Psychopathy can be used in conjunction with a short self-report test for incarcerated felons who want rehabilitation (3 assignments+)

Addendum to Anger teaches that there are a variety of angry feelings that can be expressed and controlled in more constructive ways than in the past (7 assignments)

Addendum to Social Training is written from the viewpoint of how many acting-out individuals think (10 assignments)

Anger Expression is based on the research by Forgays, Forgays, and Spielberger about the factor-structure of the STAXI-2 (5 assignments+)

Anger, Hostility and Aggression is derived from the work of Eckhardt, Deffenbacher, Spielberger, and his associates (the AHA syndrome) (5 assignments+)

Gambling covers how individuals with this addiction think about it (3 assignments+)

Social Training consists of 20 terms that control behavior and force respondents to think before they act (20 assignments)

Temper is based on the original (1982) questionnaire with the same name developed by C. Spielberger and P. London (7 assignments+)

b. For Internalization Disorders

Addendum to Phobias teaches people to learn to express and control their fears (5 assignments)

Anxiety follows the *DSM-IV* definition of this condition (6 assignments)

Anxiety, Depression, Fears are the major emotions that are difficult to control and use positively. This workbook teaches how to control these fears (3 assignments+)

Beck Anxiety and Physiological Hyperarousal is based on the tripartite model of depression and anxiety (3 assignments+)

Beck Depression Inventory-II is based on the latest revision of this much-used inventory (3 assignments+)

Co-dependency helps partners of addicted individuals to set limits (13 assignments)

Dependent Personality deals with items that describe characteristics that put dependent personalities at risk for depression (3 assignments+)

Dissociative Experiences: Form BA was developed from research by L. R. Goldberg targeted specifically at individuals with dissociative experiences (3 assignment+)

Dissociative Experiences: Form TDE was developed from research by L. R. Goldberg targeted specifically at individuals with dissociative experiences (3 assignments+)

Emotional Competence is based on the work by C. Saarni on how to become a more competent individual emotionally (10 assignments)

Emotional Expression teaches individuals who find it hard to express feelings to do so in a more appropriate and helpful fashion than in the past (3 assignments+)

Hamilton's Anxiety Scale uses the items from this scale to develop assignments relevant to learning to cope with anxiety (3 assignments+)

Hamilton's Depression Scale uses the items from this scale to develop assignments on learning how to cope with depression (3 assignments+)

Loneliness helps individuals to deal with feelings that make them unable to develop meaningful relationships on their own (6 assignments)

Moodiness is an all-purpose workbook that teaches individuals to express a great many memories that affect their moods (12 assignments)

Overdependency and Self-Critical Attitudes comprise two basic aspects of depression according to S. Blatt's model

Personality Disorders are extremely resistant to talk-based interventions. Perhaps through the writing medium and computer-assisted interventions like this workbook these disorders may become more amenable to change (3 assignments+)

Procrastination helps individuals become more aware and perhaps learn to deal with and control their procrastination (6 assignments)

Sexual Abuse is for victims of sexual abuse who need to complete it in conjunction with support or therapy groups (9 assignments)

c. For Both Internalization and Externalization Disorders

Brief Psychiatric Rating Scale permits a very quick confrontation of most symptoms of psychiatric disturbance (3 assignments+)

Post-traumatic Stress Disorder is based on the latest factor analytic study of the scale by the same name (3 assignments+)

Post-traumatic Stress Symptoms helps people who suffer from painful experiences from their pasts that are still affecting them in the present (3 assignments+)

Social Growth can be used as an all-purpose approach to a variety of clinical and borderline conditions (14 assignments)

Symptom Scale 77 (SS-77) covers most severe psychiatric conditions, many already covered by the PAI (2 assignments+)

d. For Normative Experiences

Multiple Abilities is based on the theories of H. Gardner, R. J. Sternberg, and P. Salovey about multiple intelligences (15 assignments)

Normative Experiences: Form PSC was developed from research by L. R. Goldberg and is generic and neutral enough to be administered to relatively well-functioning individuals, perhaps on a post-psychotherapy basis (3 assignments+)

Normative Experiences: Form IPIP was developed from research by L. R. Goldberg and is generic and neutral enough to be administered to relatively well-functioning individuals, perhaps on a post-psychotherapy basis (3 assignments+)

Normative Experiences: Form AB5C was developed from research by L. R. Goldberg and is generic and neutral enough to be administered to relatively well-functioning individuals, perhaps on a post-psychotherapy basis (3 assignments+)

Social Skills is based on the inventory by the same name developed by M. Lorr, R. P. Youniss, and E. C. Stefic (3 assignments+)

II. WORKBOOKS FOR COUPLES

A. Based on Psychological Test Profiles

Improving Relationships deals with the most frequent issues in committed, prolonged, and close relationships (6 assignments)

Marital Satisfaction is based on one of the most frequently administered inventories commercially available (13 assignments)

Problems in Relationships program includes a workbook and a 240-item computer-scored scale to pinpoint major discrepancies among 20 scales of potentially conflictful areas with matching assignments for each of the 20 areas (22 assignments + scale)

Relationship Conflict covers most stressful areas of conflict, including abuse and fighting (14 assignments)

B. Based on Referral Question

Arguing and Fighting consists of description, positive reframing, and prescription of seven different aspects of abusive behavior (10 assignments+)

Depression in Couples teaches them to become aware of how defeating depression develops from past family patterns that produce deadly triangles (8 assignments)

Intimacy teaches couples to care, see the good, forgive, and share joys, hurts, and fears of being hurt, qualities that are the essence of love (6 assignments)

Marital Violence teaches partners to control their violence through cognitive processing of their actions. It can be used complementarily with the *Partner Violence* workbook (3 assignments+)

Negotiation is a step-by-step process that teaches couples to learn it anew because few learned it from their families of origin (9 assignments)

Partner Violence teaches partners to control their violence and learn to express their feelings in more helpful ways (3 assignments+)

Premarital Preparation helps partners clarify reasons for their wanting to get married (3 assignments+)

Stand Up for Yourself! teaches partners to express themselves in a more constructive fashion than they have done heretofore (5 assignments)

III. WORKBOOK FOR FAMILIES

A. Based on Psychological Test Profiles

Arguing between Parent and Child pinpoints specific patterns of arguing that lead to stress and breakdown in family relationships (3 assignments+)

Arguing between Parent and Parent pinpoints sources of disagreement between parents and how to solve these disagreements (3 assignments+)

Family Environment Scale links lessons with areas of family functioning that are low in their test profile (3 assignments+)

Family Profile Form contains nine dimensions of family living that correlate highly with other measures of marital and family functioning (3 assignments+)

B. Based on Referral Question

Binge Eating consists of three assignments focused on description, positive reframing, and prescription of this symptom in children and teenagers (3 assignments)

Divorce Adjustment for Children, developed by Karin B. Jordan, Ph.D., for elementary school-aged children whose parents are divorcing (7 assignments)

Domestic Violence and Child Abuse consist of three assignments focused on description, positive reframing, and prescription of this symptom (3 assignments)

Foster or Adoptive Families is for those who need training, instructions, and suggestions in how to cope with oftentime novel and difficult responsibilities (8 assignments)

Initial Family Interviews & Feelings helps families confront feelings and emotions that many people do not know how to express (5 assignments)

Lying consists of three assignments focused on description, positive reframing, and prescription of this symptom in children (3 assignments)

Negativity in Families consists of three assignments focused on description, positive reframing, and prescription of this behavior (3 assignments)

Relationship Styles is based on the Elementary Pragmatic model developed by Piero De Giacomo, M.D. (3 assignments+)

Revised Temper Tantrums is for parents of children from preschool to adulthood (4 assignments)

Shyness in Children consists of three assignments focused on description, positive reframing, and prescription of this symptom (3 assignments)

Sibling Rivalry consists of three assignments focused on description, positive reframing, and prescription of this symptom (3 assignments)

Stealing consists of three assignments focused on description, positive reframing, and prescription of this symptom (3 assignments)

Time-Out Procedures is for parent(s) of preschool and elementary school children (4 assignments)

Verbal Abuse consists of three assignments focused on description, positive reframing, and prescription of this symptom (3 assignments)

REFERENCES

Albee, G. W. (1997). The radicals made us do it! Or is mental health a socialist plot! *Contemporary Psychology, 42*, 891–892.

Allport, G. W. (1942). *The use of personal documents in psychological science*. New York: Social Science Research Council.

Birren, J. E., & Hedlund, B. (1987). Contributions of autobiography to developmental psychology. In N. Eisenberg (Ed.), *Contemporary topics in developmental psychology* (pp. 394–415). New York: Wiley.

Bloom, B. L. (1992). Computer-assisted psychological intervention: A review and commentary. *Clinical Psychology Review, 12*, 169–197.

Bradley, V. A., Welch, J. L., & Skilbeck, C. E. (1993). *Cognitive retraining using microcomputers*. Hillsdale, NJ: Erlbaum.

Chaiken, S., & Trope, Y. (Eds.). (1999). *Dual-process theories in social psychology*. New York: Guilford.

Clemens, M., & Hales, D. (1997, September). How healthy are we? *Parade Magazine, 7*, 4–6.

Esterling, B. A., L'Abate, L., Murray, E. J., & Pennebaker, J. W. (1999). Empirical foundations for writing in prevention and psychotherapy: Mental and physical health outcomes. *Clinical Psychology Review, 19*, 79–96.

Hays, K. E. (1999). *Working it out: Using exercise in psychotherapy*. Washington, DC: American Psychological Association.

Jensen, P. S., Josephson, A. M., & Frey, J., III. (1989). Informed consent as a framework for treatment: Ethical and therapeutic considerations. *American Journal of Psychotherapy, 48*, 378–386.

Johnston, T. B., Levis, M. M., & L'Abate, L. (1987). Treatment of depression in a couple with systematic homework assignments. *Journal of Psychotherapy and the Family, 2*, 117–128.

Jordan, K. B., & L'Abate, L. (1995). Programmed writing and therapy with symbiotically enmeshed patients. *American Journal of Psychotherapy, 49*, 225–236.

L'Abate, L. (1984). Beyond paradox: Issues of control. *American Journal of Family Therapy, 12*, 12–20.

L'Abate, L. (1986). *Systematic family therapy*. New York: Brunner/Mazel.

L'Abate, L. (1990). *Building family competence: Strategies of primary and secondary prevention*. Thousand Oaks, CA: Sage.

L'Abate, L. (1991). The use of writing in psychotherapy. *American Journal of Psychotherapy, 45*, 87–98.

L'Abate, L. (1992). *Programmed writing: A self-administered approach for interventions with individuals, couples, and families*. Pacific Grove, CA: Brooks/Cole.

L'Abate, L. (1994). *A theory of personality development*. New York: Wiley.

L'Abate, L. (1997a). Distance writing and computer-assisted training. In S. R. Sauber (Ed.), *Managed mental health care: Major diagnostic and treatment approaches* (pp. 133–163). Bristol, PA: Brunner/Mazel.

L'Abate, L. (1997b). *Manual: Distance writing and computer-assisted interventions in mental health.* Atlanta, GA: Workbooks for Better Living.

L'Abate, L. (1997c). *The self in the family: A classification of personality, criminality, and psychopathology.* New York: Wiley.

L'Abate, L. (1999a). Increasing intimacy in couples through distance writing and face-to-face approaches. In J. Carlson & L. Sperry (Eds.), *The intimate couple* (pp. 328–340). Philadelphia, PA: Brunner/Mazel.

L'Abate, L. (1999b). Structured enrichment and distance writing with couples. In R. Berger & M. T. Hannah (Eds.), *Preventive approaches in couples therapy* (pp. 106–124). Philadelphia, PA: Brunner/Mazel.

L'Abate, L. (1999c). Taking the bull by the horns: Beyond talk in psychological interventions. *The Family Journal: Counseling and Therapy for Couples and Families, 7,* 206–220.

L'Abate, L., Boyce, J., L. Fraizer, & Russ, D. (1992). Programmed writing: Research in progress. *Comprehensive Mental Health Care, 2,* 45–62.

Marks, I., Shaw, S., & Parkin, R. (1998). Computer-aided treatments of mental health problems. *Clinical Psychology: Science and Practice, 5,* 151–170.

Maruish, M. E. (1st ed. 1994, 2nd ed. 1999). *The use of psychological testing for treatment planning and outcome assessment.* Mahwah, NJ: LEA.

Nickelson, D. W. (1998). Telehealth and the evolving health care system: Strategic opportunities for professional psychology. *Professional Psychology: Research and Practice, 29,* 527–535.

Ornstein, R. (1997). *The right mind: Making sense of the hemispheres.* New York: Harcourt Brace.

Pearson, L. (Ed.). (1965). *The use of written communications in psychotherapy.* Springfield, IL: Thomas.

Pennebaker, J. W. (1997). *Opening up: The healing power of confiding in others.* New York: Guilford.

Phillips, E. L., & Wiener, D. N. (1966). *Short-term psychotherapy and structured behavior change.* New York: McGraw-Hill.

Riordan, R. J. (1996). Scriptotherapy: Therapeutic writing as a counseling adjunct. *Journal of Counseling & Development, 74,* 263–269.

Schiffer, F. (1998). *Of two minds: The revolutionary science of dual-brain psychology.* New York: The Free Press.

Schwartz, M. C. (1984). *Using computers in clinical practice: Psychotherapy and mental health applications.* New York: Haworth.

Shapiro, D. H., Jr., & Astin, J. (1998). *Control therapy: An integrated approach to psychotherapy, health, and healing.* New York: Wiley.

Smyth, J. M. (1998). Written emotional expression: Effect sizes, outcome types, and moderating variables. *Journal of Consulting and Clinical Psychology, 66,* 174–178.

Stamm, B. H. (1998). Clinical applications of telehealth in mental health care. *Professional Psychology: Research and Practice, 29,* 536–542.

Torrey, E. F. (1997). *Out of the shadows: Confronting America's mental health crisis.* New York: Wiley.

Wiener, D. J. (Ed.). (1999). *Beyond talk therapy: Using movements and expressive techniques in clinical practice.* Washington, DC: American Psychological Association.

CHAPTER 2

Explorations into the Health Benefits of Disclosure: Inhibitory, Cognitive, and Social Processes

James W. Pennebaker

Writing or talking about upsetting experiences can have a profound effect on individuals' emotional, physical, and social worlds. The remarkable impact of disclosure is only now starting to be appreciated. Indeed, among those of us examining this phenomenon, the direct and subtle effects of disclosure have only gradually come to light over the past several years. Although it is now clear that writing or talking about emotional upheavals can improve physical and mental health, it is still not clear how and why it works. Over the past several years, three factors have surfaced as likely processes that may influence the disclosure-health link: reductions in inhibition, changes in the cognitive structure of an event, and, most recently, alterations in individuals' social worlds. In this chapter, a brief history of the disclosure research is introduced. As will be seen, inherent in this history are attempts to better understand the inhibitory, cognitive, and social correlates of disclosure.

Beginning in the late 1970s, my research team was studying how people perceive their physical symptoms and emotions. This work naturally led us to explore how we come to know whether we are hungry or not. As part of this work, I had a large number of students helping me. One day, a student came by my office to describe how her roommate was eating large amounts of food and then vomiting it as a way to maintain her weight. I was shocked, and later told my research group about this story. This, of course, turned out to be bulimia. In any case, we started a large-scale questionnaire survey to explore the eating habits of students on campus. The questionnaire we developed was 12 pages long and included a large number of very personal questions that people usually don't ask. Among the items, we included the following: "Prior to the age of 17, did you ever have a traumatic sexual experience: ____yes ____no."

We were amazed by the response we got. Approximately 15% of the respondents answered yes. Although the response to the question was not related to bulimia, it was strongly related to people's reports of health. That is, those who said that they had had a childhood sexual trauma were far more likely to have been to the doctor for a variety of health problems. About this time, I was contacted by the popular magazine, *Psychology Today*, because they were doing a special issue on health. I asked them to include the traumatic sexual abuse question. We received over 24,000 responses, and this time found that 22% of females and 11% of males reported that they had had a sexual trauma. Again, those who responded yes to the item were far more likely to have been hospitalized in the past year, to have been diagnosed with cancer, high blood pressure, ulcers, flu, both major and minor health problems.

After getting these first results, we asked the question: What was unique about traumatic sexual experiences? Was it that any issues surrounding sexuality provoked illness? Or was it something about sexual issues, such as their secretiveness, that resulted in stress? Later surveys indicated that it wasn't sexual experiences per se. Rather, sexual traumas were somewhat unique in that people were far less likely to talk with others about their experiences. In fact, when we surveyed hundreds of adults and students, we discovered that it didn't make any difference what kind of trauma the person had experienced. Rather, it was whether or not they had talked about it that determined their long-term health.

Our surveys have consistently found that people who do not confide about traumatic experiences are at greater risk for health problems than people who have had the same traumas but who did confide them. And both groups are at greater risk than those who have not had a trauma (for a summary of the research on trauma surveys, confiding, and health, see Pennebaker, 1993, 1997).

THE BEGINNING: INHIBITION THEORY

This and several other surveys led us to begin to develop a general theory of inhibition. Although I now realize that this explanation is only partially correct (we now think that inhibition is only part of the problem), it served as an excellent starting point. We will also be exploring both the cognitive and social dimensions of this problem later. For the time being, however, the inhibition theory works like this:

To actively inhibit ongoing thoughts, emotions, or behaviors requires work—physiological work. We can see the work of inhibition in autonomic nervous system activity as well as brain and even hormonal activity. Over time, inhibition serves as a long-term, cumulative, low-level stressor that affects the body. This inhibitory stress, then, can cause or exacerbate a number of psychosomatic illnesses. The reverse side of this theory is that if we can get people to stop inhibiting, their health should improve.

Beginning in the mid-1980s, we wanted to test this idea experimentally. To do this, we decided to bring people into the laboratory and have them disclose deeply upsetting experiences that they had previously been inhibiting. We went on the assumption that all people have had upsetting experiences that they have not been able to confide openly with others. However, if given the opportunity to disinhibit or in some way disclose, they should show health improvements.

The basic technique was straightforward. Students were brought into the laboratory and were told that they would be participating in a study wherein they would write about an assigned topic for four consecutive days for 15 minutes each day. They were assured that their writing would be anonymous and that they would not receive any feedback on it. As far as they knew, the purpose of the project was to learn more about writing and psychology. The only rule about the writing assignment was that once they began writing, they were to continue to do so without stopping without regard to spelling, grammar, or sentence structure. Participants were then randomly assigned to either an experimental group or a control group.

Those in the experimental group were asked to spend each session writing about one or more traumatic experiences in their lives. In the words of the experimenter:

For the next four days, I would like for you to write about your very deepest thoughts and feelings about the most traumatic experience of your entire life. In your writing, I'd like you to really let go and explore your very deepest emotions and thoughts. You might tie your topic to your relationships with others, including parents, lovers, friends, or relatives, to your past, your present, or your future, or to who you have been, who you would like to be, or who you are now. You may write about the same general issues or experiences on all days of writing or on different traumas each day. All of your writing will be completely confidential.

Those in the control condition were asked to write about nonemotional topics for 15 minutes on all four days of the study. Examples of their assigned writing topics included describing the laboratory room in which they were seated or their own living room. One group, then, was encouraged to delve into their emotions and the other was to describe objects and events dispassionately.

The first writing study yielded astounding results. Most striking was that beginning college students immediately took to the task of writing. Although many in the experimental condition cried, the vast majority reported that they found the writing to be extremely valuable and meaningful. Indeed, 98 percent of the experimental participants said that, if given the choice, they would participate in the study again. Most surprising was the nature of the writing itself. The students, who tended to come from upper-middle-class backgrounds, described

Figure 2–1
Monthly Health Center Visits: Across Four Studies

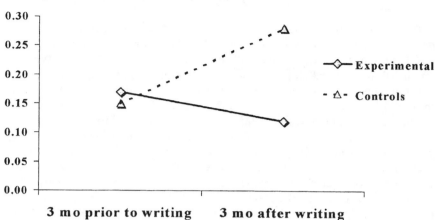

a painful array of tragic and depressing stories. Rape, family violence, suicide attempts, drug problems, and other horrors were common topics. Indeed, approximately half of the people wrote about experiences that any clinician would agree were truly traumatic (for summary of this research, see Pennebaker, 1997).

What made this first experiment so compelling, however, was not just the narratives themselves. Rather, we were primarily interested in how the writing exercise influenced physical health. During the school year, we followed the students' illness visits to the university health center in the months before and after the experiment. We discovered that those who had written about their thoughts and feelings drastically reduced their doctor visit rates after the study compared to control participants who had written about trivial topics (Figure 2–1). Confronting traumatic experiences had a salutary effect on physical health.

Soon after this first study, we sought to learn if writing affected more than just physician visits. Did it directly influence biological processes? To test this idea, I was able to team up with Jan Kiecolt-Glaser and Ron Glaser, two highly regarded psychoneuroimmunologists from Ohio State University. We conducted another writing study with 50 students wherein half wrote about traumas and the other half about superficial topics for 20 minutes on four consecutive days. In the study, we also drew blood from participants before writing, after the last day of writing, and again six weeks later. The blood was sent to Ohio State University, where the laboratory first separated out the white blood cells and then put a fixed number of these cells from each person into 81 separate tiny dishes. At this point, different "foreign agents" or mitogens were placed in the tiny dishes and allowed to incubate for two days. We were able to learn the degree to which certain white blood cells—t-helper lymphocytes—were able to grow in response to the mitogens. As predicted, participants who wrote about traumatic topics showed significant enhancements in t-lymphocyte growth compared to controls (Pennebaker, Kiecolt-Glaser, & Glaser, 1988).

The writing paradigm, then, proved to be affecting not just physician visits but basic biological processes related to the immune system. At this point, we started to investigate how writing was influencing people's behavior. For example, we conducted one study asking new college students to write about their thoughts and feelings about coming to college. In that study, we found that not only did writing influence doctor visits, but the students made better grades than those in our control groups.

It was about this time that I was contacted by Stephanie Spera, a psychologist who worked at an outplacement company in Dallas. Outplacement companies are quite popular during economic hard times. An outplacement company is an independent company that makes a contract with a large corporation that is in the process of laying people off because of economic difficulties in the company. The outplacement company agrees to take those people who have been laid off and give them small offices with telephones and help them find new jobs. When Spera called me, she had been dealing with a group of about 100 male engineers who had recently been laid off by a large computer company. Three months after the layoff, none had found jobs. She was curious if writing would help them in coping with their job loss.

We joined together and recruited 63 engineers, with a mean age of about 50 years old, to write about either their deepest thoughts and feelings about getting laid off or about how they used their time (the control condition) for five consecutive days for 30 minutes a day. In addition, we had a no-writing control condition as well. (As a side note here, asking people to write about using their time was an idea that has become very popular in the United States—a strategy called time management. Over the years, I have struggled with this movement because it has been accepted uncritically as being valuable when, in fact, it has never helped anyone in our studies. Indeed, we now use it as our standard control group because people think it works, even though it doesn't.)

In this project, we found that those who wrote about their deepest thoughts and feelings were far more successful at finding jobs. Three months after writing, about one-third of the men in the experimental group had jobs compared with only about 5% of those in the controls. Eight months after the study, 52% in the experimental group and only about 20% of those in the control groups had jobs. Interestingly, the outplacement company kept detailed records on the people in our study. The three groups did not differ on number of days they came into the office, number of letters sent, number of phone calls, and, most important, number of job interviews they went to. The only difference among the three groups was number of job offers they received (Spera, Buhrfeind, & Pennebaker, 1994).

We think the secret to this study was anger. All of these men were extremely angry about being laid off by their company. In all likelihood, writing about the emotional aspects of losing their jobs helped them to come to terms with the experience. The control subjects, however, continued to be bitter and angry. When they went to job interviews, at some point they probably expressed their anger at their old company. This behavior probably made them much less attractive prospective employees.

Taken together, these studies are all painting the same picture: writing about emotional experiences can have positive effects on physical health, biological activity, and behaviors. These studies were some of the first that we conducted. In the past ten years, it has been very exciting to see a number of projects conducted by many labs around the world replicate and extend these findings. Let me very briefly summarize some of these newer studies.

Benefits across different populations. Writing benefits a variety of groups of individuals beyond undergraduate college students. Positive health and behavioral effects have been found with maximum security prisoners, medical students, community-based samples of distressed crime victims, asthma and arthritis sufferers, men laid off from their jobs, and women who have recently given birth to their first child. These effects have been found in all social classes and major racial/ethnic groups in the United States, and in samples in Mexico City, New Zealand, French-speaking Belgium, the Netherlands, Spain, and Japan. For a recent summary of some of these studies, see Smyth (1998).

Impact on the immune system. Writing influences more than just physician visits. Four different laboratories report that writing produces positive effects on blood markers of immune function. Several studies have also found that writing or talking about emotional topics influences immune function in beneficial ways, including t-helper cell growth, antibody response to the Epstein-Barr virus, antibody response to hepatitis B vaccinations, raw t-lymphocyte counts, and even liver enzyme function (cf. Petrie, Booth, & Pennebaker, 1998; Smyth, 1998).

Short- and long-term mood effects of writing. Despite the clear health and behavioral effects, writing about traumatic experiences tends to make people feel more unhappy and distressed in the hours after writing. These emotions, in many ways, can be viewed as appropriate to the topics the individuals are confronting. When questionnaires are administered to participants at least two weeks after the studies, however, experimental volunteers report being as happy or happier than controls. Interestingly, among highly distressed samples, such as the unemployed engineers, writing about losing their jobs produced immediate improvements in moods compared to controls. Emotional state after writing depends on how participants are feeling prior to writing: the better they feel before writing, the worse they feel afterward and vice versa.

BEYOND INHIBITION: COGNITIVE ORGANIZATION

Although I am now convinced that writing about upsetting experiences has profound effects on health, it is clear that our original ideas about inhibition were inadequate. When we would try to tap the degree to which people were inhibited or changed in their inhibitions from before to after writing, our effects rarely came out. Something more was going on. Indeed, when we talked to participants in the weeks and months after writing, they said it was helpful because it helped them to understand themselves, their situation, or their emotions better. They kept using words like "understanding," "realize," "come to terms," "getting past" at high rates. There was something very cognitive going on besides just a reduction in inhibition.

As we began to study the ways people wrote, it was clear that the act of constructing stories is a natural human process that helps individuals to understand their experiences and themselves. This process allows one to organize and remember events in a coherent fashion, while integrating thoughts and feelings. In essence, this gives individuals a sense of predictability and control over their lives. Once an experience has structure and meaning, it would follow that the emotional effects of that experience are more manageable. Constructing stories facilitates a sense of resolution, which results in fewer ruminations and eventually allows disturbing experiences to gradually subside from conscious thought. Painful events that are not structured into a narrative format may contribute to the continued experience of negative thoughts and feelings. Indeed, one of the most prevalent reasons why people begin therapy is because they report suffering from emotional distress. Disclosure is unequivocally at the core of therapy. Psychotherapy usually involves putting together a story that will explain and organize major life events causing distress.

One of our first systematic approaches to understanding the potential cognitive benefits of writing was to examine the essays themselves. Independent raters initially compared the writing samples of people whose health subsequently improved after the experiment with those whose health remained unchanged. Essays from those who improved were judged to be more self-reflective, emotionally open, and thoughtful. Not being content with clinical evaluations, we decided to subject the essays to computer text analyses to learn if language use could predict improvements in health among people who had written about emotional topics.

No standard computer programs existed that specifically measured emotional and cognitive categories of word usage. Martha Francis and other students and I spent three years developing a computer program called Linguistic Inquiry and Word Count (LIWC) that analyzed essays in text format (Pennebaker & Francis, 1999). LIWC was developed by having groups of judges evaluate the degree to which over 2,000 words or words stems were related to each of several dozen categories. Although there are now over 70 word categories in the most recent version of the LIWC program, only four were of primary interest to us. Two of the categories were emotion dimensions and two were cognitive. The emotion categories included negative emotion words (e.g., sad, angry) and positive emotion words (e.g., happy, laugh).

Although using this methodology to assess emotional expression is not without flaws, it does provide a systematic index of the extent to which the two categories of emotion words are used by subjects. The two cognitive categories, causal and insight words, were intended to capture the degree to which participants were actively thinking in their writing. The casual words (e.g., because, reason) were included because they implied people were attempting to put together causes and reasons for the events and emotions that they were describing. The insight words (e.g., understand, realize) reflected the degree to which individuals were specifically referring to cognitive processes associated with thinking. For each essay that a person wrote, we were able to quickly compute the percentage of total words that these and other linguistic categories represented.

The LIWC program allowed us to go back to previous writing studies and link word usage among individuals in the experimental conditions with various health and behavioral outcomes. To date, the most extensive reanalysis of data concerns six writing studies: two studies involving college students writing about traumas where blood immune measures were collected, two studies where first-year college students wrote about their deepest thoughts and feelings about coming to college, one study by maximum security prisoners in a state penitentiary, and one study using professionals who had unexpectedly been laid off from their jobs after over 20 years of employment.

Analyzing the use of negative and positive emotion words, two important findings were revealed. First, the more that people used positive emotion words, the more their health improved. Negative emotion word use also predicted health changes, but in an unexpected way. Individuals who used a moderate number of negative emotions in their writing about upsetting topics evidenced the greatest drops in physician visits in the months after writing. That is, those people who used a very high rate of negative emotion words and those who used very few were the most likely to have continuing health problems after participating in the study. Further, the use of the two types of emotion words was uncorrelated, and the rates of usage did not tend to change appreciably over the days of writing. In other words, those people who tended to use many words in the positive category and a moderate amount in the negative category had the greatest health improvements.

In many ways, these findings are consistent with other literatures. Individuals who tend to use few negative emotion words are undoubtedly most likely to be characterized as repressive copers—people who have been defined as poor at being able to identify and label their emotional states. Those who overuse negative emotion words may well be the classic high neurotic or, high negative affect individuals. These individuals are people who ponder their negative emotions in exhaustive detail and who may simply be in a recursive loop of complaining without attaining closure. Indeed, this may be exacerbated by the inability of these individuals to develop a story or narrative. A high rate of positive emotion word use coupled with some negative emotion words suggests there is an acknowledgement of problems with a concomitant sense of optimism.

Although the findings concerning emotion words use (shown in Figure 2–2) were intriguing, the results surrounding the cognitive word categories were even more robust. Recall that in our studies, people wrote for three to five days, 15 to 30 minutes per day. As they wrote, they gradually changed what they said

Figure 2–2
Language Dimensions Predicting Health

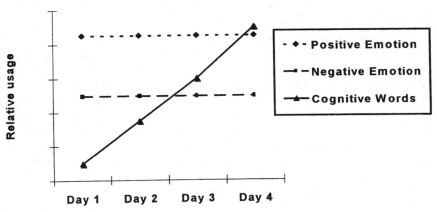

and how they said it. The LIWC analyses showed strong and consistent effects for changes in insight and causal words over the course of writing. Specifically, people whose health improved, who got higher grades, and who found jobs after writing went from using relatively few causal and insight words to using a high rate of them by the last day of writing. In reading the essays of people who showed this pattern of language use, it became apparent that they were constructing a story over time. Building a narrative, then, seemed to be critical in reaching understanding. Interestingly, those people who started the study with a coherent story that explained some past experience did not benefit from writing.

These findings are consistent with current views on narrative and psychotherapy in suggesting that it is critical for clients to confront their anxieties and problems by creating a story to explain and understand past and current life concerns. The story can be in the form of an autobiography or even a third-person narrative. Interestingly, our data indicate that merely having a story may not be sufficient to ensure good health. A story that may have been constructed when the person was young or in the midst of a trauma may be insufficient later in life when new information is discovered or broader perspectives are adopted. In our studies, as in narrative therapies, then, the act of constructing the stories is associated with mental and physical health improvement. A constructed story, then, is a type of knowledge that helps to organize the emotional effects of an experience as well as the experience itself.

Toward a Theory of Social Integration

Consider what has been discussed so far. Having a traumatic experience can be tremendously disruptive for many reasons. If the person is unable to talk about it, he or she must actively hold back from telling others—a form of inhibition. But not talking is also blocking a basic cognitive process. That is, if I can't tell you about my traumatic experience, it will be much more difficult to reach some kind of cognitive meaning or understanding. Clearly, both the increased inhibitory work along with the failure to come to some kind of cognitive closure or coherence will be additional stress.

But there is something equally troublesome. If I have a traumatic experience and can't tell anyone about it, no one in my social world will know what I'm thinking and feeling. I will be preoccupied with the emotional event. The longer I have to live with this secret, the more detached I will be from others in my social world. Almost by definition, I will become more and more isolated. I'll be a poor listener, and will be guarded in my discussions with others.

The sociologist Émile Durkheim (1951) talked about this phenomenon in his analysis of suicide. That is, people who became less socially integrated were the ones most likely to kill themselves. Social integration, then, is a key to psychological and, I think, physical health. Is it possible that one of the health benefits from writing is that people are better able to connect or integrate with others afterward? If so, how do we capture this?

This past year, we have been developing a new measurement technique that attempts to catch how people naturally talk and interact with others in their world. Working with an engineer, we have developed the Electronically Activated Recorder (EAR). The EAR is a simple tape recorder with a small computer chip attached to it. The EAR is activated and records for about 30 seconds and then goes off for about 12 minutes. This cycle continues for two days or as long as the participants wear it. The EAR is small, light in weight, and not intrusive. Because of the small external microphone, we are able to pick up snippets of people's conversations as well as determine where they are and what they are doing.

The EAR technology is fascinating because, for the first time, we are able to see how people might change after participating in the writing study. Our first experiment using this technique was conducted by Matthias Mehl and me this past year. Approximately 50 students wrote about either traumatic or time management topics for three days. Two weeks before writing and again two weeks after writing, students wore the EAR for two consecutive days. The EAR recordings were later transcribed and judged by the transcribers about the settings and actions of the EAR-wearers. At this time, we only have complete data sets for the first 18 participants. Even with this small initial sample, however, we are finding significant effects.

The first standard finding is that people who wrote about traumatic experiences are demonstrating significant drops in resting levels of both systolic and diastolic blood pressure from two weeks before to two weeks after writing. Similarly, as in other studies, the emotional writing is associated with markers of better psychological and physical health.

More striking, however, are the results from the EAR. In analyzing people's language in their natural conversation, trauma writers are evidencing an increasing use of positive emotion words and laughter from before to after writing. Similarly, writing about emotion is getting these first-year college students to talk more in the present tense and less in the past. In other words, when people are able to come to terms with past experiences, they no longer focus on the past to the same degree. Finally, and in many ways most important, trauma writers are spending a significantly greater amount of time talking to other people from before to after writing. In short, writing about traumatic experiences is having a direct impact on people's social lives. They are more integrated and connected with others.

This most recent research is extremely encouraging on several levels. It is the first time we have been able to show relatively long-term and concrete effects on normal social behavior. In some ways, these measures are striking because we do not find self-reported differences. That is, when we ask students about their interactions with others both before and after writing, they don't see or report any differences. Although they don't detect any differences, we are detecting them.

Discussion: Putting It All Together

Since the beginning of our inhibition research in the 1980s, we have made a full circle. We began with the observation that a traumatic experience that was not confided served as a significant health risk. This failure to confide was often the result of intense social pressures to maintain secrecy or, in some way, the status quo of family relationships, friendships, or saving face. This not confiding required a great deal of inhibitory work.

By the same token, not confiding blocked the natural cognitive processes normally associated with talking about important experiences. We know that putting emotional experiences into words helps to organize and understand them. Not confiding, by definition, hampered this process. Indeed, all our work on language use when people wrote pointed to the importance of writing and thinking about things in particular ways. Further, the failure to adequately put events into language prolonged health problems.

And now we are discovering that not confiding important topics is associated with social disintegration—the inability to be honest and open with others, contributing to a sense of social isolation. By putting emotional events into language, we are now finding that we are completing the circle. When we write about upsetting experiences, we no longer need to inhibit, we find cognitive coherence and closure, and we are able to return to our normal, healthy social lives.

NOTE

Preparation of this chapter was aided by a grant from the National Institutes of Health (MH 52391).

REFERENCES

Durkheim, E. (1951). *Suicide*. New York: Free Press.

Pennebaker, J. W. (1993). Mechanisms of social constraint. In D. M. Wegner & J. W. Pennebaker (Eds.), *Handbook of mental control* (pp. 200–219). Englewood Cliffs, NJ: Prentice Hall.

Pennebaker, J. W. (1997). *Opening up: The healing power of expressing emotions* (Rev. ed.). New York: Guilford.

Pennebaker, J. W., & Francis, M. E. (1999). *Linguistic Inquiry and Word Count (LIWC): A computer-based text analysis program*. Mahwah, NJ: Erlbaum.

Pennebaker, J. W., Kiecolt-Glaser, J., & Glaser, R. (1988). Disclosure of traumas and immune function: Health implications for psychotherapy. *Journal of Consulting and Clinical Psychology, 56*, 239–245.

Pennebaker, J. W., & King, L. A. (1999). Linguistic styles: Language use as an individual difference. *Journal of Personality and Social Psychology, 77*, 1296–1312.

Pennebaker, J. W., Mayne, T. J., & Francis, M. E. (1997). Linguistic predictors of adaptive bereavement. *Journal of Personality and Social Psychology, 72*, 863–871.

Petrie, K. P., Booth, R. J., & Pennebaker, J. W. (1998). The immunological effects of thought suppression. *Journal of Personality and Social Psychology, 75*, 1264–1272.

Smyth, J. M. (1998). Written emotional expression: Effect sizes, outcome types, and moderating variables. *Journal of Consulting & Clinical Psychology, 66*, 174–184.

Smyth, J. M., Stone, A. A., Hurewitz, A., & Kaell, A. (1999). Effects of writing about stressful experiences on symptom reduction in patients with asthma or rheumatoid arthritis: A randomized trial. *JAMA: Journal of the American Medical Association, 281*, 1304–1309.

Spera, S. P., Buhrfeind, E. D., & Pennebaker, J. W. (1994). Expressive writing and coping with job loss. *Academy of Management Journal, 37*, 722–733.

PART II

Research Foundations

CHAPTER 3

Focused Expressive Writing, Immune Functions, and Physical Illness

Brian A. Esterling and James W. Pennebaker

The role of emotional expression in the study and practice of psychology has been considered essential to improved mental and physical health outcomes, whereas inhibition of emotion has been considered deleterious (e.g., Breuer & Freud, 1895/1966; Rachman, 1980; Scheff, 1979), as already reviewed in the previous chapter. However, it bears repeating that this hypothesis has been further supported by recent evidence suggesting that emotional expression has salutary health effects (e.g., Esterling, Antoni, Kumar, & Schneiderman, 1990; Kelley, Lumley, & Leisen, 1997; Murray, Lamnin, & Carver, 1989; Spiegel, Bloom, Kraemer, & Gottheil, 1989), while emotional inhibition has detrimental effects (e.g., Jamner, Schwartz, & Leigh, 1988; Jensen, 1987; Larsen, 1990). One mechanism of emotional expression, which has recently been investigated, is focused expressive writing (FEW)—writing about one's past and present traumas. FEW allows one to organize and remember events in a coherent fashion, while integrating thoughts and feelings. In essence, this process gives individuals a sense of predictability and control over their lives. FEW facilitates a sense of resolution, which results in less rumination and eventually allows disturbing experiences to gradually subside from conscious thought. Painful events that are not structured into a narrative format may contribute to the continued experience of negative thoughts and feelings.

Since 1986, studies have explored the value of FEW for dealing with past traumatic experiences and enhancing physical health outcomes. Across the various studies, it has become evident that the FEW paradigm was quite powerful in bringing about clinically meaningful effects. For instance, experimental respondents asked to write about traumatic experiences evidenced significant drops in physician visits in the six months following study completion compared with various control groups (Pennebaker & Beall, 1986). Using this same basic paradigm, Greenberg and Stone (1992) found a drop in physician visits for students who wrote about deeply traumatic events compared with control respondents who wrote about either relatively mild traumas or superficial topics. Using a sample of 41 university employees, Francis and Pennebaker (1992) found that those who wrote about traumas once a week for four consecutive weeks had fewer absentee days and improved liver enzyme function (serum glutamic-oxaloacetic transaminase and serum glutamic-pyruvic transaminase) in the two months after writing, compared to controls. Recently, Smyth (1998) has reported the results of a meta-analysis of over a dozen writing studies conducted across multiple labs and has found that the effect size for physical health outcomes of the writing intervention are comparable to those of psychotherapy.

Despite these beneficial effects of writing, it is not entirely clear why writing brings about such striking physical health changes. A number of investigators point to the critical role of cognitive changes brought about by writing. In two studies by Murray and his colleagues (Donnelly & Murray, 1991; Murray et al., 1989), reviewed in greater detail in Chapter 4, students either wrote or talked to a therapist about a trauma or about superficial topics. In addition to greater emotional expression in the two trauma conditions, students who wrote or talked about upheavals evidenced greater cognitive changes across the four days of the study. Cognitive change was measured by judges who evaluated transcripts on the degree to which they exhibited better understanding of the problem and the awareness of alternative explanations for the upheavals. Post-experimental self-reports of cognitive change were also apparent in the groups writing or talking about traumas. Other studies bolster these findings in that respondents who write about traumas spontaneously report that writing forced them to think about the events differently (Pennebaker, 1989).

In understanding the broad issue of cognitive change, it is imperative to appreciate that a traumatic experience affects individuals on multiple levels, including attempts to understand the meaning and significance of the event itself as well as the emotional responses to it (Silver, Boon, & Stones, 1983). Cognitive processing must incorporate both emotions and perceived objective features of the event. For example, Pennebaker and Beall (1986) asked students to write about a traumatic event from one of three perspectives: focus only on the facts surrounding the trauma, focus only on the emotions, or focus on both. Respondents who only wrote about the facts were indistinguishable from controls that wrote about superficial topics across a variety of outcomes. The emotion-focus group reported the study to be valuable but showed no long-term physical health improvements. Only those people who wrote about both the facts of the trauma and their emotional responses exhibited long-term mental and physical health benefits.

For researchers, the definition and measurement of long-term cognitive change as the mediator of greater physical health outcomes is a daunting task. One problem has been defining what dimensions of mental activity best predict long-term improvement. For example, does writing about an event and its associated emotions help to form a coherent schema of it? Once the schema has been formed and reinforced, the individual may be able to efficiently assimilate trauma-related reminders or experiences (Markus, 1977). Therefore, less effortful processing may be associated with lower chronic stress levels and thus less physical illness.

A related cognitive factor relevant to the FEW procedure concerns the nature of chronic construct accessibility. Several researchers have reported that constructs that are chronically accessible to individuals may remain for weeks or even years (Higgins, 1989; Higgins, King, & Mavin, 1982; Fazio, 1986). Furthermore, chronically accessible constructs have been shown to guide the processing of information in a stable manner over time (Lau, 1989). On the surface, one would assume that writing about an event would make the event more broadly accessible. That is, after writing, individuals should be able to identify and recall more dimensions of the traumatic experience. It would also follow that heightened accessibility over time would become automatic, thereby associated with less effortful, conscious processing of the written trauma.

A third cognitive factor relevant to FEW was that the mere act of writing might alter the way the event is represented and organized in memory. Indeed, a basic assumption of conversation is that when ideas are communicated, they require coherence, self-reflection, and the use of multiple perspectives (Clark, 1993; Freyd, 1993). Coherence subsumes several characteristics, including structure, use of causal explanation, repetition of themes, and an appreciation of the listener's perspective. Furthermore, conveying of stories to others typically requires an ordered sequence of events (Labov & Fanshel, 1977). Writing, like talking, forces a structure on an otherwise overwhelming and oftentimes chaotic experience.

In addition to using language to understand and explain events, translating emotions into language alters inchoate feeling states into conscious verbal labels. In fact, recent research suggests that the mere labeling of an emotion may actually reduce its perceived intensity (Berkowitz & Troccoli, 1990; Keltner, Locke, & Audrain, 1993; Schwarz, 1990). In everyday speech, the labeling of emotional experience should be apparent by simply analyzing the use of emotion words (e.g., angry, sad, happy, love).

Beginning in 1989, a series of studies were designed to get a better understanding of writing on physical health outcomes (Pennebaker, 1989). However, several hypotheses failed to adequately explain the value of FEW. Initially, it was hypothesized that FEW could provide positive outcomes by fostering healthier behaviors or lifestyles. Analyses of self-reports from several writing studies, however, failed to confirm this explanation (Pennebaker, 1993). That is, people continued to smoke, exercise, and sleep at rates comparable to control respondents. A second hypothesis was that FEW caused individuals to change the ways in which trauma-relevant events were represented in memory or consciousness. However, no effects emerged on a reaction time task even though health improvements were found (Pennebaker & Francis, 1996). The third hypothesis was that people who got better after FEW wrote about different topics than those who did not get better. Content analyses of the chosen topics from several studies again failed to yield any links between the topic chosen and any physical health or behavioral outcome measure.

The most encouraging explanation for the effects of FEW was that the act of converting emotions and images into words changed the way the person organized and thought about the trauma. Further, part of the distress caused by the trauma lay not just in the events but in the person's emotional reactions to them. By integrating thoughts and feelings, then, the person could more easily construct a coherent narrative of the experience. Once formed, the event could then be summarized, stored, and forgotten more efficiently. Tests of this general idea are still in progress. However, preliminary findings are encouraging.

One of the first systematic approaches to understanding the potential cognitive benefits of FEW was to examine the essays themselves. Independent raters initially compared writing samples of people whose physical health subsequently improved after writing with those whose physical health remained unchanged. Essays from those who improved were judged to be more self-reflective, emotionally open, and thoughtful. Not being content with clinical evaluations, Pennebaker and colleagues decided to subject the essays to computer text analyses to learn if language use could predict improvements in physical health among people who had written about emotional topics.

To address this issue, Pennebaker and Francis (1999) created a computer program called LIWC, which analyzed essays in text format. LIWC had been developed by having groups of judges evaluate the degree to which about 2,000 words or word stems were related to each of several dozen. The categories included negative emotion words (sad, angry), positive emotion words (happy, laugh), causal words (because, reason), and insight words (understand, realize). For each essay that a person wrote, the program was able to quickly compute the percentage of total words that represented these and other linguistic categories.

Analyzing the use of negative and positive emotion words, two important findings were revealed (Pennebaker, Mayne, & Francis, 1997). First, the more that people used positive emotion words, the more their physical health improved. Negative emotion words use also predicted physical health changes but in an unexpected way. Individuals who used a moderate number of negative emotions in their writing about upsetting topics evidenced the greatest drops in physician visits in the months after FEW. That is, those respondents who used a very high rate of negative emotion words and those who used very few were the most likely to have continuing physical health problems after participating in the study.

In many ways, these findings are consistent with other literatures. Individuals who tend to use very few negative emotion words are undoubtedly most likely to be characterized as repressive copers—people whom Weinberger, Schwartz, and Davidson (1979) have defined as poor at being able to identify and label their emotional states. Those who overuse negative emotion words may well be the classic high neurotic or high negative affect (Watson & Clark, 1984) individuals. These individuals are people who ponder their negative emotions in exhaustive detail and who may simply be in a recursive loop of complaining without attaining closure. Indeed, this may be exacerbated by the inability of these individuals to develop a story or narrative.

Although the findings concerning emotion word use were intriguing, the results surrounding the cognitive word categories were even more robust. In these studies, respondents wrote for three to five days, 15 to 30 minutes per day. As they wrote, they gradually changed what they said and how they said it. The LIWC analyses showed strong and consistent effects for changes in insight and causal words over the course of FEW. Specifically, respondents whose physical health improved, who got higher grades, and who found jobs after writing went from using relatively few causal and insight words to using a high rate of them by the last day of writing. In reading the essays of respondents who showed this pattern of language use, it became apparent that they were constructing a story over time. Building a narrative, then, seemed to be critical in reaching understanding. Interestingly, those people who started the study with a coherent story that explained some past experience did not benefit from writing (see Mahoney, 1995; Meichenbaum & Fong, 1993; Gergen & Gergen, 1988).

The language analyses are particularly promising in that they suggest that certain features of essays predict long-term physical health. Further, these features are congruent with current view on narratives in psychology. The next issue that is currently being addressed is the degree to which cohesive stories or narratives predict changes in real-world cognitive processes. That is, does a coherent story about a trauma produce improvements in physical health by reducing ruminations or flashbacks? Does a story ultimately result in the assimilation of an unexplained experience that allows people to get on with their lives?

MECHANISMS LINKING WRITING TO PHYSICAL HEALTH

Several studies have found that specific autonomic nervous system measures were associated with the inhibition and disclosure of thoughts and emotions. Wegner and his colleagues (e.g., Wegner, 1992; Wegner, Shortt, Blake, & Page, 1990) have found that the experimentally induced suppression of specific thoughts was associated with increased skin conductance level (SCL), an autonomic index associated with behavioral inhibition. Similarly, Levenson and his colleagues (e.g., Levenson, Carstensen, Friesen, & Ekman, 1991; Gross & Levenson, 1993) found that the suppression of emotions was associated with increased SCL as well as various cardiovascular changes (e.g., heart rate, pulse transit time). Finally, general disclosure of deeply traumatic experiences has been found to be linked to drops in SCL relative to the same subjects' discussing superficial topics (Pennebaker, Hughes, & O'Heeron, 1987). Interestingly, SCL appears to be more closely linked to trauma disclosure than heart rate among Holocaust survivors (Pennebaker, Barger, & Tiebout, 1989) and college students (Pennebaker et al., 1987). None of these studies, however, have focused on specific verbal content and autonomic activity.

To address the association between word usage and autonomic activity, Pennebaker and Uhlmann (1994) recruited individuals who were instructed to type their thoughts and feelings for 15 minutes into a computer. This procedure linked each word to the respondents' concurrent autonomic levels, such as SCL and heart rate. Independent judges rated each phrase along multiple dimensions based on both word usage (e.g., positive or negative emotion words) and clinical judgment (e.g., use of psychological defenses), and these data were regressed against their SCL and heart rate (Hughes, Uhlmann, & Pennebaker, 1994). The resulting analyses yielded beta weights for each respondent that allowed the determination of independent mathematical links between each linguistic dimension and autonomic level.

In these studies, SCL was found to be much more closely linked to language than was heart rate. Indeed, virtually all respondents had several significant SCL-text beta weights. The majority of respondents evidenced significant relationships with SCL, including word order in the sentence, as well as use of negative emotion and positive emotion words within phrases, causal statements, and insight statements. However, there were large individual differences in the direction of these significant effects. The expression of negative emotions was associated with increased SCL whereas the expression of positive emotions were associated with decreased SCL, suggesting that expressing something positive was safe and briefly relaxing. Causal and insight phrases were equally powerful in provoking both increased and decreased SCL.

Therefore, the effects of the typing analyses offer a promising parallel to the LIWC and judges' rating studies. Written disclosure of negative emotions tended to bring about immediate, short-term arousal whereas positive emotions provoked immediate drops in SCL. Further, cognitive phrases were strongly linked to SCL but varied in direction from person to person, a finding that is not surprising given that this dimension is only related to health over time (i.e., change, not overall effect).

Given that writing about emotions regarding a previous trauma was related to improved physical and psychological health, and that it may be mediated by changes in the autonomic nervous system, other studies have examined the impact of FEW on other moderators of physical health, namely, the immune system. Changes in behavioral and emotional states that accompany the perception of, and the effort to adapt to, environmental circumstances are accompanied by complex patterns of neuroendocrine changes. Animal and human studies implicate psychosocial factors in the predisposition to, and initiation and progression of, various pathophysiological processes, including infectious, bacterial, allergic, autoimmune, and neoplastic diseases that involve alterations in immunological defense mechanisms (Ader, Cohen, & Felten, 1991). The chain of psychophysiological events has not yet been firmly established, but changes in several components of antibody- and cell-mediated immunity have been associated with naturally occurring and experimentally induced behavioral and emotional states associated with writing.

Several studies have shown that there exists a wide degree of individual differences in the way people express emotions (e.g., Asendorpf & Scherer, 1983; Esterling, Antoni, Kumar, & Schneiderman, 1993). Such stylistic differences (e.g., repressive personality and anger suppression) have been found to be associated with greater subclinical disease progression (Antoni & Goodkin, 1991) and poorer clinical course in patients with certain types of carcinomas (Jensen, 1987; Levy, Herberman, Lippman, & d'Angelo, 1987; Pettingale, Morris, Greer, & Haybittl, 1985). In fact, metastatic breast cancer patients participating in a year-long psychosocial intervention designed, in part, to modulate emotional expression in a supportive group environment survived twice as long as those randomized to standard medical care only (Spiegel et al., 1989). Because progression of some neoplastic diseases may be mediated by cell-mediated and natural immune responses, it was reasoned that it was important to examine how emotional response styles might relate to shifts in immunologic status.

One such marker was the immune system's control over the reactivation of latent Epstein-Barr virus (EBV). EBV is widespread in the general population, which is at least 90% seropositive (Sumaya, 1986). In addition to being among the most efficient of the opportunistic pathogens, the most remarkable feature of herpes viruses such as EBV is their ability to persist in the host indefinitely (Rinaldo, 1990). When an individual is infected with EBV, seroconversion and latency results, with or without the presence of clinical disease. Under certain conditions, the latent virus will lytically replicate, although the mechanisms of reactivation are unknown. This latent state can be established in the presence of high levels of circulating antibody, suggesting that the cellular immune response is primarily responsible for controlling the latent infection.

In healthy individuals, EBV can reactivate spontaneously, and often in the absence of clinical symptoms. EBV reactivation is usually accompanied by a significant increase in specific antibody to the reactivating EBV as a consequence of antigen expression on the cell surface, even in the absence of infectious virus. Under chronic states of cellular immunodeficiency, such as in persons infected with HIV-1 or in those undergoing immunosuppressive therapy for transplantation, reactivation of EBV may result in severe morbidity and mortality (Ernberg, 1986; Rinaldo, 1990). Moreover, EBV has been shown to suppress a wide number of immunologic functions, including cytokine production and lymphocyte blastogenesis to mitogens (Rinaldo, 1990).

In one study, stable interpersonal coping styles and differential written disclosure responses indicative of emotional repression to a standardized stimulus among healthy college students were assessed. These differing styles were related to their EBV antibody response (Esterling et al., 1990). It was hypothesized that those individuals displaying less emotional disclosure on a writing task and a personality style characterized by low emotional expressivity would have the highest antibody titers to EBV (suggesting poorer immune function and greater reactivation of latent virus). Respondents completed a personality inventory and were also asked to write for 30 minutes describing a stressful/traumatic event that had happened to them previously, but which they had not yet fully disclosed to others.

Respondents with repressive personality styles (i.e., tend to deny negative feelings, attempt to appear content in the face of problems, and commonly engage in self-sacrificing behaviors) had higher levels of antibody to EBV compared to those with sensitizer styles (i.e., tend to present to others as being overbearing and aggressive, having a low frustration tolerance, and who are quick to express their negative feelings). Similarly, those who used a smaller percentage of emotional words (low disclosers) in FEW had higher antibody titers as compared to those with a higher percentage of emotional words. Interestingly, personality style interacted with behavioral performance of the written emotional disclosure task in predicting EBV antibody titers. Specifically, within the repressive personality group, the level of emotional disclosure evidenced through writing was not associated with differences in antibody titers to EBV. However, within the sensitizer personality group, those who engaged in a high degree of emotional disclosure through FEW evidenced the greatest degree of immunological control (i.e., lowest EBV antibody titers). However, the low-disclosing sensitizers had antibody levels as high as those classified as repressors. These associations held even after controlling for medication use, recent sleep loss, physical activity levels, lean body mass, caloric intake, and alcohol and recreational drug use.

These findings suggested that if individuals were aware of but chose not to disclose the emotional intensity of the stressful events through FEW because of embarrassment, fear of punishment, or other reasons, the consequence may have been to hold back or inhibit their thoughts, feelings, and behaviors from others. In fact, this pattern of inhibition may have been most salient for individuals who were especially sensitive to and aware of the impact of previously encountered environmental and emotional stressors (i.e., sensitizers). These findings supported the hypotheses that inhibiting emotional material in the face of discussing a stressful/traumatic event was associated with impaired control of latent EBV. Further, individual differences in interpersonal style (characterized by emotional repression) were associated with this immunologic measure in a similar fashion, and these two factors interacted in determining EBV antibody titers. What these findings suggested was that for individuals dealing with major stressors (e.g., HIV-1 infected gay men, couples experiencing divorce), coping strategies such as written emotional disclosure and confrontation (rather than denial) of the stressor may be associated with a normalization of immunologic control over herpes viruses such as EBV.

To test the effects of experimentally manipulating emotional expression through different mechanisms of arousal on antibody titers to EBV, an experimental study was subsequently designed. Respondents were asked to either write or talk about a stressful event in three separate emotional disclosure sessions occurring once per week over a three-week period, or write about trivial topics (Esterling, Antoni, Fletcher, Margulies, & Schneiderman, 1994). After completing demographic and behavioral questionnaires, blood was sampled just prior to randomization to groups and again one week after the final emotional disclosure session. In each of the trauma conditions, respondents were asked to recall and focus on a stressful/traumatic event that had happened to them and that they had not disclosed to many people.

As in previous work (Esterling et al., 1990), respondents were classified into one of three personality groups, and ratings of the percentages of total emotional words served as the index of emotional expressiveness on this behavioral task. Two emotional expression indices were computed with respect to valence (positive and negative emotional word use). Content ratings were also conducted on all written and verbal disclosures, using a form modified from Murray, Lamnin, and Carver (1989). Specifically, all disclosures were scored for positive cognitive appraisal change (e.g., Were alternative explanations discussed and to what degree, or was there evidence of better understanding of the problem and to what degree?), self-esteem improvements (e.g., Was there evidence that the subject felt better about or less down on himself or herself, and to what degree?), and degree to which adaptive coping strategies were discussed (e.g., Was there evidence that the respondent expressed feelings to people, became more assertive, or took more interpersonal risks?). In addition, the seriousness of the event was rated on each respondent's disclosure.

Overall, participation in either the written or verbal emotional disclosure intervention significantly decreased EBV antibody titers over the four-week observation period. Although equivalent at baseline, individuals assigned to the verbal/stressful group showed significantly lower EBV antibody titer values (i.e., better immune function) after the intervention compared to those in the written/stressful group, who had significantly lower values compared to controls. Further, it was found that respondents assigned to the written/stressful group expressed significantly more total and negative emotional words than the verbal/stressful and control groups at each time point. However, the verbal/stressful group was rated higher in cognitive change, self-esteem improvements, and adaptive coping strategies as compared with the other groups. These results suggested that ventilation of negative feelings may be the important event in written disclosure, whereas cognitive reappraisal, enhanced self-esteem, and generation of adaptive coping strategies may be achieved through verbal expression. Finally, consistent with previous studies, individuals classified as having a repressive personality style had significantly higher EBV antibody titers compared to sensitizers, suggesting a poorer immune response and greater reactivation of the latent virus. Furthermore, the fact that an interaction between personality classification and group assignment was not found suggested that both FEW and speaking about stressful events might have beneficial physiological effects independent of personality factors related to emotional proclivities.

In understanding the interactions between FEW and immune function, the literature suggests that immune function and physical health are differentially modulated depending on whether individuals are subjected to emotionally arousing situations or have an appropriate outlet for the expression of those feelings. For example, anxiety-provoking events (e.g., medical school examinations, marital disruption, or antibody testing for HIV-1) have all been associated with increased reactivation of latent EBV (i.e., poorer immune function). Therefore, these and previous data suggest that the experience of an emotion (e.g., anxiety) does not by itself have a beneficial effect on the immune response against latent viruses such as EBV; in fact, the opposite seems to be the case. On the one hand, experiencing heightened emotion without the opportunity to release or express it in a constructive manner may be detrimental to various components of the cellular immune system. On the other hand, if with heightened emotion there is an easily accessible and comfortable route of expression (e.g., FEW), disclosure may have beneficial effects in controlling EBV reactivation and, perhaps, ultimately physical symptom development.

In addition to EBV, other studies have supported the use of FEW in improving the immune system using other immune outcome markers. For example, Pennebaker, Kiecolt-Glaser, and Glaser (1988) had respondents write about either traumatic experiences or superficial topics for 15 to 20 minutes on four consecutive days; they were followed up six weeks later. Immune function was assessed by stimulating lymphocytes with one of two nonspecific mitogens, which provide a measure of global cellular immune functioning. Respondents assigned to the trauma group evidenced significant improvements in two independent markers of cellular immune function across the study period. Consistent with previous studies (Pennebaker & Beall, 1986), these respondents evidenced a drop in physician visits relative to controls. Similarly, trauma respondents reported being significantly happier than controls at the three-month follow-up. With respect to individual differences, these investigators found that within the trauma writing group, those respondents who could be classified as high-disclosers wrote significantly more emotional words and evidenced greater cellular immune function compared to their low-disclosing counterparts. These outcomes were consistent with other studies (e.g., Esterling et al., 1990, 1994), suggesting that FEW could be effective in improving cellular immune function and that those individuals who disclose a high degree of emotions through FEW may receive the greatest immune benefit. Further, there is support for the evidence that the immune outcomes may have been translated to clinical health in that those respondents who wrote about traumatic events also reported greater physical health.

To date, there has been only one study that has investigated the role of FEW on the immunological response to a viral challenge (Petrie, Booth, Pennebaker,

Davison, & Thomas, 1995). In this study, investigators studied whether written emotional expression of traumatic experiences influenced the immune response to a hepatitis B vaccination program. In this study, hepatitis B negative respondents were randomly assigned to write about personal traumatic events or control topics during four consecutive daily sessions. The day after completion of the FEW, respondents were given their first hepatitis B vaccination, with booster injections at one and four months following the writing sessions. Compared to the control group, respondents in the emotional expression group showed significantly higher antibody levels against hepatitis B at the four- and six-month follow-up periods, suggesting greater immune responsivity to the viral challenge.

CONCLUSION

There is growing support for the therapeutic and preventive use of FEW, suggesting that this process can improve mental and physical health. FEW may be providing its benefits through its association with increased insight, self-reflection, optimism, sense of control, and self-esteem. In addition, there is evidence that FEW improves organization as well as developing adaptive coping strategies. Another equally plausible explanation is that the disclosure taking place through FEW is merely another form of exposure to traumatic stimuli. In this case, respondents are reexposed time and again to the same traumatic stimuli, permitting the development of greater insight and control. Together, these changes may result in decreased depression and anxiety, as well as changes in autonomic nervous system activity. Furthermore, there is growing evidence suggesting that these changes (i.e., cognitive, behavioral, emotional), as a function of FEW, improve immune system function (e.g., reduce reactivation of latent viruses), which may be related to reductions in physical symptoms and physician visits. Given the evidence that the nervous system has been linked to immune system in a number of studies (Black, 1994a, 1994b), a mechanism exists whereby FEW may have direct effects on physical health.

REFERENCES

Ader, R., Cohen, N., & Felten, D. L. (1991). *Psychoneuroimmunology* (2nd ed.). New York: Academic.

Antoni, M. H., & Goodkin, K. (1991). The interaction of viral and psychosocial factors in the promotion of cervical neoplasia. In J. ten Have-deLabije & H. Balner (Eds.), *Coping with cancer and beyond* (pp. 99–134). Amsterdam: Swets & Zeileiner.

Asendorpf, J. B., & Scherer, K. R. (1983). The discrepant repressor: Differentiation between low anxiety, high anxiety, and repression of anxiety by autonomic-facial-verbal patterns of behavior. *Journal of Personality and Social Psychology, 45*, 1334–1346.

Berkowitz, L., & Troccoli, B. T. (1990). Feelings, direction of attention, and expressed evaluations of others. *Cognition and Emotion, 4*, 305–325.

Black, P. H. (1994a). Central nervous system-immune system interactions: Psychoneu-
roendocrinology of stress and its immune consequences. *Antimicrobial Agents
and Chemotherapy, 38,* 1–6.

Black, P. H. (1994b). Central nervous system-immune system interactions: Effect and
immunomodulatory consequences of immune system mediators on the brain. *Antimicrobial Agents and Chemotherapy, 38,* 7–12.

Breuer, J., & Freud, S. (1895/1966). *Studies on hysteria.* New York: Avon.

Clark, L. F. (1993). Stress and the cognitive-conversational benefits of social interaction.
Journal of Social and Clinical Psychology, 12, 25–55.

Donnelly, D. A., & Murray, E. J. (1991). Cognitive and emotional changes in written
essays and therapy interviews. *Journal of Social and Clinical Psychology, 10,*
334–350.

Ernberg, I. (1986). The role of Epstein-Barr virus in lymphomas of homosexual males.
In E. Klein (Ed.), *Acquired immunodeficiency syndrome* (pp. 301–318). Basel:
Karger.

Esterling, B. A., Antoni, M. H., Fletcher, M. A., Margulies, S., & Schneiderman, N.
(1994). Emotional disclosure through writing or speaking modulates latent
Epstein-Barr virus reactivation. *Journal of Consulting and Clinical Psychology,
62,* 130–140.

Esterling, B. A., Antoni, M. H., Kumar, M., & Schneiderman, N. (1990). Emotional
repression, stress disclosure responses, and Epstein-Barr viral capsid antigen titers. *Psychosomatic Medicine, 52,* 397–410.

Esterling, B. A., Antoni, M. H., Kumar, M., & Schneiderman, N. (1993). Defensiveness,
trait anxiety, and Epstein-Barr viral capsid antigen antibody titers in healthy college students. *Health Psychology, 12,* 132–139.

Fazio, R. H. (1986). How do attitudes guide behavior? In R. M. Sorrentino & E. T.
Higgins (Eds.), *Handbook of motivation and cognition: Foundations of social
behavior* (pp. 204–243). New York: Guilford.

Francis, M. E., & Pennebaker, J. W. (1992). Putting stress into words: The impact of
writing on physiological, absentee, and self-reported emotional well-being measures. *American Journal of Health Promotion, 6,* 280–287.

Freyd, J. J. (1993). Five hunches about perceptual processes and dynamic representations.
In D. E. Mayer & S. Kornblum (Eds.), *Attention and performance 14: Synergies
in experimental psychology, artificial intelligence, and cognitive neuroscience*
(pp. 99–119). Cambridge, MA: MIT.

Gergen, K. J., & Gergen, M. M. (1988). Narrative and the self as relationship. In L.
Berkowitz (Ed.), *Advances in experimental social psychology* (Vol. 21, pp. 17–
56). New York: Academic.

Greenberg, M. A., & Stone, A. A. (1992). Writing about disclosed versus undisclosed
traumas: Immediate and long-term effects on mood and health. *Journal of Personality and Social Psychology, 63,* 75–84.

Gross, J., & Levenson, R. W. (1993). Emotional suppression: Physiology, self-report,
and expressive behavior. *Journal of Personality and Social Psychology, 64,* 970–
986.

Higgins, E. T. (1989). Knowledge accessibility and activation: Subjectivity and suffering
from unconscious sources. In J. S. Uleman & J. A. Bargh (Eds.), *Unintended
thought* (pp. 75–123). New York: Guilford.

Higgins, E. T., King, G. A., & Mavin, G. H. (1982). Individual construct accessibility and subjective impressions and recall. *Journal of Personality and Social Psychology, 43,* 35–47.

Hughes, C., Uhlmann, C., & Pennebaker, J. W. (1994). The body's response to psychological defense. *Journal of Personality, 62,* 565–585.

Jamner, L., Schwartz, G., & Leigh, H. (1988). The relationship between repressive and defensive coping styles and monocyte, eosinophile, and serum glucose levels: Support for the opiod peptide hypothesis of repression. *Psychosomatic Medicine, 50,* 567–575.

Jensen, M. (1987). Psychobiological factors predicting the course of breast cancer. *Journal of Personality, 55,* 317–342.

Kelley, J. E., Lumley, M. A., & Leisen, J. C. (1997). Health effects of emotional disclosure in rheumatoid arthritis. *Health Psychology, 16,* 331–340.

Keltner, D., Locke, K. D., & Audrain, P. C. (1993). The influence of attributions on the relevance of negative feelings to personal satisfaction. *Personality and Social Psychology Bulletin, 19,* 21–29.

Labov, W., & Fanshel, D. (1977). *Therapeutic discourse.* New York: Academic.

Larsen, D. (1990). Self-concealment: Conceptualization, measurement, and health implications. *Journal of Social and Clinical Psychology, 9,* 439–455.

Lau, R. R. (1989). Construct accessibility and electoral choice. *Political Behavior, 11,* 5–32.

Levenson, R. W., Carstensen, L. L., Friesen, W. V., & Ekman, P. (1991). Emotion, physiology, and expression in old age. *Psychology and Aging, 6,* 28–35.

Levy, S., Herberman, R., Lippman, M., & d'Angelo, T. (1987). Correlation of stress factors with sustained depression of natural killer cell activity and predicted prognosis in patients with breast cancer. *Journal of Clinical Oncology, 5,* 348–353.

Mahoney, M. J. (Ed.). (1995). *Cognitive and constructive psychotherapies: Theory, research, and practice.* New York: Springer.

Markus, H. (1977). Self-schemata and processing information about the self. *Journal of Personality and Social Psychology, 35,* 63–78.

Meichenbaum, D., & Fong, G. T. (1993). How individuals control their own minds: A constructive narrative perspective. In D. M. Wegner & J. W. Pennebaker (Eds.), *Handbook of mental control* (pp. 473–490). Englewood Cliffs, NJ: Prentice Hall.

Murray, E. J., Lamnin, A., & Carver, C. (1989). Emotional expression in written essays and psychotherapy. *Journal of Social and Clinical Psychology, 8,* 414–429.

Pennebaker, J. W. (1989). Confession, inhibition, and disease. In L. Berkowitz (Ed.), *Advances in experimental social psychology* (Vol. 22, pp. 211–244). New York: Academic.

Pennebaker, J. W. (1993). Putting stress into words: Health, linguistic, and therapeutic implications. *Behavior Research and Therapy, 31,* 539–548.

Pennebaker, J. W., Barger, S. D., & Tiebout, J. (1989). Disclosure of traumas and health among Holocaust survivors. *Psychosomatic Medicine, 51,* 577–589.

Pennebaker, J. W., & Beall, S. K. (1986). Confronting a traumatic event: Toward an understanding of inhibition and disease. *Journal of Abnormal Psychology, 95,* 274–281.

Pennebaker, J. W., & Francis, M. E. (1999). *Linguistic Inquiry and Word Count (LIWC): A computer-based text analysis program.* Mahwah, NJ: Erlbaum.

Pennebaker, J. W., Hughes, C. F., & O'Heeron, R. C. (1987). The psychophysiology of confession: Linking inhibitory and psychosomatic processes. *Journal of Personality and Social Psychology, 52,* 781–793.

Pennebaker, J. W., Kiecolt-Glaser, J., & Glaser, R. (1988). Disclosure of traumas and immune function: Health implications for psychotherapy. *Journal of Consulting and Clinical Psychology, 56,* 239–245.

Pennebaker, J. W., Mayne, T. J., & Francis, M. E. (1997). Linguistic predictors of adaptive bereavement. *Journal of Personality and Social Psychology, 72,* 863–871.

Pennebaker, J. W., & Uhlmann, C. (1994). A technique for the simultaneous recording of typing and biological responses: The CARMEN machine. *Behavior Research Methods, Instruments, and Computers, 26,* 28–31.

Petrie, K. J., Booth, R. J., Pennebaker, J. W., Davison, K. P., & Thomas, M. G. (1995). Disclosure of trauma and immune response to a hepatitis B vaccination program. *Journal of Consulting and Clinical Psychology, 63,* 787–792.

Pettingale, K. W., Morris, T., Greer, S., & Haybittl, J. L. (1985). Mental attitudes to cancer: An additional prognostic factor. *Lancet, 1,* 750.

Rachman, S. J. (1980). Emotional processing. *Behavior Research and Therapy, 18,* 51–60.

Rinaldo, C. R. (1990). Immune suppression by herpes viruses. *Annual Reviews of Medicine, 41,* 331–338.

Scheff, T. J. (1979). *Catharsis in healing, ritual, and drama.* Berkeley: University of California Press.

Schwarz, N. (1990). Feelings as information: Informational and motivational functions of affect. In E. T. Higgins & R. M. Sorrentino (Eds.), *Handbook of motivation and cognition: Foundations of social behavior* (Vol. 2, pp. 527–561). New York: Guilford.

Silver, R. L., Boon, C., & Stones, M. H. (1983). Searching for meaning in misfortune: Making sense of incest. *Journal of Social Issues, 39,* 81–102.

Smyth, J. M. (1998). Written emotional expression: Effect sizes, outcome, types, and moderating variables. *Journal of Consulting and Clinical Psychology, 66,* 174–184.

Spiegel, D., Bloom, J. R., Kraemer, H. C., & Gottheil, E. (1989). Effect of psychosocial treatment on survival of patients with metastatic breast cancer. *Lancet, ii,* 888–891.

Sumaya, C. V. (1986). Epstein-Barr virus serologic testing: Diagnostic indications and interpretations. *Pediatric Infectious Disease, 5,* 337–342.

Watson, D., & Clark, L. A. (1984). Negative affectivity: The disposition to experience aversive emotional states. *Psychological Bulletin, 96,* 465–490.

Wegner, D. M. (1992). You can't always think what you want: Problems in the suppression of unwanted thoughts. In M. Zanna (Ed.), *Advances in experimental social psychology* (Vol. 25, pp. 193–225). San Diego, CA: Academic.

Wegner, D. M., Shortt, J. W., Blake, A. W., & Page, M. S. (1990). The suppression of exciting thoughts. *Journal of Personality and Social Psychology, 58,* 409–418.

Weinberger, D., Schwartz, G. E., & Davidson, R. J. (1979). Low-anxious, high-anxious, and repressive coping styles: Psychometric patterns and behavioral and physiological responses to stress. *Journal of Abnormal Psychology, 88,* 369–380.

CHAPTER 4

Comparison of Distance Emotional Expression with Psychotherapy

Daniel L. Segal and Edward J. Murray

A tragedy is the imitation of an action that is serious and also, as having magnitude, complete in itself . . . with incidents arousing pity and fear, wherewith to accomplish its catharsis of such emotions.

Aristotle, *Poetics*

The expression of deep, powerful, and often intensely painful feelings has been linked with the process of psychotherapy since the origins of modern psychotherapy traceable to Sigmund Freud's work in the 1890s (e.g., Breuer & Freud, 1895/1966). In recent years, theorists and researchers have begun to suggest that the mere expression of emotions (i.e., writing in a journal) can be psychologically and physically beneficial in the *absence* of interpersonal contact with a psychotherapist (e.g., Esterling, Antoni, Fletcher, Margulies, & Schneiderman, 1994; Esterling, Antoni, Kumar, & Schneiderman, 1990; Greenberg & Stone, 1992; L'Abate, 1992; Pennebaker & Beall, 1986; Pennebaker, Kiecolt-Glaser, & Glaser, 1988). The purpose of this chapter is to discuss the similarities and differences in process and outcome between the pure expression of feelings without a clinician present (distance emotional disclosure) and psychotherapy. We begin with a brief historical overview of the role of emotional expression in psychotherapeutic change and then review a series of laboratory studies in which psychotherapy was compared to various forms of distance emotional disclosure.

EMOTIONAL EXPRESSION AND PSYCHOTHERAPY

Historical Overview

Since the origins of modern psychotherapy, massive proliferation of therapeutic schools and approaches has occurred. A common thread linking all of
these approaches is the belief that the outpouring of feelings about traumatic
life events plays a crucial role in the therapeutic process. The term "catharsis"
has historically been used to indicate an intense affective discharge as a way to
provide emotional relief. Catharsis has been viewed by many as a common
operational factor in psychotherapy (e.g., Marmor, 1976). In their incisive review, Nichols and Zax (1977) wrote, "catharsis is generally included in lists of
the underlying curative factors common to all forms of psychotherapy" (203).
Even current textbooks on systems of psychotherapy typically cite catharsis as
one of the important common factors of therapy (e.g., Prochaska & Norcross,
1999). Currently, the concept of catharsis is enjoying a renaissance among social
and clinical psychologists, particularly concerning its role in psychotherapeutic
change and the mechanisms by which it operates.

Catharsis as a vehicle of therapeutic change has a long history. Etymologi-
cally, catharsis comes from the Greek *katharsis*, which means purgation or pu-
rification. Aristotle believed that listening to certain kinds of music or observing
a tragedy led to the release of emotions. He believed that the artistically produced emotional release served to purge the listeners of their own grief, sadness,
and fear. Even before the Greeks, however, catharsis was an important component in healing rituals of primitive societies (Frank, 1973; Nichols & Zax,
1977; Scheff, 1979). Catharsis has also played a prominent role in mesmerism
and hypnotherapy, religious revivals, and rituals of mourning (Nichols & Efran,
1985).

In its modern psychotherapeutic context, the cathartic method was first described by Josef Breuer and Sigmund Freud (1895/1966). This discovery high-
lighted the beginning of both psychoanalysis and modern emotive therapies.
Breuer discovered that hysterical patients were relieved of their conversion
symptoms (e.g., blindness, paralysis) when they recalled and psychologically
reexperienced traumatic events while under hypnosis. Breuer encouraged his
patients to recall the upsetting events that initially provoked the symptoms, as
well as the accompanying emotions. When traumatic memories and emotions
were resurrected, the patient's symptoms disappeared. The process was termed
abreaction, and was believed by Breuer and Freud to be a cheap, easy, and
effective way to treat hysterics. Thus, early psychoanalysis was based on the
idea that buried conflictual feelings could be recovered or released through the
cathartic process. Use of abreaction or catharsis as a treatment was congruent
with Freud's hydraulic model of emotions, in which unacceptable feelings can
be blocked from direct expression. Pressure from these stored-up unexpressed
emotions could then seek expression through indirect means such as physical

symptoms (e.g., headaches, ulcers, and other psychosomatic illnesses). Relief occurred when emotions were discharged more directly; thus, clients were encouraged by their psychotherapists to cathart, abreact, emote, or ventilate.

In his later work, Freud abandoned catharsis in favor of free association and interpretation, which he believed were more effective ways to overcome repression (Nichols & Efran, 1985; Nichols & Zax, 1977). The hydraulic model was replaced with the conflict theory of neurosis. Although catharsis was relegated to a subsidiary role in traditional psychoanalysis, it became a central feature in many modern analytic therapies (e.g., Davanloo, 1980; Greenson, 1967). Catharsis also played a primary role in many emotive therapies that came into vogue in the 1960s, including psychodrama (Moreno, 1958), bioenergetics (Lowen, 1967), Gestalt therapy (Perls, 1969), primal therapy (Janov, 1970), reevaluation counseling (Jackins, 1965), and new identity therapy (Casriel, 1972). Catharsis also was a central component in many of the fad encounter groups of the early 1970s, in which group leaders would often use drastic techniques to break down psychological defenses and provoke intense emotions in participants (Blatner, 1985).

While historical accounts, clinical theory, and clinical testimonials attest to the potency of catharsis as a therapeutic tool, only recently has a meaningful body of empirical evidence accumulated on the topic (e.g., see recent review by Littrell, 1998). Despite recent investigative attention, exact descriptions of the nature of catharsis and its therapeutic implications have been elusive, with no model gaining widespread acceptance (Nichols & Efran, 1985). Even the question of whether a cathartic experience is beneficial or hurtful has not convincingly been answered (Biaggio, 1987). Indeed, this controversy is one of the oldest issues in psychology, possibly rivaling the nature versus nurture issue in importance. To make matters worse, extensive differences in terminology when referring to emotional expression have perennially existed, resulting in confusing and overlapping terms and definitions of catharsis. For example, catharsis has historically been associated with a variety of terms, such as "abreaction" (Breuer & Freud, 1895/1966), "explosion" (Perls, 1969), and "primal scream" (Janov, 1970). These terms all describe an intense expression of negative feelings, and, like the term "catharsis," imply therapeutic relief or relief of symptoms. Currently, the term "emotional processing" is preferred by many researchers to describe the cathartic phenomenon (Rachman, 1980; Greenberg & Safran, 1987).

Theoretical Background

According to Guinagh (1987), most current psychotherapies can be subsumed under two main approaches: cathartic and cognitive. Guinagh suggests that the cathartic approach encourages emotional expression and is based on the notion that psychological difficulties are best treated by encouraging clients to ventilate repressed or pent-up emotions such as sadness, anger, and grief. The two main approaches to psychotherapy, cathartic and cognitive, are not mutually exclusive; rather, it is possible that they produce increased beneficial results if used together.

Indeed, many recent theories of catharsis posit the importance of a cognitive component for positive cathartic results. For example, Greenberg and Safran (1987) devised an integrative model of emotion, in which emotion, cognition, and behavior are fused. All three are vital aspects of human functioning that influence each other via feedback loops. In line with their integrative model, they note that the term "catharsis" is too general to describe the complex affective, cognitive, and expressive phenomena that occur in therapy. Rather than focusing solely on emotional expression, the theorists outline several categories of affective change processes that they believe describe the emotional processing in which therapy clients become involved. In general, the change processes involve a shift from negative to positive emotion in conjunction with some form of cognitive reorganization of the client's view of the world. In their model, the arousal and expression of affect can produce adaptive cognitive changes, such as a new self-image or finding meaning in a traumatic experience or event. Similarly, cognitive experiences such as new interpretations of events can influence our emotional experiences.

Nichols and Efran (1985) described a two-stage model of emotional processing or catharsis. The first phase is termed activation, which occurs when a person's goal is blocked. The person subsequently becomes aroused and works on solving the problem. The second phase is called recovery, in which the obstacle is overcome or the person's goal is given up. Only during the recovery phase can one experience emotion. The theorists note that "all forms of 'emotional discharge' have in common that they are preceded by an activating event (stage one) and are then part of a recovery phase (stage two)" (52). Therapists are implored to encourage the recovery processes to occur (i.e., give the client permission to cry or scream). Catharsis is defined as "a label for completing (some or all of) a previously restrained or interrupted sequence of self-expression" (55). It is useful in that it can help the client express a natural reaction to some event where the reaction was thwarted or restrained at the time it naturally should have occurred. The client can then proceed to the recovery stage that previously was blocked, and emotions are properly shed. Thus, it is not the mere expressing of feelings that is curative, but the emotional ventilation leads to the completion of an interrupted action sequence.

Murray (1985) proposed and researched a model of therapeutic change that joins the two prominent components in most psychotherapies: cognitions and affect. Murray suggested that a combination of the two results in a more complete therapeutic experience. In a series of controlled laboratory studies, Murray and his associates found that emotional ventilation in conjunction with cognitive reinterpretation was more effective in reducing anger and aggression than either factor in isolation. His model asserts that catharsis as used therapeutically involves more than just affective release—there must be an accompanying cognitive reinterpretation of the event for long-range positive cathartic effects to be realized.

Pennebaker (1985, 1989) has proposed a model that links cathartic expression, behavioral inhibition, and psychosomatic disease processes. Pennebaker theorized that inhibiting feelings (a form of behavioral inhibition) about traumatic or upsetting events takes physiological work and is physically stressful. With chronic inhibition of feelings there is an increased probability of obsessing about the event, increased stress on the body, and an associated increase in rates of illness and physical symptoms. Pennebaker proposed that volitional emotional disclosure (the opposite of inhibiting feelings) serves to reduce the work of inhibiting, reduce stress on the body, and therefore enhance positive long-term health consequences.

Empirical Research

In support of his model, Pennebaker (1985) showed in a laboratory study that the active inhibition of behavior was associated with physiological activity, such as increased skin conductance, heart rate, and blood pressure. In a series of survey studies with various populations, Pennebaker and his associates found that childhood traumatic experiences, particularly those that were never discussed, were highly correlated with increased health problems. Recent traumas (i.e., death of a spouse) that were not discussed were likewise linked with increased health problems and increased ruminations about the traumas (Pennebaker & Hoover, 1985; Pennebaker & Susman, 1988).

Following the survey research, Pennebaker and his associates (e.g., Pennebaker & Beall, 1986; Pennebaker et al., 1988) devised an interesting and influential experimental paradigm for systematically and directly testing the impact of revisiting trauma or disclosing emotional experiences on physical and mental health. The Pennebaker procedure entails instructing participants to write about or talk privately (usually 15- to 30-minute disclosure sessions) about personally traumatic or depressing experiences over several days (usually three to five consecutive days) while comparison participants describe superficial events. Consistent with their behavioral inhibition model, the researchers hypothesized that allowing individuals to divulge traumatic events (the opposite of inhibiting those thoughts and feelings) would have the positive effect of reducing long-term stress and stress-related disease.

Across many studies, therapeutic mental and physical health effects of focused writing or focused talking were substantial (Esterling, L'Abate, Murray, & Pennebaker, 1999). Notably, these "confession" studies and experimental tests of catharsis have generated a substantial body of literature about emotional processing or catharsis, and the model has been studied and modified by many other research teams. Pennebaker's theory has evolved as well, focusing now more on the effects of emotional expression leading to the transduction of the emotional experience into a linguistic structure that promotes cognitive assimilation of the material and emotional improvements (Pennebaker, 1993). Although a full review of Pennebaker-inspired studies will not be provided here (see Chapter 3 in this book), results from many studies have prompted researchers to reliably conclude that the expression of emotions has a salubrious impact on emotional and physical functioning and is a valuable form of therapy. In their early review article summarizing several studies, Pennebaker and Susman (1988) concluded that "these data offer support that confiding about traumatic experience, although depressing in the short run, appears to have positive physical and psychological effects in the long run" (330). More recently, a meta-analysis (Smyth, 1998) indicated that effect sizes of written emotional expression were clinically meaningful and similar to those generated by other psychological or behavioral interventions (mean weighted effect size across all studies and outcomes was $d=0.47$, indicating a 23% improvement in the experimental group over the control group). Perhaps most important, it became apparent that these positive effects can and do occur in the *absence* of interpersonal contact with a psychotherapist. This intriguing notion prompted Murray's research team to conduct a series of studies comparing private emotional disclosure with psychotherapy, and these will be discussed next.

DISTANCE EMOTIONAL DISCLOSURE VERSUS PSYCHOTHERAPY

It seems clear from many Pennebaker studies that emotional processing can take place by simply writing or talking about traumatic events. Importantly, this notion seems to challenge the essential role of the therapist, or interpersonal relationship between therapist and client, in the therapeutic enterprise. Notably, in none of Pennebaker's studies did participants actively engage in interpersonal transactions with a live therapist who offered any type of feedback or support. The distance emotional disclosure procedure (written or verbal expression) does, however, offer an interesting comparison to psychotherapy. Writing, for example, relies a good deal on some sort of cathartic process without the interpersonal aspect of psychotherapy. The processes of support, empathy, feedback, confrontation, interpretation, and so on that are believed to be crucial to effective therapy are eliminated in writing therapy (Donnelly & Murray, 1991; Murray, Lamnin, & Carver, 1989; Murray & Segal, 1994; Segal & Murray, 1994).

It seemed incredible to this research team that simply writing about traumatic events could generate outcomes that seemed as impressive as those produced by even brief psychotherapy. Thus, several studies were devised to address two questions: (1) If writing were as effective as psychotherapy, what mechanisms of change could be involved? (2) In what ways were the processes in writing therapy and psychotherapy similar and different?

Writing Versus Psychotherapy

To examine these issues, the traditional Pennebaker paradigm was modified to include a psychotherapy condition (Murray et al., 1989; Donnelly & Murray,

1991). Undergraduate participants were randomly assigned to either write about a traumatic event (i.e., describe the most upsetting experience of your life), write about a superficial event (i.e., describe your room), or talk to a therapist about a traumatic event over several days. Clinical psychology graduate students served as psychotherapists, and they were trained to reflect and reframe the emotional content in a warm, empathic, and supportive manner. Dependent measures included a post-experimental questionnaire (PEQ) about cognitive and emotional changes, mood scales administered immediately before and after each session, and an independent content analysis of the written or taped sessions. Thus, in these two studies, our modification allowed for a brief generic "active listening" form of psychotherapy to be directly compared to writing therapy. This was done so that the complex cognitive and emotional processing presumed to occur in psychotherapy could be compared to written emotional processing.

The design of the first study (Murray et al., 1989) called for two 30-minute experimental sessions, separated by one day. Fifty-six students (equal number of males and females) completed the study. Results suggested a small advantage of psychotherapy over written traumatic expression. Specifically, participants in the psychotherapy condition reported more attitudinal change at the end of the experiment as measured by the PEQ. Content analysis results for session 1 showed that, during the intervention, the written expression condition aroused high levels of stressful emotions, while the psychotherapy condition aroused somewhat less emotion. However, the psychotherapy condition was more effective in producing positive changes in cognition, self-esteem, and adaptive behavior. By the second session the greater effectiveness of psychotherapy over written expression disappeared, although both groups were significantly more therapeutic than the control group. Overall, the most striking results were that both writing and psychotherapy showed strong evidence of therapeutic changes in cognition, self-esteem, and adaptive behavior in the content analysis.

The second study (Donnelly & Murray, 1991) increased the number of sessions to four and increased the number of participants to 102. Overall, results showed that psychotherapy and writing essays were equally effective in ameliorating traumatic experiences. Both conditions showed important therapeutic changes relative to controls. Specifically, the PEQ indicated that both treatment groups reported feeling significantly better about themselves and about their topic relative to the control group. The treatments also reduced the extent to which participants perceived their topic as being painful and upsetting. Furthermore, the content analysis showed that both treatment groups expressed more positive emotion and less negative emotion than controls, and also showed more cognitive, self-esteem, and behavioral changes. Over the course of the four sessions, both treatment groups increased in the expression of positive emotion and decreased in negative emotion. Both groups also increased over days in self-esteem and adaptive cognitive changes compared to controls.

Taken together, these two studies suggest that writing therapy can produce meaningful therapeutic changes that are quite comparable to those produced by brief psychotherapy. Although there might be an initial advantage for psychotherapy, this advantage disappeared over a four-session period. These conclusions are based on content analysis and PEQ results. Notably, the mood measure results revealed a surprisingly different picture.

In contrast to the other measures, there were dramatic differences in the measures of positive and negative mood generated by the written expression and psychotherapy groups. Mood was assessed immediately before and immediately after each session. After each writing session, there was a consistent upsurge in negative mood and a consistent decline in positive mood. In sharp contrast, the mood after the psychotherapy sessions was typically positive. In spite of the upsurge in negative mood after each session in the writing therapy, writing participants did report feeling more positive overall by the end of the study. Yet, each writing session left participants in an unpleasant emotional state while each psychotherapy session left participants in a positive mood. In explaining these results, Donnelly and Murray (1991) concluded that "initially, facing a stressful or traumatic event is disturbing to subjects in both treatment groups, although it might be necessary for therapeutic outcome. In the written condition, subjects continue to experience the session in a negative way, in spite of the fact that they are making therapeutic progress. In other words, the task is aversive even though it is being accomplished. In the psychotherapy condition, the therapist seems to ameliorate the aversiveness of the task, in some unspecified way" (349).

Thus, both writing and psychotherapy show strong evidence of significant emotional processing of traumatic experiences. This evidence includes a shift from negative to positive feelings over time, as well as cognitive, self-esteem, and adaptive behavioral changes. Indeed, these findings support Murray's (1985) model of psychotherapeutic change, suggesting that catharsis as used therapeutically is never just emotional ventilation, but includes cognitive components as well. Yet the dramatic differences in mood produced by the two interventions suggests that different mechanisms may be involved. Specifically, it would seem that the therapist plays a role in bringing about the more positive mood after psychotherapy sessions, suggesting that an important function of the therapist is to provide emotional support as the client faces his or her emotional trauma.

Writing Versus Talking (Vocal Expression)

In comparing psychotherapy and written expression (as in the previous two studies) it became apparent that two important factors were necessarily confounded. First, psychotherapy involves an interpersonal interaction. The therapist may have ameliorated the residual negative mood experienced in the writing therapy intervention. Such an effect might have been important in keeping a person dealing with an emotional trauma until emotional processing was complete. Second, psychotherapy differs from written expression in that psychotherapy involves *vocal* emotional expression while the other does not. In psychoanalytic therapy, it has been suggested that the vocal expression of feelings is therapeutic in its own right (Bady, 1985). Therefore, it is possible that vocal emotional expression may play some role in emotional processing when talking to a therapist.

Thus, the third study (Murray & Segal, 1994) was conducted to test the hypothesis that the differential effects of psychotherapy and written expression on residual negative mood after each session were due to the vocal expression inherent in psychotherapy. Participants ($n = 120$) were randomly assigned to either write or talk (speak into a tape recorder) about a traumatic event while alone in a room or to write or talk about a trivial event. Participants completed 20-minute sessions daily for four consecutive days. In this study, we eliminated the brief psychotherapy condition in order to compare directly the effects of vocal versus written expression of feelings about traumatic events. The same basic procedure and measures from the earlier research were used. Consistent with previous studies, both writing and talking about the traumatic experiences resulted in positive therapeutic effects. For example, painfulness of the topic decreased steadily over the four days. At the end, both traumatic groups (writing and talking) felt better about their topic and themselves and showed positive cognitive changes compared to trivial conditions. Both groups also showed positive changes on the content analysis. Vocal expression produced more emotional expression than the written material, but this effect was probably due to the difference in the sheer amount of verbal production between vocal and written expression.

Interestingly, after both writing sessions and vocal expression sessions, the mood scales showed an upsurge in negative mood and a decrease in positive mood after each session. These results are similar to those found earlier (Murray et al., 1989; Donnelly & Murray, 1991). The fact that the vocal expression group showed the same upsurge in negative mood after each session supported the idea that the differences between written expression and psychotherapy were due to the interpersonal aspect of psychotherapy rather than the vocal expression aspect. Therefore, written essays and talking into a tape recorder about traumatic events seem to have equally effective outcomes. In addition, both procedures produced the paradoxical upsurge in negative mood after each session, which was not found with psychotherapy.

Vocal Expression Versus Cognitive Therapy

The fourth and most recent study in this series (Segal & Murray, 1994) was designed to provide a more powerful test of the hypothesis that psychotherapy is more effective than distance emotional expressive techniques. First, a more structured, active form of therapy, cognitive therapy, was employed since there is strong evidence that cognitive therapy is a particularly effective brief treatment for emotional problems (Beck, Rush, Shaw, & Emery, 1979; Burns, 1985). Cognitive therapy is not passive or unstructured. Rather, it involves an active structured collaboration between therapist and client to challenge the client's cognitive distortions that, in theory, underlie the client's emotional problems. Second, a more distressed group of participants was selected to approximate a true clinical sample. Only those respondents who indicated on a pre-screening questionnaire that a traumatic event in their lives was still disturbing to them were eligible for the study. Third, for ethical reasons, the trivial topics control condition used in previous studies was eliminated. Since previous studies using this control procedure have repeatedly shown few psychological or health effects, it did not seem necessary to further replicate them, and we did not feel comfortable placing any of these distressed participants in a control condition that would not address any of their concerns. Fourth, the comparison group to cognitive psychotherapy was vocal expression (talking into a tape recorder while alone in a room) so as to control for various elements (i.e., more words are produced when participants talk about upsetting events compared to writing for the same time period; easier to judge emotion through vocal channels; both groups include vocal emotional processing). Presumably, the only difference is that the psychotherapy condition involves an interpersonal dimension that the vocal condition does not. Thus, a vocal expression group was used as it seemed to be a more appropriate comparison group than a written expression group. Fifth, updated assessment measures were used and several additional measures were added to help understand the underlying mechanisms in the two interventions.

The basic procedure of earlier research with 20-minute sessions, once per day over four successive days, was again continued. In a preliminary survey, 648 students were pre-screened. A total of 86 eligible students (who were currently distressed about a past traumatic experience) were contacted, 63 students (73%) agreed to enter the study, and 60 students participated in the intervention: 30 in the psychotherapy group, and 30 in the vocal expression group. At one-month follow-up, 37 participants were maintained (psychotherapy, n = 18; vocal expression, n = 19). Seven advanced clinical psychology graduate students served as therapists. They received specific training in the therapy techniques, were familiar with basic cognitive therapy techniques through coursework and clinical experience, and were supervised by an expert in cognitive therapy.

Results clearly indicated that both cognitive therapy and simply talking into a tape recorder were highly effective in helping participants emotionally process a traumatic experience. Both procedures were equally effective in reducing negative thoughts and feelings about the traumatic event. Cognitive therapy was somewhat more effective on the PEQ, although both interventions produced positive outcomes.

In spite of similar outcomes, there were important differences in what actually happened in the treatment sessions of the two groups. In vocal expression, participants focused persistently on negative emotional content over the four-day period. Concurrently with this focus, they experienced an upsurge in negative feelings after each session. In contrast, the cognitive therapists, by design, shifted the focus from the expression of unpleasant and distressing emotions to the examination of negative thoughts and cognitive distortions. Concurrently with this shift in focus, these participants experienced positive feelings after each session. Thus, cognitive therapy seemed to be a more positive experience.

Aside from the immediate upsurge in negative feelings in vocal expression, both groups experienced a good deal of negative affect, particularly at the start of treatment. Interestingly, correlational analyses showed that both the overall summed total amount of negative affect and the post-session upsurge in negative affect were related primarily to negative rather than positive outcomes on the PEQ. Thus, the sheer arousal of negative affect by itself does not seem to be therapeutically valuable, as might be expected from simple catharsis theories. Moreover, correlational analyses also suggested that cognitive processes were more directly involved in cognitive therapy than vocal expression. Cognitive changes during therapy were more closely related to positive outcomes for cognitive therapy than for vocal expression.

Thus, talking into a tape recorder seems to be almost as effective as cognitive therapy in a brief analogue intervention dealing with interpersonal traumatic experiences. In both procedures, the reduction of negative thoughts and feelings rather than the level of emotional arousal was associated with positive outcomes at the end of the study. Both procedures resulted in a reduction of negative thoughts and feelings. Despite similarities in outcome, correlational analyses did suggest that the two interventions seemed to operate by different mechanisms.

Examples of Traumatic Experiences and Typical Responses

Participants in our studies and other studies following the Pennebaker disclosure paradigm were asked to engage in a rather unusual activity, namely, to express their deepest thoughts and feelings about a traumatic event in their lives. What kind of topics did participants choose to divulge? It was apparent across studies that most participants took the task seriously and typically chose to focus on extremely painful, hurtful, and poignant experiences. It was abundantly clear that this procedure evokes powerful and deep emotions in most participants.

Common themes included traumatic personal losses (e.g., death of beloved relative or friend; divorce of parents), rape or sexual assault, family conflicts, relationship failures, rejections, and lowered self-esteem. For example, one female participant described the sudden death of her grandfather whom she perceived as the only supportive person in her life. She cried when describing how she would never be able to feel his hugs again. A young man divulged his story of being the intoxicated driver and sole survivor of a car crash that killed his two best friends. His guilt and despair were palpable and moving. Another male participant expressed his fear and rage about being gang raped in a junior high school locker room by a group of boys. Another example involved the embarrassment of a young woman who was caught by her devoutly religious father as she was engaging in intercourse with her boyfriend. Another woman vowed never to trust a man when her father cheated and her parents divorced. A final example involved a young man who was unable to date for a very long time after being rejected and humiliated by his girlfriend. Although our studies included college students (not clinical cases), the emotional pain of the participants was typically significant and affecting. It was not uncommon for participants to cry during and at the end of the sessions. It was clear that the experiences participants described in disclosure studies were real and important to them.

SUMMARY AND CONCLUDING COMMENTS

Catharsis or emotional processing has a long tradition of being viewed as a central process in psychotherapeutic change. Laboratory studies of emotional processing over the past 15 years have attempted to document the effects of emotional expression and tease out the mechanisms by which emotional disclosure may work. Many recent studies indicate that expressive methods, such as writing and talking into a tape recorder, seem to be as effective or nearly as effective as several types of psychotherapy. But expressive methods are not a panacea. The major drawback to these expressive methods is that they result in an upsurge in negative emotions after each disclosure session. This effect could produce an avoidance of expressive methods. Since a therapist seems to ameliorate the upsurge in negative moods, the use of a combination of expressive sessions and regular therapy sessions might be therapeutically optimal as well as cost-effective. How exactly this combination plays out is an empirical question that deserves future research attention. It is also likely that distance emotional expression techniques can be used para-preventively as a secondary prevention tool for those who need some kind of intervention but are not yet at a crisis phase. As suggested by L'Abate (1992) expressive techniques can be used before, during, and after either preventive or therapeutic interventions.

We hope that future research will apply distance emotional expression techniques to diverse populations (e.g., elderly, minorities) and to diverse clinical and social problems to assess new and potentially important therapeutic uses of the techniques. In fact, a recent study (Segal, Bogaards, Becker, & Chatman 1999) applied distance emotional disclosure techniques to bereaved older adults who were struggling with the death of their spouse (n = 30; mean age = 67.0). In this study, elderly participants were randomly assigned to treatment (four 20-minute vocal expression sessions within a two-week period) or delayed treatment. During the sessions, the older adult participants disclosed deep and painful feelings about their adjustment to their loss. A battery of outcome measures were administered at baseline, post-experimentally, and at one-month follow-up. Results showed that participants receiving treatment showed a decrease in hopelessness, while participants in delayed treatment showed an increase in hopelessness from baseline to the end of the intervention. After treatment was provided to the delayed treatment group, combined data from both groups indicated significant decreases in hopelessness, avoidance, intrusive thoughts, and depression from baseline to one-month follow-up. Moreover, feelings of painfulness and negative affect decreased steadily over sessions. These results suggest that emotional expression was a powerful therapeutic tool for these elders.

It is clear that the use of writing, either alone or in conjunction with traditional psychotherapy, has increased substantially in recent years (Esterling et al., 1999), and we believe that this trend will continue. Notably, sensible guidelines for the use of therapeutic writing as an adjunct to traditional face-to-face psychotherapy have been recently provided (Riordan, 1996). Finally, it is readily apparent that distance emotional disclosure techniques can arouse deep and painful emotions that previously were hidden, forbidden, or repressed. One caution with this approach that should be emphasized, however, is that these newly recognized or experienced feelings can potentially cause an emotional crisis in the individual if he or she is not able to cope with them. A key role of the psychotherapist may be to help distressed persons stay with and manage their affect and eventually integrate the new emotions and accompanying role functions. Our research suggests that it may be emotionally easier to reveal threatening emotions and aspects of oneself in the presence of a supportive and warm other who can accept, validate, and encourage the person to grow and change.

REFERENCES

Bady, S. L. (1985). The voice as a curative factor in psychotherapy. *Psychoanalytic Review, 72*, 479–490.

Beck, A. T., Rush, A. J., Shaw, B. F., & Emery, G. (1979). *Cognitive therapy of depression.* New York: Guilford.

Biaggio, M. K. (1987). A survey of psychologists' perspectives on catharsis. *Journal of Psychology, 121*, 243–248.

Blatner, A. (1985). The dynamics of catharsis. *Journal of Group Psychotherapy, Psychodrama and Sociometry, 37*, 157–166.

Breuer, J., & Freud, S. (1966). *Studies on hysteria.* New York: Avon. (Original work published 1895).

Burns, D. D. (1985). *Intimate connections.* New York: Morrow.

Casriel, D. (1972). *A scream away from happiness.* New York: Grosset & Dunlap.

Davanloo, H. (1980). A method of short-term dynamic psychotherapy. In H. Davanloo (Ed.), *Short-term dynamic psychotherapy.* New York: Jason Aronson.

Donnelly, D. A., & Murray, E. J. (1991). Cognitive and emotional changes in written essays and therapy interviews. *Journal of Social and Clinical Psychology, 10*, 334–350.

Esterling, B. A., Antoni, M. H., Fletcher, M. A., Margulies, S., & Schneiderman, N. (1994). Emotional disclosure through writing or speaking modulates Epstein-Barr virus antibody titers. *Journal of Consulting and Clinical Psychology, 62*, 130–140.

Esterling, B. A., Antoni, M. H., Kumar, M., & Schneiderman, N. (1990). Emotional repression, stress disclosure responses, and Epstein-Barr viral capsid antigen titers. *Psychosomatic Medicine, 52*, 397–410.

Esterling, B. A., L'Abate, L., Murray, E. J., & Pennebaker, J. W. (1999). Empirical foundations for writing in prevention and psychotherapy: Mental and physical health outcomes. *Clinical Psychology Review, 19*, 79–96.

Frank, J. D. (1973). *Persuasion and healing.* Baltimore: Johns Hopkins University Press.

Greenberg, L. S., & Safran, J. D. (1987). *Emotion in psychotherapy.* New York: Guilford.

Greenberg, M. A., & Stone, A. A. (1992). Emotional disclosure about traumas and its relation to health: Effects of previous disclosure and trauma severity. *Journal of Personality and Social Psychology, 63*, 75–84.

Greenson, R. R. (1967). *The technique and practice of psychoanalysis.* Vol. I. New York: International Universities Press.

Guinagh, B. (1987). *Catharsis and cognition in psychotherapy.* New York: Springer.

Hunt, M. G. (1998). The only way out is through: Emotional processing and recovery after a depressing life event. *Behaviour Research and Therapy, 36*, 361–384.

Jackins, H. (1965). *The human side of human beings.* Seattle: Rational Island.

Janov, A. (1970). *The primal scream.* New York: Putnams.

L'Abate, L. (1992). *Programmed writing: A self-administered approach for interventions with individuals, couples, and families.* Pacific Grove, CA: Brooks/Cole.

Littrell, J. (1998). Is the reexperience of painful emotion therapeutic? *Clinical Psychology Review, 18*, 71–102.

Lowen, A. (1967). *The betrayal of the body.* New York: Macmillan.

Marmor, J. (1976). Common operational factors in diverse approaches to behavior change. In A. Burton (Ed.), *What makes behavior change possible?* (pp. 3–12). New York: Brunner/Mazel.

Moreno, J. L. (1958). *Psychodrama.* Vol. II. New York: Beacon House.

Murray, E. J. (1985). Coping and anger. In T. M. Field, P. M. McCabe, & N. Schneiderman (Eds.), *Stress and coping* (pp. 243–261). Hillsdale, NJ: Erlbaum.

Murray, E. J., Lamnin, A. D., & Carver, C. S. (1989). Emotional expression in written essays and psychotherapy. *Journal of Social and Clinical Psychology, 8*, 414–429.

Murray, E. J., & Segal, D. L. (1994). Emotional processing in vocal and written expression of feelings about traumatic experiences. *Journal of Traumatic Stress, 7*, 391–405.

Nichols, M. P., & Efran, J. S. (1985). Catharsis in psychotherapy: A new perspective. *Psychotherapy, 22*, 46–58.

Nichols, M. P., & Zax, M. (1977). *Catharsis in psychotherapy.* New York: Gardner.

Pennebaker, J. W. (1985). Traumatic experience and psychosomatic disease: Exploring the role of behavioral inhibition, obsession, and confiding. *Canadian Psychology, 26*, 82–95.

Pennebaker, J. W. (1989). Confession, inhibition and disease. In L. Berkowitz (Ed.), *Advances in experimental social psychology* (Vol. 22, pp. 211–244). New York: Academic.

Pennebaker, J. W. (1993). Putting stress into words: Health, linguistic, and therapeutic implications. *Behaviour Research and Therapy, 31*, 539–548.

Pennebaker, J. W., & Beall, S. K. (1986). Confronting a traumatic event: Toward an understanding of inhibition and disease. *Journal of Abnormal Psychology, 95*, 274–281.

Pennebaker, J. W., Colder, M., & Sharp, L. K. (1990). Accelerating the coping process. *Journal of Personality and Social Psychology, 58*, 528–537.

Pennebaker, J. W., & Hoover, C. W. (1985). Inhibition and cognition: Toward an understanding of trauma and disease. In R. J. Davidson, G. E. Schwartz, & D. Shapiro (Eds.), *Consciousness and self-regulation*. New York: Plenum.

Pennebaker, J. W., Kiecolt-Glaser, J., & Glaser, R. (1988). Disclosure of traumas and immune function: Health implications for psychotherapy. *Journal of Consulting and Clinical Psychology, 56*, 239–245.

Pennebaker, J. W., & O'Heeron, R. C. (1984). Confiding in others and illness rate among spouses of suicide and accidental-death victims. *Journal of Abnormal Psychology, 93*, 473–476.

Pennebaker, J. W., & Susman, J. R. (1988). Disclosure of traumas and psychosomatic processes. *Social Science and Medicine, 26*, 327–332.

Perls, F. S. (1969). *Gestalt therapy verbatim*. Moab, UT: Real People.

Prochaska, J. O., & Norcross, J. C. (1999). *Systems of psychotherapy: A transtheoretical analysis* (4th ed.). Pacific Grove, CA: Brooks/Cole.

Rachman, S. (1980). Emotional processing. *Behaviour Research and Therapy, 18*, 51–60.

Riordan, R. J. (1996). Scriptotherapy: Therapeutic writing as a counseling adjunct. *Journal of Counseling and Development, 74*, 263–269.

Scheff, T. J. (1979). *Catharsis in healing, ritual, and drama*. Berkeley: University of California Press.

Segal, D. L., Bogaards, J. A., Becker, L. A., & Chatman, C. (1999). Effects of emotional expression on adjustment to spousal loss among older adults. *Journal of Mental Health and Aging, 5*, 297–310.

Segal, D. L., & Murray, E. J. (1994). Emotional processing in cognitive therapy and vocal expression of feeling. *Journal of Social and Clinical Psychology, 13*, 189–206.

Smyth, J. M. (1998). Written emotional expression: Effect sizes, outcome types, and moderating variables. *Journal of Consulting and Clinical Psychology, 66*, 174–184.

CHAPTER 5

A Meta-analytic Evaluation of Workbook Effectiveness in Physical and Mental Health

Joshua M. Smyth and Luciano L'Abate

There is a growing movement to use supplements or alternatives in the direct delivery of mental and physical health care. Supplements have included FEW in its expressive form, as already covered in Chapters 2, 3, and 4 (Esterling, L'Abate, Murray, & Pennebaker, 1999; Riordan, 1996; Smyth, 1998), and PDW, as in workbooks. Elsewhere, L'Abate and Kern (in press) argued that these workbooks constitute the software for structured (in contrast to less structured) CAI (L'Abate, 1992; this volume, Chapter 1). Workbooks may be used on their own, without any additional intervention, in preventive or para-preventive activities. L'Abate (1990) has argued that workbooks constitute a secondary prevention strategy, because they are *targeted* rather than *universal* (primary prevention), and can be used in conjunction with or as alternatives to primary or tertiary prevention, that is, face-to-face, talk-based psychotherapy (*necessary*).

Proponents of these supplements have argued that face-to-face delivery of verbal treatment is inherently inefficient. It dramatically limits the number of respondents (individuals, couples, and families) that can receive treatment from mental health professionals. Through replacing or supplementing traditional psychotherapeutic treatments with DW in its various structures and CAI, a great deal of the therapeutic process can be achieved outside the limits prescribed by direct, verbal, face-to-face contact between a professional and a respondent (client, patient, consumer). The inclusion of these supplements and alternatives, then, hopefully will lead to more cost-effective treatments. Through DW and CAI, it should be possible to treat greater numbers of respondents with fewer sessions and on an outpatient basis, at a distance from the professional (L'Abate, 1999a).

A critical assumption of this argument, however, is whether DW/CAI and workbooks are effective. Will the use of DW/CAI or workbooks, as supplements to or replacements for more traditional therapies, actually lead to improvement? The goal of this chapter will be to examine this assumption within the limited domain of workbooks. It attempts to determine to what degree workbooks lead to improvements in mental and/or physical health. It should be noted that the use of nonmanualized writing assignments (writing about emotionally traumatic experiences) has been shown to be effective in promoting health and well-being in both healthy and chronically ill individuals, as summarized in Chapters 2, 3, and 4 and in Smyth (1998) and Smyth, Stone, Hurewitz, and Kaell (1999). A notable limitation in the provision of such writing assignments is the difference between controlled, experimental research (*efficacy*) and the reality of clinical application (*effectiveness*). Although efficacy studies are necessary to establish causal effect and specific treatment benefits, they often do so at the cost of external validity. For example, in a trial of a written disclosure intervention, certain aspects of the patient included may be limited (e.g., age, disease severity, drug use, etc.). It remains likely, then, that the intervention—although effective in randomized trial—will not work as successfully among diverse practitioners operating under real-world constraints. The current analysis will look at the much more ecologically valid approach to writing assignments: the use of workbooks, which have a long history in the context of clinical care.

Prior to examining the efficacy of workbooks, it is important to establish some sense of their prevalence. A recent annotated bibliography of mental health workbooks (L'Abate, Odell, & Medlock, 1999) reported on over 60. As shown in Appendix C in Chapter 1, the Workbooks for Better Learning (WFBL) has available over 80 workbooks, covering a variety of topics including, but not limited to, the management and expression of externalizing and internalizing disorders in individuals (children, teenagers, and adults), couples, and families, as well as normalization of behavior. Workbooks have been targeted to patients with bipolar disorder (Pollack, 1995), asthma (Bailey et al., 1990; Wilson et al., 1993), hearing-impaired adults (Tye-Murray, 1992), and mildly retarded young adults (Cuvo, Davis, & Gluck, 1991). Workbooks have also been used as teaching aids more generally, being used to train caretakers of individuals with disabilities (Glassman, Miller, Wozniak, & Jones, 1994), promote communication skills in hospital pharmacists (Summers & Summers, 1991), train health care workers for community participation (Shoo, 1991), and train medical students (Hendrick, Neuhauser, Melnikow, & Vanek, 1991).

Finally, workbooks have been used to promote behavior change, particularly within the domain of potentially health-threatening behaviors, such as smoking (O'Hara, Gerace, & Elliott, 1993) and obesity (Miller, Eggert, Wallace, Lindeman, & Jastremski, 1993; Wylie-Rosett et al., 1994), although more general behaviors, such as academic performance in high school students (Lewis, 1995) have also been examined. More recently, there has been a plethora of workbooks covering agoraphobia (Craske & Barlow, 1994), anxiety (Barlow & Craske, 1994), depression (Weissman, 1995), drug and alcohol problems (Daley & Marlatt, 1997), eating disorders (Apple & Agras, 1997), obsessive-compulsive disorder (Foa & Kozak, 1997), phobias (Antony, Craske, & Barlow, 1995), sexuality (Wincze & Barlow, 1997), and stopping anxiety medication (Otto, Pollack, & Barlow, 1995), among the many available commercially.

Despite this prevalence, few workbooks have established an empirical basis for their preventive or clinical use. Such support would need to include demonstration of both efficacy and efficiency. An efficacious intervention is one that produces results above and beyond those that would occur without intervention. The group that receives an intervention should show a "better" improvement than a control group that did not receive the same intervention. By "better" is meant greater improvement and, optimally, longer lasting effects. An efficient intervention, however, is one that can produce the same results with fewer costs than a more expensive intervention. Costs can be evaluated on a number of factors, but include such things as the number of sessions needed to produce results, the type of personnel (professional versus para-professional) needed to produce those results, and the setting where the treatment is taking place (inpatient versus outpatient). Given interventions that produce the same results, the intervention that requires a fewer number of sessions, uses para-professionals over professionals (assuming the formers' time costs less), or can take place on an outpatient basis (assuming inpatient treatment is more expensive than outpatient treatment) is more efficient. Treatments that are both effective and efficient are highly desirable from both ethical and economic perspectives (L'Abate, 1999).

Current changes and trends in the health care system (for both mental and physical health) suggest that treatments that fail to meet increasingly stringent cost-effectiveness criteria will not be made available, or will not receive reimbursements from insurance and managed care companies. Conversely, those treatments that are demonstrated to be cost-effective will become commonplace in the arsenal of managed care. Cost-effectiveness, therefore, becomes a critical concept as the combination of both effectiveness and efficiency. Although the nature of workbooks makes them inherently low-cost and mass-produced, we remain confronted with the bugaboo of effectiveness. To justify the continued use of workbooks in clinical settings, as well as to promote more stringent empirical examination of this issue, this chapter will examine if workbooks show any effectiveness.

The question becomes: "How do we determine if workbooks are effective?" There are several concerns facing us in our evaluation. One is the paucity of controlled studies, and the other consists of problems inherent in subjective reviews. By subjective review is meant the typical strategy of reviewing a specific literature on a given topic—studies are grouped, the direction and statistical significance of findings is noted, and conclusions are drawn from the number and consistency of the findings (e.g., Esterling et al., 1999; Riordan, 1996). This approach has a number of limitations, including the fact that individual studies present mixed results (Lipsey & Wilson, 1993). That is, study participants may show improvement on some measures but no change or even decrement on others. This subjective approach is also heavily influenced by the report of statistical significance tests. Although beyond the scope of this chapter to review, there is extensive evidence that such reliance on statistical significance can lead to interpretive problems. This issue is most clearly articulated by Schmidt (1996), who argued that the preferred method is to use techniques common to meta-analysis, most notably, the establishment of effect sizes and confidence intervals rather than statistical significance. (The interested reader is again referred to Schmidt, 1996.)

Meta-analytical methods for the cumulation and examination of research studies can thus provide an alternative, and in many ways preferable, approach to evaluate a research literature (Cooper & Hedges, 1994). Meta-analysis is a statistically based approach for generating effect size estimates (e.g., for the effectiveness of workbooks) by aggregating effect size information from all available sources (i.e., research studies). There are, however, some unique difficulties posed by the literature on workbooks. Vast differences exist between studies in overall design and quality of the methods and statistics used. A comprehensive discussion of the problems caused by poor data quality is not feasible here, but interested readers are referred to Cooper and Hedges (1994) and to Yeaton, Langenbrunner, Smyth, and Wortman (1995). Most notable among the problems caused by this uneven literature is the relative paucity of randomized trials examining the effectiveness of workbooks. Rather, the majority of studies lack control groups, thus making estimates of effect size problematic.

There are, however, a relatively small number of studies that contrast workbooks to a control condition (often a delayed treatment condition). Some of these studies used workbooks as a component of a total rehabilitation program or as a supplement to other forms of treatment. Such approaches do not provide objective evidence for the unique contribution of workbooks beyond that of other treatments included. Accordingly, it is not readily possible to strictly evaluate the unique effectiveness of workbooks from multimodal approaches. Rather, we attempt to ascertain the effectiveness of workbooks by cumulating information across a variety of studies. By generating and comparing effect sizes for studies that examine workbooks alone, as well as workbooks plus other therapies, it will be possible to generate preliminary estimates of the relative contribution of workbooks to improvement. Although we recognize that this is not the definitive answer to the question of workbook effectiveness, we do believe it is a necessary first step. We further hope that this analysis provides an impetus to future research that more carefully evaluates the unique contribution of workbooks to the therapeutic armamentarium.

LITERATURE SEARCH

Studies on the effectiveness of workbooks were located through a computer search of *Psychological Literature Medline, PsychInfo* (Psychological Abstracts), and *Citation Index*. Various permutations of keywords were used from the following: writing, workbook, written, and manual. All sources found in this manner were used to perform a backward search of the references for additional articles. Furthermore, several authors who have published studies on the use of workbooks were contacted and requested to supply information on any other published or unpublished articles (including dissertations) on this topic. The total group of articles collected in this fashion was then examined to determine if they met the necessary inclusion criteria for this review. As this review specifically focused on the use of workbooks as therapy or supplement to therapy, all studies had to include the use of a workbook in conjunction with, or solely as, therapy (with the explicit aim of producing positive change on some outcome measure). The study was also required to contain some outcome measure of health, although, for the purposes of this chapter, we defined health in the broadest possible terms. Such health outcomes could be in the domain of either mental or physical health, or more general measures of performance (e.g., student grades, cognitive performance). Studies also had to contain statistical information necessary to calculate an effect size.

Following these criteria, 18 studies were included in this analysis. It should also be noted that there were some cases where study results were presented in several sources or at different times (e.g., dissertation and subsequent publication, pilot work, and final results). Care was taken to not duplicate information in this analysis. Generally, the final (i.e., most recent) source was included in the analysis. The exception to this approach was when earlier reports included data unreported in subsequent publications reporting on the same subjects and intervention. In these cases, the earlier information was integrated into the final report and analyzed as a single study.

GENERAL EFFECT SIZES

All results, taken from a variety of inferential statistics, were transformed into Cohen's d as the measure of effect size. Cohen's d is a standardized mean difference estimate (Hedges & Olkin, 1985). Most transformations and analyses were conducted on the software DSTAT (Johnson, 1990), and followed procedures used previously by the first author (e.g., Smyth, 1998). All transformations and analyses not covered in DSTAT were accomplished using the techniques described in Cooper and Hedges (1994). In cases where no inferential or descriptive information was provided, but an effect was noted as nonsignificant, analyses assumed an effect size of zero (Rosenthal, 1984). A conservative approach was taken in that when multiple comparisons were implied, but not explicitly reported, multiple effect sizes of zero were inferred.

The magnitude and significance of the overall mean weighted effect size was computed for all outcomes and all studies. All outcomes were scored so that when the workbook group was superior to the control group, the effect size was in the positive direction, regardless of whether high or low scores on the measure were desirable. Following established guidelines, the homogeneity of effect sizes was examined. If the homogeneity test is significant, it suggests that the d's (i.e., effect sizes) vary more than would be expected by sampling error. Significant variance among effect sizes suggests that additional variables should be examined that may moderate the effect under observation (Hedges & Olkin, 1985). Noncontinuous moderator variables were tested by comparing the mean effect sizes between groups (formed on the basis of study qualities). This between group test results in the goodness of fit, Qb, with an approximate chi-square distribution with p-1 degrees of freedom (p = number of groups; Hedges & Olkin, 1985).

EFFECTIVENESS OF WORKBOOKS

Studies using workbooks included in this study examined a wide array of topics. Samples were drawn from couples in seminaries to firefighters to 9th grade math students. The outcomes evaluated in these studies were similarly wide-ranging. Such outcomes included mental health outcomes such as anxiety and depression, physical health outcomes such as cholesterol levels and weight loss, and more general performance measures such as student grades and cognitive functioning. An overview of the primary topics and primary outcome measures from each study included is shown in Table 5–1.

The magnitude and significance of the overall mean weighted effect size was computed for all outcomes (averaged within study) and all studies. That is, one effect size was computed for each study by generating effect sizes for each outcome in the study, and then averaging across all outcomes. These study effect sizes were then cumulated across all studies (corrected for bias) for an overall effect size of workbooks. It must be noted that this approach is quite conservative, in that all outcomes were weighted equally. In cases where more exploratory outcomes were included, effect sizes were weighted as much as primary outcomes. This process likely results in an underestimation of the overall effect size, as exploratory outcomes are presumably less likely to be influenced by workbook intervention. In this preliminary examination of workbook effectiveness, however, this conservative approach was deemed most appropriate.

The effect sizes and 95% confidence intervals for each of the included studies is shown in Table 5–2. The overall effect size across all outcomes and all studies was $d = 0.30$ ($r = 0.15$; 95% CI +0.21 / +0.39, p <0001). There was considerable variability in effect sizes between studies, ranging from −0.22 to +1.16. The test for homogeneity of effect sizes was significant ($Qw(17) = 30.8$,

Table 5–1
Goals and Outcomes of Studies Included in This Analysis

Study	Primary Goals and Outcomes
ASML90	Depression treatment in adolescents; depression, cognition
B92	Improvement of self-esteem, self-disclosure, and coping; self-esteem, self-disclosure, coping
BRBet90	Self-management of asthma; medication use and adherence, symptoms, emergency care
BSFPG97	Anxiety treatment; anxiety
FGSet87	Energy conservation in arthritis patients; exercise behaviors
JS95	Depression treatment; depression, cognition
L95	Self-determination and goal achievement in 9th grade math students; attributions, goals, grades
LBFR92	Depression and anxiety reduction; depression, anxiety
M92	Anticipation training for adults with hearing impairment; speech recognition
M97	Marital adjustment for couples in seminary; marital adjustment, satisfaction
MEWLJ93	Weight loss; weight, body fat
OGE93	Smoking cessation for firefighters; cessation rates
PCT76	Meditation for anxiety reduction; anxiety
RG93	Cognitive remediation in alcoholics; cognitive performance
SJG89	Depression treatment; depression, cognition
TMHet96	Smoking cessation; cessation rates
WL77	Enrichment and written homework assignments with couples
WSPet94	Weight reduction; weight loss, cholesterol

Note: Studies are noted by the first letter of each author's last name ("et" indicates multiple authors not listed) and the two-digit year associated with the study.

$p = 0.02$), suggesting that examination of moderator variables would be appropriate.

One potential moderator was the use of workbooks alone versus in conjunction with other therapy. Effect size estimates were conducted, following the same procedures, for the conditions of workbook only and workbook plus other therapy to provide estimates of the effect size for workbooks alone and in conjunction with additional therapeutic intervention. The effect size for workbooks alone was $d = 0.36$ ($r = 0.15$; 95% CI $+0.22$ / $+0.50$), whereas the effect size for workbooks used in conjunction with other treatment was $d = 0.26$ ($r = 0.13$; 95% CI $+0.15$ / $+0.37$). The difference between these two effect sizes was not significant ($Qb(1) = 1.27$, $p = 0.26$). It must also be noted that the

Table 5–2
Effect Sizes for Studies Included in This Analysis

Study	d	95% CI	r	p
ASML98	+0.7241	+0.45/+1.00	+0.34	0.0001
B92	+0.2317	−0.31/+0.78	+0.12	0.4049
BRBet90	+0.3308	+0.07/+0.60	+0.16	0.0137
BSet97	+0.6920	+0.44/+0.94	+0.33	0.0001
FGSet87	+0.2050	−0.57/+0.98	+0.11	0.5877
JS95	+0.9116	+0.69/+1.13	+0.42	0.0001
L95	+0.1481	−0.29/+0.59	+0.08	0.5084
LBFR92	+0.4359	−0.16/+1.03	+0.22	0.1009
M92	−0.0183	−0.89/+0.86	−0.01	0.9672
M97	−0.0116	−0.37/+0.35	−0.01	0.9492
MEWLJ93	+1.1020	+0.33/+1.87	+0.49	0.0006
OGE93	−0.2225	−0.64/+0.20	−0.11	0.3008
PCT76	+0.1759	−0.14/+0.49	+0.09	0.2685
RG93	+0.5307	+0.02/+1.04	+0.26	0.0416
SJG97	+0.3312	+0.12/+0.54	+0.16	0.0010
TMHet96	+0.2001	+0.04/+0.36	+0.10	0.0124
WL77	+1.1600	+0.41/+1.91	+0.51	0.0024
WSPet94	+0.3345	+0.12/+0.55	+0.17	0.0027
Overall	+0.2992	+0.21/+0.39	+0.15	0.0001

studies differed on a number of other important dimensions. Most notably, they were not similar in terms of the outcomes under assessment. Consequently, any comparison of effect sizes must be taken most cautiously. For example, it is possible that multimodal approaches (using workbooks in conjunction with other therapeutic approaches) are used when targeting outcomes that are more difficult (or resistant) to change. Nonetheless, this very preliminary comparison suggests that workbooks alone are a viable intervention, and it is not necessary to use them in the context of additional treatment.

Another potential moderator was the domain of outcome assessment. As noted earlier in this chapter, and elsewhere throughout this volume, the use of workbooks in both mental health and physical health treatment is of particular interest. Effect size estimates were made for two classes of outcomes, mental health and physical health. Health behaviors (e.g., weight loss, smoking rates) were included in the physical health category despite the fact that they are notoriously difficult to change (and thus may result in an underestimation of the effect size for workbooks on more malleable physical health outcomes). Effect sizes were computed for each study including only those outcomes within the category (i.e., mental or physical health). The overall effect sizes for mental health and physical health outcomes were then computed by cumulating across all studies containing relevant outcomes in the fashion used previously.

The effect size for mental health outcomes was $d = 0.44$ ($r = 0.21$, 95% CI +0.29 / +0.59), substantially higher than the overall effect size generated from all available outcomes. This effect size is quite similar to that observed in other meta-analyses of psychological, educational, and behavioral interventions (e.g., Lipsey & Wilson, 1993). Additionally, the test for homogeneity of effect sizes was not significant ($Qw(10) = 15.3$, $p = 0.12$), suggesting that moderator variables are not significantly influencing this effect size.

In contrast to the larger effect size observed for mental health outcomes, the effect size for physical health outcomes was similar (albeit slightly lower) than the overall effect size drawn from all outcomes. The effect size of workbooks on physical health outcomes was $d = 0.25$ ($r = 0.12$, 95% CI +0.14 / +0.35). Also unlike the mental health outcomes, the test for homogeneity of effect sizes was significant ($Qw(5) = 10.79$, $p = 0.05$). This suggests that there is considerable variability between the contributing studies to this overall effect size and other variables are likely moderating this effect. In other words, there seem to be individuals, outcomes, or situations, for whom or in which workbooks would have a relatively more—or less—pronounced impact on physical health. Future research should certainly examine such factors influencing the effectiveness of workbooks on physical health and health-related behaviors.

DISCUSSION

The goal of this chapter was to determine if there exists empirical support for the use of workbooks. That is, do workbooks lead to improvements in mental and/or physical health? In brief, this analysis suggests that workbooks do seem to lead to health improvements. In spite of our most conservative approach (including all outcomes and studies lacking a theoretical justification for the use of workbooks) there was clear evidence that the use of workbooks leads to reliable improvements in health outcomes broadly defined. The enormous breadth of samples and outcomes, even in this limited analysis, suggests the robustness and intuitive appeal of workbooks as helpful. This robustness also suggests that the effectiveness of workbooks is much more likely to generalize to new samples, outcomes, and processes. That is, if workbooks only appeared to be helpful for a certain class of individuals (e.g., students) or for a certain outcome (e.g., depression), we would be much less confident in inferring that workbooks might work for a variety of individuals and outcomes. Future research can clarify for what samples and outcomes workbooks are most effective. Along these lines, the progression of research will increase our understanding of what elements of workbooks are effective commensurably. This understanding will, in turn, facilitate the development of increasingly effective and efficient workbooks.

It is also clear that the current use of workbooks leads to considerable variability in the effect sizes observed from study to study. Such variability may be related to many factors, including—but not limited to—workbook content, sample selection, and outcome type(s). We specifically examined two such potential moderators: outcome type (mental health and physical health) and the use of workbooks by themselves or in conjunction with other therapeutic interventions.

The examination of mental and physical health outcomes separately suggested higher effect sizes for mental, but not physical, health measures. It is important to note, however, that both outcome types were significantly improved by the use of workbooks. Also, the indication of moderating variables in the physical health outcomes suggests that additional research and more stringent methodologies are needed to better understand and use workbooks to influence physical health outcomes. Clearly, this is strictly a pilot analysis because of the limited number of studies used. However, they indicate and support future research, suggesting that preventive and clinical practice using workbooks could take place within the context recommended repeatedly by the second author: informed consent, pre- and post-intervention evaluation, and long-term follow-up (L'Abate, 1990, 1992, 1999).

Another issue this analysis raises relates to the combination of workbooks used on their own versus the combination of workbooks with other therapeutic intervention (e.g., face-to-face therapy, phone counseling, etc.). The analysis indicates that workbooks do, in fact, seem to produce improvement when used alone. As noted earlier, the differences between the samples and outcomes used in studies preclude an accurate comparison of the relative efficacy of workbooks on their own and workbooks combined with other therapy. This distinction would best be made by future research contrasting workbooks and workbook multimodal therapies on the same outcomes using the same samples. There are also a number of other methodological approaches to disentangling the unique contribution of the components of multimodal therapies (e.g., dismantling) that could be used. Regardless of the approach used, this becomes an important issue when attempting to determine cost-effectiveness. If the two approaches are equally effective, as indicated by this analysis, then the more cost-effective intervention—workbooks alone—should be preferable. A more complicated scenario is that perhaps multimodal therapies are both more efficacious (as they utilize more therapeutic approaches) and more expensive. The relative trade-off between the increased cost and increased benefit in this case would have to be carefully examined in future research.

Another issue that must be kept in the foreground refers to the nature of the respondents. In many cases, especially studies with mental health workbooks, research examined undergraduate students. What would happen if and when a clinical population were used? Would the same results be obtained? It is certainly plausible that clinical samples would be differently motivated to use workbooks (although in what direction may depend in turn on the specific clinical sample). Additionally, workbooks might show even greater effects if baseline levels of pathology and/or symptomatology is higher than in student samples. At this point, research on applications of workbooks to clinical populations is needed to demonstrate their usefulness, as generalizations from results with nonclinical populations to clinical ones seem unwarranted. Clearly, the examination of this issue is a foremost concern for future research.

The major implication of these results pertains to the traditional practice of psychotherapy. If the latter does show major effects in its own right, then the combination of face-to-face, talk-based psychotherapy with workbooks should lead to synergistic results. These results would produce more cost-effective interventions than either approach would obtain on its own (L'Abate, 1986). Hence, the traditional practice of psychotherapy may need changing in view of arguments that it might be limited to specific populations and ineffective with other ones. For instance, results of traditional psychotherapy with offenders and acting-out character disorders (Chapter 9) are notoriously negative. Could it be that using a different medium, namely DW/CAI, might produce more cost-effective outcomes? Even if the outcome is negative, at least there would not be an expense of professional time and energy involved.

Although the results of this analysis are supportive of the efficacy of workbooks, clearly there remains much we do not know. This promising first step underscores the need for additional, high-quality research on the use of workbooks. Both therapists and consumers are faced with the questions of whether or not to use workbooks and, if so, which workbooks to use. The review presented here suggests that, in fact, the answer to the first question is yes—workbooks seem to help and are thus a viable therapeutic tool. Hopefully, this preliminary evidence that workbooks are effective will provoke additional research and, eventually, this analysis can be replicated with a larger number of studies. This review also underscores the relative dearth of information from research to address the latter question—which specific workbooks are appropriate for use? We hope that this (and future) analyses increase the pressure on the purveyors of workbooks to provide empirical support for the clinical utility of workbooks. This will allow therapists and consumers a basis on which to choose a workbook for use. Additionally, increasing expectations for such efficacy information may be helpful in dissuading authors and publishers from flooding the market with poorly designed and theoretically unsound workbooks merely for the motive of profit.

CONCLUSION

Workbooks seem to produce a medium effect size in mental health and a somewhat lower effect size for physical health (although there was great variability for such outcomes). This analysis supports the use of workbooks as additions or as alternatives in preventive and psychotherapeutic practices, making them tools for secondary prevention. Furthermore, as long as they are external to traditional psychotherapeutic practices, they are not yet part of the mental or physical health mainstream. It behooves practitioners using them to include informed consent and pre- and post-objective evaluation as standard operating procedures in their preventive and clinical practices. Finally, we explicitly encourage future research on the use of workbooks.

REFERENCES

Antony, M. M., Craske, M. G., & Barlow, D. H. (1995). *Mastery of your specific phobia*. San Antonio, TX: The Psychological Corporation.

Apple, R. F., & Agras, W. S. (1997). *Overcoming eating disorders: A cognitive-behavioral treatment for bulimia nervosa and binge-eating disorder*. San Antonio, TX: The Psychological Corporation.

Bailey, W. C., Richards, J. M., Jr., Brooks, C. M., Soong, S. J, Windsor, R. A., & Manzella, B. A. (1990). A randomized trial to improve self-management practices of adults with asthma. *Archives of Internal Medicine, 150*, 1664–1668.

Barlow, D. H., & Craske, M. G. (1994). *Mastery of your anxiety and panic*. San Antonio, TX: The Psychological Corporation.

Bird, G. F. (1992). *Programmed writing as a method for increasing self-esteem, self-disclosure and coping skills*. Unpublished doctoral dissertation. Department of Counseling and Psychological Services, Georgia State University, Atlanta, GA.

Cooper, H., & Hedges, L. (1994). *The handbook of research synthesis*. New York: Russell Sage Foundation.

Craske, M. G., & Barlow, D. H. (1994). *Mastery of your anxiety and panic II: Agoraphobia supplement*. San Antonio, TX: The Psychological Corporation.

Cuvo, A. J., Davis, P. K., & Gluck, M. S. (1991). Cumulative and interpersonal task sequencing in self-paced training for persons with mild handicaps. *Mental Retardation, 29*, 335–342.

Daley, D. C., & Marlatt, G. A. (1997). *Managing your drug or alcohol problem*. San Antonio, TX: The Psychological Corporation.

Esterling, B. A., L'Abate, L., Murray, E. J., & Pennebaker, J. W. (1999). Empirical foundations for writing in prevention and psychotherapy: Mental and physical health outcomes. *Clinical Psychology Review, 19*, 79–96.

Foa, E. B., & Kozak, M. J. (1997). *Mastery of obsessive-compulsive disorder*. San Antonio, TX: The Psychological Corporation.

Glassman, P., Miller, C., Wozniak, T., & Jones, C. (1994). A preventive dentistry training program for caretakers of persons with disabilities residing in community residential facilities. *Special Care Dentistry, 14*, 137–143.

Hedges, L. V., & Olkin, I. (1985). *Statistical methods for meta-analysis*. Orlando, FL: Academic.

Hendrick, L., Neuhauser, D., Melnikow, J., & Vanek, E. (1991). Introducing quality improvement thinking in medical students: The Cleveland asthma project. *Quality Review Bulletin, 17*, 254–260.

Jamison, C., & Scogin, F. (1995). Outcome of cognitive bibliotherapy with depressed adults. *Journal of Consulting and Clinical Psychology, 63*, 644–650.

Johnson, B. T. (1990). *DSTAT: Software for the meta-analytic review of research literatures*. Hillsdale, NJ: Erlbaum.

Kendall, P. C. (1990). *The coping cat workbook*. Merion Station, PA: Author.

L'Abate, L. (1986). *Systematic family therapy*. New York: Brunner/Mazel.

L'Abate, L. (1990). *Building family competence: Primary and secondary prevention strategies*. Newbury Park, CA: Sage.

L'Abate, L. (1992). *Programmed writing: A self-administered approach for interventions with individuals, couples, and families.* Pacific Grove, CA: Brooks/Cole.

L'Abate, L. (1999). Taking the bull by the horns: Beyond words in psychological interventions. *The Family Journal: Counseling and Therapy with Couples and Families, 7,* 6–20.

L'Abate, L., Boyce, J., Fraizer, L., & Russ, D. A. (1992). Programmed writing: Research in progress. *Comprehensive Mental Health Care, 2,* 45–62.

L'Abate, L., & Kern, R. (in press). Workbooks as software for structured computer-assisted interventions. In S. J. Lepore & J. M. Smyth (Eds.), *The writing cure: How expressive writing promotes health and emotional well being.* Washington, DC: American Psychological Association.

L'Abate, L., Odell, M., & Medlock, A. (1999). *An annotated bibliography of selected self-help workbooks.* Atlanta, GA: Workbooks for Better Learning.

Lewis, R. E. (1995). *A write way: Programmed writing effects on high-school math students' attendance, homework, grades, and attribution.* Unpublished doctoral dissertation, University of San Francisco.

Lipsey, M., & Wilson, D. (1993). The efficacy of psychological, educational, and behavioral treatment: Confirmation from meta-analysis. *American Psychologist, 48,* 1181–1209.

McMahan, O. (1997). *Programmed distance writing as an intervention for seminary couples.* Unpublished doctoral dissertation. Department of Counseling and Psychological Services, Georgia State University, Atlanta, GA.

Miller, W. C., Eggert, K. E., Wallace, J. P., Lindman, A. K., & Jastremski, C. (1993). Successful weight loss in a self-taught, self-administered program. *International Journal of Sports Medicine, 14,* 401–405.

O'Hara, P., Gerace, T. A., & Elliott, L. L. (1993). Effectiveness of self-help smoking cessation guides for firefighters. *Journal of Occupational Medicine, 35,* 795–799.

Otto, M. W., Pollack, M. H., & Barlow, D. H. (1995). *Stopping anxiety medication: Panic control therapy for benzodiazepine discontinuation.* San Antonio, TX: The Psychological Corporation.

Platt-Furst, G., Gerber, L. H., Smith, C. C., Fisher, S., & Shulman, B. (1987). Program for improving energy conservation behaviors in adults with rheumatoid arthritis. *American Journal of Occupational Therapy, 41,* 102–111.

Pollack, L. E. (1995). Treatment of inpatients with bipolar disorders: A role for self-management groups. *Journal of Psychosocial Nursing and Mental Health Services, 33,* 11–16.

Puryear, H. B., Cayce, C. T., & Thurston, M. A. (1976). Anxiety reduction associated with meditation: Home study. *Perceptual and Motor Skills, 43,* 527–531.

Riordan, R. J. (1996). Scriptotherapy: Therapeutic writing as a counseling adjunct. *Journal of Counseling & Development, 74,* 263–269.

Roechrich, L., & Goldman, M. S. (1993). Experience-dependent neuro-psychological recovery and the treatment of alcoholism. *Journal of Consulting and Clinical Psychology, 61,* 812–821.

Rosenthal, R. (1984). *Meta-analytic procedures for social research.* Beverly Hills, CA: Sage.

Schmidt, F. L. (1996). Statistical significance testing and cumulative knowledge in psychology: Implications for training of researchers. *Psychological Methods, 1,* 115–129.

Scogin, F., Jamison, C., & Davis, N. (1990). A two-year follow-up of the effects of bibliotherapy for depressed older adults. *Journal of Consulting and Clinical Psychology, 58,* 665–667.

Scogin, F., Jamison, C., & Gochneaur, K. (1989). The comparative efficacy of cognitive and behavioral bibliotheraphy for mildly and moderately depressed older adults. *Journal of Consulting and Clinical Psychology, 57,* 403–407.

Shoo, R. (1991). Training primary health care workers to foster community participation. *World Health Forum, 12,* 55–62.

Smyth, J. (1998). Written emotional expression: Effect size, outcome types, and moderating variables. *Journal of Consulting and Clinical Psychology, 66,* 174–184.

Smyth, J., Stone, A., Hurewitz, A., & Kaell, A. (1999). Writing about stressful events produces symptom reduction in asthmatics and rheumatoid arthritics: A randomized trial. *Journal of the American Medical Association, 281,* 1304–1309.

Stipek, D., Milburn, S., & Clements, D. (1992). Parents' beliefs about appropriate education for young children. *Journal of Applied Developmental Psychology, 13,* 293–310.

Summers, R. S., & Summers, B. (1991). Evaluation of a communications skills workshop for hospital pharmacists. *Journal of Clinical and Pharmaceutical Therapy, 16,* 215–219.

Taylor, C. B., Miller, N. H., Herman, S., Smith, P. M., Sobel, D., Fisher, L., & DeBusk, R. F. (1996). A nurse-managed smoking cessation program for hospitalized smokers. *American Journal of Public Health, 86,* 1557–1560.

Tye-Murray, N. (1992). Preparing for communication interactions: The value of anticipatory strategies for adults with hearing impairment. *American Speech-Language-Hearing Association, 35,* 430–435.

Wagner, V., & L'Abate, L. (1977). Enrichment and written homework assignments with couples. In L. L'Abate. *Enrichment: Structured interventions with couples, families, and groups* (pp. 184–202). Washington, DC: University Press of America.

Weissman, M. M. (1995). *Mastering depression through interpersonal psychotherapy.* San Antonio, TX: The Psychological Corporation.

Wilson, S. R., Scamagas, P., German, D. F., Hughes, G. W., Lulla, S., Coss, S., Chardon, L., Thomas, S. R., Starr-Schneidkraut, N., & Stancavage, F. B., et al. (1993). A controlled trial of two forms of self-management education for adults with asthma. *American Journal of Medicine, 94,* 564–576.

Wincze, J. P., & Barlow, D. H. (1997). *Enhancing sexuality: A problem-solving approach.* San Antonio, TX: The Psychological Corporation.

Wylie-Rosett, J., Swencionis, C., Peters, M. H., Dornelas, E. A., Edlen-Nezin, L., Kelly, L. D., & Wassertheil-Smoller, S. (1994). A weight reduction intervention that optimizes use of practitioner's time, lowers glucose level, and raises HDL cholesterol level in older adults. *Journal of the American Dietary Association, 94,* 37–42.

Yeaton, W., Langenbrunner, J., Smyth, J., & Wortman, P. (1995). Exploratory research synthesis: Methodological considerations for addressing limitations in data quality. *Evaluation and the Health Professions, 18* (3), 283–303.

PART III

Clinical Applications

CHAPTER 6

A Feedback-Driven Computer Program for Outpatient Training

Roger L. Gould

This chapter is about the use of the computer as a psychotherapeutic agent, a concept that is foreign to most therapists, anathema to many, and mystifying to most who have not used such programs.

"COMPUTER AS THERAPIST"

The image of a plastic, metal, wired, and impersonal computer is in strong contrast to a patient's positive expectation of a warm, intelligent, caring therapist, experienced in the mysteries of the unconscious mind. How can a computer do what therapists do when we therapists know how hard it is to understand the complexity of any single life, how impossible it is at times to get through a patient's resistance to change or fully understand the meaning of what is being said, and how difficult it is to interpret accurately and therapeutically what is not being said?

The answer to these questions is simple. A computer, or more accurately, a computer program, cannot do what a therapist can do. A computer program cannot even understand natural language sufficiently well to reliably engage in the process, although much progress has been made in this area during the past 30 years. The human intelligence is of a different order than machine intelligence, and there will always be a gap between any program and a human therapist. Therapists cannot be re-created in purely electronic form.

However, therapists may still have to worry about being partially displaced in some circumstances. Computer programs can perform some functions that therapists cannot. Ken Colby expressed this quite well in 1986:

The advantage of a computer psychotherapist would be several. It does not get tired, angry, or bored. It is always willing to listen and to give evidence of having heard. It can work at any time of day or night, every day and every month. It does not have family problems. It does not try to perform when sick or hungover. It has no facial expressions of contempt, shock, surprise, etc. It is polite, friendly, and always has good manners. It is comprehensible and has a perfect memory. It does not seek money. It will cost only a few dollars a session. It does not engage in sex with its patients. It does what it is supposed to do and no more. (414–415)

In addition to the above, computer programs can print accurate verbatim summaries that can be handed to the patient at the end of the session so the therapeutic work can continue between sessions.

Do computers actually help patients do psychotherapeutic work? If effective, how do they do it? In this chapter, I answer these questions based on 18 years on the frontier.

A LITTLE HISTORY

The arc of my professional career is important background for understanding the work described here. From each phase of this arc comes the values and perspectives used to compose the Therapeutic Learning Program (TLP).

I started my professional career in psychiatry as a professor at UCLA responsible for outpatient services and community psychiatry. At the same time I was becoming a psychoanalyst. It was like living in two worlds simultaneously—the narrow and deep world of intrapsychic functioning, and the broad public health arena with concern for vast underserved at-risk populations.

From psychoanalysis came a deep appreciation for the fine and complex processes of thinking, and the many different ways that problems can be creatively resolved once insight is combined with a dedication to understanding the reality of a particular situation. I also learned to appreciate that although the past is important in theory, it is contemporaneous issues that occupy the bulk of the analytic hour, where the present is palpable and the potential future is at stake. Furthermore, I was forced to clarify the difference between the intrapsychic struggles and the more obvious interpersonal dynamics. Publicly, we live primarily in an interpersonal environment. Each interpersonal relationship creates numerous intrapsychic conflicts that have to be resolved. Even under the best of circumstances, when one falls deeply in love and enjoys all the glories of that state, he or she still has to deal with the conflict of competing needs for family, friends, work, and alone time. He or she has to decide about accommodating behavior and attitudes in order to have a finer fit with his or her partner. He or she has to undergo an internal separation event from former love objects, including parental imagos. When circumstances are difficult the intrapsychic struggle is more intense, and that in itself often leads to maladaptive behavior, making the circumstances even worse.

The community psychiatry challenge forced me to think about how to help the 20% of the population in distress deal with these finely grained cyclical intrapsychic and interpersonal conflicts. In those days, in the early 1970s, proper treatment was only intensive psychotherapy or psychoanalysis. The gap between resources and need seemed insurmountable.

My first attempt to explore this gap was in a paper entitled *Community Psychiatry and the Psychoanalytic Field Theory of Reality* (1970). This was an attempt to look at how external reality (institutions, workplace, interpersonal and small group phenomena) intersect with the dynamics of intrapsychic reality. The grandiose hope of the community psychiatry movement at the time was to make institutions and small groups more healthy as part of a "mental hygiene" approach. The outcome was supposed to be the creation of healthier individuals through a healthier environment. The paper was an attempt to outline the major highways of connection between inner and outer reality in a systematic way.

As part of that paper, I became aware that if you are going to look at inner and outer reality as an integrated dynamic, you have to take age into consideration. The outer reality of work, for example, is different for a 20-year old, a 40-year-old, and a 60-year-old. Work obviously has different meaning and importance at different times in the life cycle.

That led me to review Erik Erikson's work and to embark on empirical studies of adult development. The first publication was "The Phases of Adult Life" (1972) and then a book, *Transformations* (1978), which was an attempt to integrate adult development and phase of life theory with the everyday practice of psychotherapy.

By the time I had written these three pieces, I had all of the conceptual material I needed to embark on the 18-year project that produced our current software programs. The first three-year research grant focused on converting the concepts of adult development and the practice experience of psychotherapy into an integrated structured learning program. If it was possible to translate the art form of therapy into a systematic learning model, then one could find new ways of distributing this information and mediating these important processes other than face-to-face long-term therapy. The purpose was not to eliminate psychotherapy, but to add a tool for people who had distress of a subclinical variety, or an easier-to-resolve variety. They could do it on their own or use it as an augmentation between sessions to make the psychotherapy process more efficient.

At the end of a three-year project in 1982, we had a ten-session structured group learning program with a trainer's manual and a workbook for each participant. We had good research (Gould, 1996a) to show that it was a very effective and efficient treatment method. We also had preliminary evidence indicating that the classes could be taught by educators who did almost as well as trained mental health practitioners.

Just as we were about to embark on establishing a training institute, along came the PC and we decided to put the workbook on the computer. Every participant would have firsthand contact with the material that we so meticulously developed and would therefore be more empowered. Our thinking was that over time each of the therapists or educators leading the program would eventually dilute the program content with their own particular version or slant, and by putting the program on the computer, we were certain that the participant was at least exposed to a consistent and internally coherent model of change. In this way, the therapist variable was isolated.

In 1985, we developed a fully computerized ten-session program that could be used individually or in groups and gave the patient as well as the therapist a printout for discussion. This is TLP. Since its inception, 19,000 patients have gone through the program. In 1995 we added a new iteration of the TLP: self-directed care to be delivered on the Internet as our current Mastering Stress Program.

THE ESSENTIAL STARTING POINT

From a development perspective, adulthood is a continuation of the same separation individuation processes that are central to the adolescent struggle. There are distinctive phase patterns tied to age-related demands of the life cycle and the role requirements that come with mating, parenting, working, and grand-parenting.

The demand to grow and change is relentless and normal. Growth takes place more obviously during periods of transition, when unfamiliar demands and new situations require people to change their internal image of who they are. The person who grows a step separates from something that was, and becomes a more finely defined human being. The simple act of standing up for yourself with more confidence is one that can only be sustained by a concomitant internal imagery shift representing a more fully enfranchised human being. But there is a difference between change and development. All people change with age because new priorities in the life cycle require it. New attitudes and new behaviors can be straightforward responses to new circumstances that do not require a modification of a self-definition. The reality of facts or roles or responsibility requires a new combination of action or attitudes that are already encompassed in a flexible self-definition. The person's observed change and behavior is a conflict-free adaptational response. As people get older, they necessarily go through many such adaptations and demonstrate many new behaviors and attitudes. This is overt change but not the manifestation of the development model being discussed here.

Development is initiated when the person cannot respond with the appropriate adaptational response to a situation because the appropriate response is mired in internal conflict (inhibitions, defenses, or character patterns). The immediate challenge then is to loosen the rigidities of the self-definition so as to be able to respond appropriately and effectively to the healthy demand. When that conflict is successfully resolved, the person recovers necessary functions and is more fully, finely, and flexibly redefined.

Most patients come to treatment with symptoms that are consequences of this development struggle. If they could simply respond to the adaptational demand, they would not have the intense symptoms that are associated with intrapsychic conflict. Therapists frequently observe immense struggles in patients responding to normal demands of the life cycle that require relatively simple behavior change. Sometimes being available for a single person is as impossible as asking a shy person to speak publicly. Attempts to change behavior are blocked by increasing levels of negative affect, the content of which is catastrophic predictions about potential adverse consequences such as rejection and humiliation. The patient who has so much difficulty changing a simple behavior pattern is often observed to be confusing the inherent demand of the current situation (which calls for a relatively easy and safe change of behavior) with some earlier adaptational success that rewarded the rigid protective pattern that now ought to be modernized. The patient's conflict is between two different frames of reference. The crystallization of the past as part of a rigid self-definition has more power to compel behavior than the current demand situation. I have written extensively about these issues. Readers interested in a more detailed understanding of these concepts of adult development are invited to peruse my previous work (see references). For now it will be useful to condense all the complexity of adult development into a concept, a unit of development that might be defined as follows:

1. A specific adaptational demand inherent in the situation calls for a new behavior pattern that is not within the comfort zone of the current self-definition.

2. The patient achieves the required behavioral change only after doing a significant piece of psychological work that includes sorting out the difference between current reality and past realities in order to redefine himself or herself in terms of what he or she can or cannot do.

3. The patient arrives at a clear and better grounded understanding of current reality and a new position of strength.

At the center of the unit of adult development is the question of action. Will the individual choose to try the new action required by the situation, or will he or she avoid the action because of outdated fears that are still palpable and present? We created the TLP to help people intelligently wrestle with this particular choice in the most conscious and explicit way we could design. Our task was to design a program to help a patient sustain an interior dialogue about a distressing subject, and come to know and recognize an invisible conflict that was constantly obscured by catastrophic levels of fear.

THE THERAPEUTIC LEARNING PROGRAM

We created the TLP, a ten-session computer course, to help participants define a problem, propose an action solution, and resolve their conflict about taking action. In each session the patient spends about one-half hour alone with an interactive computer program, receives a feedback printout, and talks immediately thereafter with a therapist either individually or in a group session. The printout is the basis for the discussion with the therapist and focuses the treatment process into a series of decisions. The decisions at each stage are made by the patient after discussion with the therapist, and the patient is then ready to go on to the next session. A typical decision would be the prioritization of problems at the end of the first session in order to work on one problem at a time, and the prioritization of action solutions at the end of the second session in order to focus on a particular action conflict that represents the "invisible" development conflict.

The TLP is therapy conducted by a professional therapist. The goal is to remove symptoms by a changed perspective that comes about through clarification and decision making. It is short-term rather than prolonged. Interventions from the therapist are not provided through transference interpretations, but through help in distinguishing past adaptations from present realities, and rational from irrational thinking.

The TLP Mediates an Intrapsychic Experience

When the patient is working with the interactive program directly, he or she is really having a private, controlled, interpersonal relationship with the designer of the program. The program represents a condensation of years of therapeutic experience into a very explicit development model, translated into a computer program. The intelligence of the designer-therapist is built into the program and available to the patient. Since other consultants have contributed their wisdom and experience to the program, the TLP can be said to contain over 100 years of clinical experience. In this sense, the patient is having a phantom interpersonal conversation with a collective clinical "other."

The TLP program has been designed to help the patient have a self-reflective experience and, in particular, to create a "cleavage plane" between a rational contemporary part of the self and a conflicting part of the self dominated by an irrational past history. The participants in the TLP report that they forget about the program and the computer very quickly because they become so intrigued with their own internal drama. Their emotions are stimulated and they become inward, self-absorbed, and involved in a very intense self-reflective training process. In this sense, the person is having a private experience in which the medium is largely obliterated from emotional consciousness. We use special programming techniques, particularly the use of patients' favored language patterns, to facilitate this self-reflective internal process.

So far we might summarize the process from the patient's point of view as beginning with a phantom interpersonal relationship with the program designer. It quickly leads to an articulated intrapersonal dialogue between facilitative and inhibitory aspects of the self as the patient considers an action-oriented decision that represents a new development behavior.

When the patient completes the interactive portion of the program at the end of each module, he or she receives a printout. The printout documents everything that was learned in the interaction, including all of the distinctions between rational and irrational thinking that the person discovered. The format of the printout is straightforward. The skeleton of the printout reinforces the model of learning and allows for the specifics of the individual user.

In the printout, the patient's words and choice of language are reflected. The most commonly reported experience from the user is, "That is exactly what I am thinking, but I could never have said it more clearly or as exactly!" The program and the printout help patients become more articulate, focused, and clear thinking than they could possibly have been on their own in the same amount of elapsed time (about 30 minutes). In particular, the distinction between current perceptions and past distortions is clearly made. If it is not totally accurate, it is correctable by simply using a pen or pencil to cross out what is incorrect and substitute what is more correct. This printout is a very important thinking and remembering prosthesis. Patients frequently refer back to it between sessions as well as use it as a discussion piece with their therapist.

The TLP Mediates an Interpersonal Process

In this document, the work to be accomplished by patient and therapist is subtly laid out so that the essential activities of the therapeutic relationship are helpfully contained. This serves several purposes. On one hand, the patient is helped to think more clearly because he or she does not have to understand and articulate all thoughts but only deal with that which is essential at a particular step in the process. It also gives the patient confidence that he or she can talk intelligently with a trained therapist without feeling overwhelmed by the therapist's education and experience. It helps to democratize the interpersonal relationship and convert the therapist from a potential magical guru into a teacher who can help with a specific learning task.

Because the patient only has to master a specific point in the process at the moment of interaction, the dependence of the patient on the therapist is diminished and his or her self-confidence is increased. This leads to less resistance and more open communication and revelation than would otherwise take place in unmediated communication.

For example, a therapist may have spent as little as 10 or 15 minutes with the patient in the first two sessions, yet have an almost complete working knowledge of all the things that are bothering the patient, how the major issues should be prioritized, what the symptoms are, the exact statement of the patient's perceptions, the patient's acknowledged inability to cope in specific areas, the ineffective patterns, a choice of multiple action options, ideal areas in which the patient needs to develop, exact action statements, and healthy motives for carrying out the intended action. It would literally be impossible for this much information to be gathered and shared without the use of the computer program.

The interpersonal relationship between the patient and the therapist is a different relationship because of the medium. The patient is better prepared, less dependent, looking for a different kind of help, and more articulate. The therapist is also different. He or she is face-to-face with a different kind of patient, has less of a global responsibility, is guided by the focus and the model, has a tool to help do some of the insight and clarification work, and has an infinitely greater amount of information available to in a recorded and useable fashion than he or she would otherwise have.

The therapist is a teacher and is relieved of the burdensome role of guru. However, he still achieves the one important goal of ideal psychoanalytic communication, which is to demonstrate to patients the domination of their lives by reified, internal, object-controlled irrational patterns.

This process of working on the computer, getting a printout, and having an intrapsychic experience followed by an interpersonal relationship with a therapist is repeated for each of the ten steps in the process. The patient gets deeper into intrapersonal dialogue as the modules advance into deeper psychological issues. As the issues become deeper, that is, more emotionally powerful and related to earlier training patterns, the patient gets involved in more intense and emotionally cathected states of mind. Usually, in conventional unmediated treatment, this leads to a greater dependency on the therapist for guidance. But in the TLP, that does not occur because the patient becomes progressively more skilled in making distinctions about rational and irrational processes and is able to work with the programmed "lessons" as learning topics without being overwhelmed.

As an example of the kinds of issues that are dealt with in the latter half of the program, the question of one's negative self-esteem, which is the weakest and most vulnerable part of the psyche, is the subject matter for the whole second half of the course. When patients gain a new perspective on these deep fears, they become more independent and more anchored to their current time frame. They are then ready to leave the TLP course with a greater sense of control.

Description of the TLP Session

There are unique objectives for each of the ten TLP sessions. They are as follows:

1. Identifying stress-related problems, conflicts, and symptoms

    a. to identify sources of stress and ineffective responses

    b. to sort out stressful issues from development stress problems

    c. to prioritize one clearly stated stress problem that calls for some action

2. Clarifying goals and focusing on action

    a. to identify the development goal that addresses the adaptational demand

    b. to clarify and define the action or behavior change that is necessary

    c. to build an action intention that represents the recovery of the underdeveloped function

3. Thinking through the consequences of taking action

    a. to distinguish real dangers from exaggerated dangers

    b. to isolate and expose the fears as predictions confused with memories

    c. to reach a conscious, cost-beneficial, positive decision about the intended action

4. Uncovering hidden motives and fears of failure and success

    a. to clarify that certain strongly felt fears are not objective dangers

    b. to weaken the hold of irrational fears

    c. to learn to identify thinking errors as a useful concept

    d. to distinguish between healthy and unhealthy motives

    e. to demonstrate that fears of failure and success rarely point to real dangers

5. Exploring anger and guilt as obstacles to action

    a. to clarify that certain strong anxiety feelings are not indicative of external dangers

    b. to demonstrate that angry feelings are controllable by rational considerations

    c. to demonstrate that the feeling of guilt is information that can be processed to continue to confirm that the intended action is safe and do-able

6. Confronting issues of self-esteem

    a. to identify and acknowledge self-esteem sensitivities

    b. to begin to accept the universality and mystery of these sensitivities

    c. to entertain the thought that this powerful inner voice represents a historical fiction

    d. to understand that the self-esteem sensitivity is the biggest block to resolving the developmental conflict

7. Examining old and detrimental patterns of behavior

    a. to identify the deepest vulnerability that is being challenged by the action intention

    b. to see how the self-doubt triggers the ineffective protective behavior

    c. to examine and demonstrate how the self-doubt system feeds itself

    d. to begin to challenge the automatic response

8. Understanding the history of the self-doubt

    a. to expose the illusion of permanent damage

    b. to see that responses to early events were limited and naturally protective

    c. to see that these early protective behaviors were automatic responses to feeling inadequate

9. Analyzing a current incident involving the self-doubt

    a. to demonstrate and diminish self-fulfilling prophecies

    b. to identify the erroneous thinking that currently feeds the powerful self-doubt

    c. to understand that feeding the doubt by misinterpretation is a choice, not a necessity

    d. to recognize that to continue to do this is to avoid growth

10. Evaluating the changes experienced during the course

    a. to see that fears are to be overcome and not submitted to

    b. to see the action intention as part of ongoing recovery of function

    c. to understand that recovery of function and individuation is necessary

    d. to consolidate new views of reality

The result of adaptational action exploration leads to experimenting with new behavior and getting positive feedback. The patient moves from relative helplessness to empowerment as he or she finds successful adaptational options and acts on well-thought-out decisions. When this happens there is not only symptom reduction and function improvement, but there are also signs of a new vibrancy and zest for life as the patient takes control of a challenge that was previously immobilizing.

The TLP form of short-term therapy based on a developmental problem can be viewed, within a life course framework, as a form of therapy that helps a person progressively develop through intermittent episodes of treatment rather than traditional, long-term, continuous treatment. An argument can be made that patients are ready for change during crisis periods and that effective help during crises is a good way of leveraging scarce economic and clinical resources.

Generalized Learning

By the time patients have completed the program they have not only resolved the identified problem, but have also generated their own unique self-help book. This computer-generated, individualized self-help book has proved to be a surprisingly valuable part of after-treatment. In fact, in a three-year follow-up study done by a major client, CIGNA Healthplan, 75% of a sample of 2,000 patients continued to use these self-help books as guides and they claim the books have made a significant difference in the way they approach and resolve problem-in-living. The TLP is a tool that extends brief therapy into the highly desired realm of generalized learning.

Does Computer-Assisted Therapy Work?

Although computer therapy and computer-assisted therapy programs have been produced and studied for over 30 years, few have come to market. Most have been products of university research that have demonstrated efficacy on a small, scientifically valid sample but have not borne the test of everyday clinical usage on a large scale. The TLP has been somewhat of an exception.

Ten separate studies have been completed over the past decade on samples totaling roughly 15% of the patient population who used the TLP. Each study supports the conclusion that the TLP is an effective short-term therapy program. Favorable comparisons have been made to a panel of clinicians who did not use the program. The most recent study done at UCLA compared patients who received ten face-to-face therapy sessions with patients who used only the TLP. Both groups did equally well at a six-month follow-up. In addition, one study already quoted strongly suggests that generalized learning continues for at least 3 years and that 65% of the users keep their printouts for reference with future problems in living. All of the TLP studies are reported in detail in Gould (1996a).

In addition to the studies on the TLP, outcome studies have been conducted on the major cognitive behavioral computer programs. There are striking findings in studies that parallel the UCLA TLP study (e.g., several self-administered smoking cessation programs demonstrated abstinence rates equivalent to well-run live programs).

Consequently, there is a growing body of evidence that computers are not only strong adjunctive treatments to ongoing therapy, but actually powerful substitutes for many. The patient accepts and utilizes the computer. Furthermore, all of the satisfaction studies in the literature, and our own reported and unreported studies, confirm that patients across treatment settings like using the computer. They find it helpful and easy to use. They tend to be more honest in their replies and more forthcoming with sensitive information when they are comfortable with the arrangements for confidentiality.

One very appreciative patient wrote the following poem about the TLP:

Ode to My Own TLP

Like a thief in the night
thou striketh fear unto hearts
of those who would not conform
to thy quiet strength

Thou listens to every
cry and thought and feeling
with such compassion and love
as each soul pleads for guidance.

Thou art a tender loving person
Who answereth prayer and
does not scorn the petition of the
Humblest of thy people.

Thou inspireth self discovery
and bringeth forth self worth and joy.
We join voices with yours in exclamation
Damn we're good.

The next big move in our journey was when we turned toward self-directed care. This was stimulated by the UCLA-Kaiser study.

Kaiser and UCLA Studies

The Kaiser Foundation funded two studies, one at UCLA and the other at the Kaiser Foundation Outpatient Center in Los Angeles (Snibbe, Dolezal, & Belar, 1995). The Kaiser study compared 54 patients treated by TLP group therapy with 55 patients treated by cognitive behavioral group therapy. The findings replicated the results on CIGNA TLP group therapy a decade earlier. This included the same high degree of satisfaction, effectiveness, and therapist rating of effectiveness.

This study added new weight to the evidence for the TLP as a treatment tool. It was a well conducted random assignment comparison study using standard pre- and post-measurement tools for depression, anxiety, and severity and sophisticated data analysis techniques. At the end of ten group sessions and at the six-month follow-up, both the experimental and control groups were significantly and equally improved. When the Kaiser study group compared TLP group effectiveness ratings to the literature on brief therapy, they found the TLP group to rate quite a bit higher at the end of ten sessions (82% versus 50%) and much quicker in achieving equal effectiveness (10 sessions versus 26 sessions).

The UCLA study (Jacobs, Christianson, Huber, Snibbe, Dolezal, & Polterock, 1995) focused on individual treatment rather than group treatment. They used essentially the same measurement tools on 100 outpatients divided into control and experimental groups. By the end of the treatment and at a six-month follow-up, both groups had improved significantly and equally.

This study adds new information about potential use of the TLP as a self-help tool as well as evidence for its effectiveness and efficiency as a therapeutic tool. The TLP was used in a unique way. The experimental group received ten

TLP sessions but only 10 to 15 minutes per session with a therapist clarifying the printout and the next steps but avoiding usual therapeutic conversations. The comparison group was given ten full therapeutic hours without the TLP.

Ending up with identical effectiveness and satisfaction after minimal expenditure of therapist time opens the door to the possible use of the TLP as a self-help tool or as a follow-up to brief therapy (many of the brief therapy control patients requested the use of the computer program during their follow-up interviews) or as an efficient way of utilizing therapist time.

IMPLEMENTATION BARRIERS TO OVERCOME

Before computer-assisted programs like the TLP can be successfully implemented, at least five major challenges have to be addressed.

- Therapist's belief in the sanctity of the "relationship"
- Financial threat to various stakeholders
- The question of rigor and quality
- Organizational resistance
- Patient resistance

I have discussed each of these in detail in a chapter on reengineering mental health (Gould, 1998). I will summarize my thoughts about the relationship challenge here.

Sanctity of the Therapeutic Relationship

There is a strong phenomenological basis for some of this resistance; it is difficult for people to conceive of the computer's being useful in an intimate relationship, especially when they visualize the computer coming between the two people. Although the perception can be quite strong, it is not consistent with the actual sequential process of how computer-assisted therapy programs are used.

Another argument against the use of computers in therapy cites research findings about the strong correlation between positive outcomes and a trusting patient-therapist relationship. This argument asserts that no patient could actually trust a computer as he or she would a therapist or other human being. However, our studies have shown that patients trust the therapist more in combination with the computer. Therefore, the program serves to enhance the therapeutic relationship. But what is not said, and what is probably the most important element of the argument, is the implicit belief that the "relationship" itself is therapeutic.

There are many theories that explain how the relationship can be therapeutic. The relationship itself provides patients with firsthand experience to which they must adapt. The therapist brings special qualities of empathy and care that foster trust. If we switch the emphasis from trust to adaptation and learning, it can be argued that during the course of the relationship, patients learn something about themselves and about new ways of looking at and resolving problems in living. Trust is the mediating factor, and learning is the therapeutic factor. The fact that learning takes place within the relationship is the change ingredient that is therapeutic.

Until this is pointed out, therapeutic trust is taken out of context and elevated to be the only therapeutic factor. Learning can take place in many different ways and through many experiences, sometimes directly with people at home and at work and at other times mediated through newspapers, television, movies, novels, self-help books, and, the most powerful self-help modality of them all, the interactive computer.

MASTERINGSTRESS.COM—OUR CURRENT FOCUS

Stimulated by the UCLA study, we set out to create a consumer-friendly Internet site where we could deliver the first part of the TLP to the public.

We chose "stress" as an umbrella word to cover the whole spectrum from aggravations of daily life to severe depression and substance abuse. We chose to start with the first two concepts of the TLP, "What's bothering you and what can you do about it," as the most immediately accessible level for the general public. Then we package this into a broader program that could serve both as a self-help program and an augmentation to employee assistant program (EAP) services. We plan on revising the program for medical visits in order to deal with the large-scale public health problem of stress in the doctor's office.

The Problem

Stress is costly to employers both directly and through inflated health plan costs. The direct cost impact on productivity has been estimated by the New York Business Group on Health to be $2 billion. They report that depression, anxiety, and stress account for the following:

• 47% of reduced productivity
• 40% of morale problems
• 40% of absenteeism
• 30% of substance abuse
• 29% of poor work quality

Health plans have to contend with the fact that 23 million Americans now have an anxiety disorder, and one in five will suffer a debilitating depression during their lifetime. When one considers the relationship between stress and addictions, as well as lifestyle and compliance with disease management routines, the size of the problem increases.

Although the figures listed earlier tell us of the magnitude of the stress problem in this country, the more immediate grounding statistic comes from the studies done by the National Institutes of Mental Health. It reports that 25% of the population is stressed each day to the same degree as those who have a diagnosable mental illness. Although 25% of the population has this high degree of distress, only 4% of the population are in treatment with either a mental health provider or an EAP practitioner. That means that 21% of the population of the United States (or 84% of those under stress) do not seek expert professional care for their stress and either find care elsewhere or go without care.

There are many barriers that keep people from going to a mental health provider or an EAP counselor: stigma, cost, inconvenience, questions of value, fear of what might happen, and worries about confidentiality, especially having personal information on their medical or employee record. Recent articles in the *New York Times* indicate that many will pay for expensive out-of-pocket mental health care to avoid having a mental record that might complicate their careers.

Where do the 84% of the distressed population go for help? They fall into four broad categories:

- *Self-medication.* People use over-the-counter medication, turn to alcohol and drugs, and use smoking and eating habits to dull their pain.

- *Alternative medication.* More and more people are seeking alternative medicine and other nontraditional approaches. It has been estimated that the amount of money spent for nontraditional health care is equal to the amount spent for health care directly. There is a recent surge of consumer demand to include nontraditional health care approaches in the health plan, in part, to solve the problem of distress.

- *Primary care physicians.* People see their primary care physicians with physical complaints and fatigue or exhausted immune systems. It has been estimated that over 50% of primary care visits are stress-related. Many studies have indicated that primary care physicians underdiagnose both substance abuse and depression, and when depression is treated, it is undertreated. Since the physician is not trained or does not have incentives to engage in sufficient dialogue with the patient to understand the causes of stress, he or she is more likely to offer palliative interventions, order marginally indicated laboratory tests to rule out organic disease, or precribe expensive medications for the stress symptoms of indigestion, heartburn, depression, and anxiety.

- *Stress endurance.* There are many people who do nothing and just endure and sometimes get worse. This part of the distressed population suffers unnecessarily long and probably contributes disproportionately to the productivity loss identified by the New York Business Group on Health in the statistics quoted earlier.

The Solution

The problem of stress and health care costs is large and complicated. There is no magical solution. But there is an almost magical starting point, which can be the beginning of a comprehensive solution. The Mastering Stress Program is the starting point where employees and HMO members can go to receive intelligent recommendations about what they can do for themselves and where they can get help that is customized to their particular set of circumstances.

The only barrier to access is the Internet or the corporate Intranet. The remaining barriers of stigma, cost, embarrassment, loss of control, inconvenience, and access are eliminated. Although the issue of trust and confidentiality cannot be entirely eliminated, those barriers are minimized in the program described here.

The Mastering Stress Program

The employer or health plan subscribes to the Mastering Stress Program and gives the employees or members an access code. Employees come to the web site and put in the employer or health plan access code. At this time, they have a choice of putting in their names or fictitious names if they are worried about confidentiality and security. Employees have access to the site 24 hours a day.

The computer program starts a "conversation" with the employee about the degree and kind of stress the employee has today. This conversation is conducted through a series of menus and feedback dialogue screens that help the employee describe, without necessarily typing in, stress level, feelings of distress, level of daily functioning, physical symptoms, mood changes, change in behavior patterns like sleeping or eating, current problems of daily life that are triggering or causing the stress, and ways in which he or she might be inadvertently making the stress worse by habitual attempts to modulate stress level.

After this brief screening conversation, the user will get a summary on screen that can be printed and used for self-monitoring. If this first-stage screening, "Stress Portrait," suggests problems that may require the attention of a professional, the computer program makes a strong recommendation that the user proceed to the "Getting Help" module.

In the "Getting Help" module, the information from the "Stress Portrait" will be the beginning of a more precise questioning protocol. The answer to the questions will be played against commonsense criteria about whether individuals should be seeing their primary physicians, their mental health providers, or their EAP practitioners, or seeking help in various community self-help and support groups such as AA or Al-Anon.

Our research with antecedent computer programs used by more than 27,000 people indicates that people are much more honest on the computer than they are in face-to-face interviews. Our findings have been corroborated by many other published reports, giving us confidence that the data provided by the user who is looking for help are uniquely valid and useful.

In addition to or instead of the recommendations to providers, the user will get self-help recommendations and may decide that a self-help effort should be made first.

In addition to the screening "Stress Portrait" and the "Getting Help" modules, there are additional self-help modules to assist the user in solving problems at work or at home as well as learning more about self-care ways of reducing tension (stress course on-line).

Benefits

There are three key benefits from using the Mastering Stress Program.

1. Early intervention, prevention, screening. There is a unique opportunity for early intervention, prevention, and screening. As employees and their families become comfortable with using the Mastering Stress Program, the opportunities increase to do screening and triage for depression, substance abuse, and the cardiac symptoms that sometimes mimic and are confused with stress symptoms.

2. Quality of care. When an employee follows through with a recommendation for care, he or she will present the provider with a printed summary of the reason he or she is there. The professional visit will be facilitated and made more efficient. It will be more likely to succeed from the patient's point of view because it starts clearly from the patient's well-documented starting point.

   This will be of particular value when the patient presents himself or herself to the primary care physician. It can increase the accuracy of diagnosis of substance abuse and depression and thereby lead to more effective treatment by the primary care physician as well as providing an appropriate rationale when referral to a mental health provider is recommended. It will be a great aid to the primary physician who does not have the time to go into the personal matters causing stress symptoms.

3. Appropriateness of stress-related medical visits. When individuals have completed the "Stress Portrait" and "Getting Help" modules and additional self-care modules, they may decide medical visits are unnecessary. Better yet, some individuals will follow through on medical visits because they believe they are necessary when they would not otherwise have gone. In either case, there is a more appropriate use of medical resources.

CONCLUSION

Throughout this chapter I have described two major programs, a history of my thinking about adult development, experiences with computer-assisted and self-directed therapy, research results, and a rationale for the value of computers in the self-help and personal development enterprise.

The central theme running throughout is the fundamental fact that both relief from stress and personal growth require the resolution of an intrapsychic conflict.

And a computer program is the perfect tool to accomplish this on a large scale. It is not advice that is delivered. It is more what a good therapist would do—facilitate a process that leads to a higher level of conscious thinking. The starting point is being "stuck" or unclear. The ending point is clarity and better reality testing. The product is consciousness, mindfulness, perspective, insight, awareness.

The computer program, delivered over the Internet, is a conscious, producing machine. That is the beacon that has guided my professional life for the past 20 years.

REFERENCES

Colby, K. M. (1986). Ethics of computer-assisted psychotherapy. *Psychatr. Ann., 16,* 414–415.

Gould, R. L. (1972, November). The phases of adult life: Study in developmental psychology. *American Journal of Psychiatry, 129* (5), 521–531.

Gould, R. L. (1978). *Transformations: Growth and change in adult life.* New York: Simon & Schuster.

Gould, R. L. (1986, September). The Therapeutic Learning Program (TLP): A computer-assisted short-term program. *Computers in Psychiatry/Psychology.*

Gould, R. L. (1989). Adulthood. In H. I. Kaplan & B. J. Sadock (Eds.), *Comprehensive textbook of psychiatry* (5th ed., Vol. 1). Baltimore: Williams & Wilkins.

Gould, R. L. (1990a). Clinical lessons from adult development. In A. Nemiroff & C. A. Colarusso (Eds.), *New dimensions in adult development.* New York: Basic Books.

Gould, R. L. (1990b). The Therapeutic Learning Program. In J. Mezirow (Ed.), *Fostering critical reflection in adulthood.* New York: Jossey-Bass.

Gould, R. L. (1990c). Therapeutic Learning Program (TLP): Computer assisted short-term psychotherapy. In Gary Gumpert & Sandra L. Fish (Eds.), *Talking to strangers: Mediated therapeutic communication.* Norwood, NJ: Ablex.

Gould, R. L. (1992). Brief psychotherapy and adult development and computer assisted therapy in an HMO setting. In *Mental health and managed care.* Washington, DC: American Psychiatric Press.

Gould, R. L. (1996a). Development, problem solving, and generalized learning: The Therapeutic Learning Program (TLP). In M. Miller, K. Hammond, & M. Hile (Eds.), *Mental health computing.* New York: Springer.

Gould, R. L. (1996b). The use of computers in therapy. In T. Trabin & M. Freeman (Eds.), *The computerization of healthcare.* San Francisco: Jossey-Bass.

Gould, R. L. (1998). Reengineering mental health. In W. Currey (Ed.), *Reengineering health.* Tampa, FL: American College of Physician Executives.

Gould, R. L., Colby, K. M., & Aronson, G. (1989). Some pros and cons of computer-assisted psychotherapy. *Journal of Nervous and Mental Diseases, 177* (2), 106–108.

Jacobs, M., Christianson, A., Snibbe, J., Dolezal, S., Huber, A., & Poletrock, A. (1995). Computer-assisted individual therapy vs. standard, brief individual therapy. Presented at the Annual Symposium of the Western Psychological Association, Los Angeles, CA.

Snibbe, J., Dolezal, S., & Belar, C. (1995). Computer-assisted psychotherapy vs. standard cognitive-behavior group therapy: Do computers have a future? Presented at the Annual Symposium of the Western Psychological Association, Los Angeles, CA.

CHAPTER 7

Computer Workbooks in Psychotherapy with Psychiatric Patients

Piero De Giacomo and Sabina De Nigris

In this chapter we describe our experiences in the creation and clinical applications of workbooks to be administered to well-functioning individuals as well as psychiatric patients (i.e., respondents) through computers. We view these workbooks as means of discovering more about how respondents' minds work and increasing their awareness of cognitive processes that would not be noticed otherwise. The completion of assignments in each workbook is intended to increase cognitive flexibility and improve the respondents' awareness and knowledge of how they relate with intimate others, as in ways of living in a relationship and relationship styles. This awareness can then be compared with how the same relational aspects are perceived by intimate others. At present, we have available a CD-ROM containing several workbooks in Italian and in English. Our purpose is to offer respondents to each workbook the possibility of observing themselves and the world around them as they perceive it or as perceived by intimate others. They are confronted by a variety of personal and interpersonal situations as well as 16 different relational functions (De Giacomo, 1994, 1995, 1996, 1999; De Giacomo & De Giacomo, 1997; De Giacomo, Storelli, De Giacomo, & Vaira, 1998).

The process is like putting on an extra pair of special lenses with which individuals can observe behaviors that occur inside and outside themselves, as seen, for instance, from at least 16 different viewpoints or nine experiences from the past. Next, respondents are encouraged to recognize and to master these 16 styles of constructing relationships by interacting with them and choosing different sequences. This process is like intellectual gymnastics that are intended to amplify cognitive and intellectual potentials and make them more flexible.

Three workbooks are designed to (1) increase *cognitive flexibility* and widen creative possibilities; (2) improve *moodiness*, aiming at the discovery and improvement of sequences in cognitive constructions; and (3) improve respondents' knowledge about *relationship styles*, how they relate with intimate others. The first and third workbooks derive directly from a model of relationships that has already been described in a number of publications (De Giacomo, 1993; De Giacomo, 1996; De Giacomo, L'Abate, & De Giacomo, 1997) reviewed by L'Abate (1994), Price (1997), and Gardner (1997). This "elementary pragmatic" model has also been compared with attachment and developmental competence models developed respectively by Bowlby (Cassidy & Shaver, 1999) and L'Abate (1997, 1998).

The elementary pragmatic model is based on four coordinates that derive from exemplary interactions between subject A (husband) and subject B (wife). The same interactions could take place between parent and child, lovers, friends, and boss and subordinate. These interactions are composed of elements that form the content of shared (common) internal and external worldviews: (1) internal-external; (2) one's worldview; (3) the other's worldview; and (4) whatever is common to the two worldviews. The process of change that results from the mutual coming together of two individuals according to these four elements forms the four coordinates of the model:

1. *Acceptance* of an event or experience that did not exist in the husband's world but that existed in the wife's world and is accepted in the interaction. For instance, when the husband says, "I don't want to watch TV," the wife replies, "Come on, in a little while a great program will be on." As a result of the wife's comment, the husband acquiesces to her proposal, and he watches TV.

2. *Maintenance* of one's own world occurring when something that existed in the husband's world but did not exist in the wife's world is accepted. For instance, he suggests "I want to watch TV," and the wife replies instead, "I want to go out," but nevertheless she then acquiesces and eventually watches TV with the husband, allowing and encouraging him to maintain his own view.

3. *Sharing* of one's world with another, when an event or experience existing in both the wife's and husband's worlds is accepted by both parties. For instance, he says, "Tonight I want to watch TV," and the wife replies, "Me too, dear," and they end up both watching TV.

4. *Antifunction*, which represents inconsistent or contradictory rejection-acceptance of a proposal that is neither world. For instance, the husband says, "I do not want to watch TV," the wife replies, "Neither do I," but nevertheless they both end up watching TV.

From the possible merging (combinations and permutations, 4 × 4) of these four coordinates, 16 relational styles, called functions (F), are derived:

F0. Emptiness of mind, when nothing is accepted and there is no acceptance of one or the other's world, nor of external elements common to the two interactants. The subject is annulled in the relationship.

F1. Sharing of part of one's world with part of the other's, when only what is common to both worlds is accepted, such as two workers who work on something they have to do when at work but who then go their separate ways after leaving work.

F2. Exclusive acceptance of one's world but not of the other's nor of whatever may be common to the two. This process implies the exclusive acceptance of one's own personal world (at the end of the interaction only what belongs to this exclusive personal world remains). Here, the subject has maintained only the intersecting space that was common to both. For instance, a self-centered individual ignores, dismisses, and discounts the other's proposal and whatever the other may have in common in the relationship.

F3. Maintenance of one's world through acceptance not only of one's own world but also of whatever is in common with the other's worldview, as seen in extremely selfish and rigidly unbending individuals who take from the other what is already in their world.

F4. Accepting the world of another without sharing it, as, for instance, in passive individuals who yield uncritically and flexibly to the other's worldview, surrendering their own worldview to the other's worldview, thus giving up their own worldview and, possibly or partially, the self.

F5. Accepting only the other's worldview and what is common to both worldviews, as, for instance, in individuals who, altruistically and gratefully, actively accept the other's proposals.

F6. Accepting one's own and the other's world without sharing it, as, for instance, in so-called selfish-altruists who hesitate to share either world.

F7. Accepting one's own and the other's world by mediating both worlds harmoniously without getting lost in the other's world.

The next eight functions are characterized by events or experiences that did not previously exist in the interacting subjects' world but are accepted ("anti-function").

F8. Accepting only what does not exist in one's own or in the other's worldview, accepting external elements of a new worldview that were not present previous to the interaction and that were not common to both worldviews. For instance, words or acts that are irrelevant or extraneous to what is going on in an interaction, such as raising the issue of the price of eggs in China while having intercourse.

F9. Accepting only what exists or does not exist in one's own and the other's worldview, as, for instance, unquestioning and uncritical sharing of what is in common in the internal and external worlds. Another example could be a couple of average people who share the decision to buy a very expensive and unusual pet, like an elephant.

F10. Accepting only what exists in one's internal worldview as well as the external world but that does not exist in the other's worldview or whatever is shared, as in "Mary, Mary, quite contrary," that is, active, systematic opposition, spiteful negativism, and continuous obstructionism.

F11. Maintaining totally one's own world with tendencies toward expansion, involving the acceptance of one's own worldview. This function includes whatever is shared with the other's worldview as well as whatever is foreign to one's and the other's worldview. An example would be an exaggerated sticking to one's own world and, if there is opposition, becoming confused while attempting to expand toward the worldview of the other, as seen in bullies, dictators, and arrogant egotists who are confronted by revolutions or powerful forces that may destroy their worldview or hegemony.

F12. Accepting only what exists in the other's worldview without sharing it but accepting also whatever does not exist in one's own worldview nor in the other's worldview—for instance, a pseudo-altruist who appears to accept the other's worldview but in reality maintains his or her own world. This process may be illustrated by martyrs who do it for their own sake and not for the sake of others, or in those who get pleasure from giving pleasure to others.

F13. Rejecting what exists exclusively in one's own worldview but accepting the other's worldview and whatever is common that does not exist in one or the other's worldview but not what is part of one's own worldview. This process is seen in an amplification of the other person's worldview while refusing only what exists exclusively in one's own worldview. For example, if one partner likes pets, the partner who hates pets gives the other a snake as a gift.

F14. Total acceptance of one's own worldview, the other's worldview, and the world external to both, without accepting shared elements, as seen in individuals who cannot focus directly and complete interactions successfully, as in premature ejaculation.

F15. Total acceptance of whatever exists in one's own and the other's worlds internally and externally, as seen in individuals who accept unselectively and inconclusively whatever exists in their and the other's worldview.

THE *MENTAL FLEXIBILITY* WORKBOOK

We have translated these 16 functions into 16 mental states, using them as springboards for reflection and the organization of thoughts. There are 16 ways to increase our awareness of relationships, sixteen variables to be filled with contents. Contents may change, but the processes remain the same. This translation was made easier by a workbook that leads to progressive widening out, "like a funnel," from the strictly formal language of the model to the common language used by people in everyday life. Before explaining how we have transformed the 16 relationship styles into 16 steps in the workbook, we must describe its organization.

To develop creativity, it is necessary, as a first step, to establish the general framework, as follows: "Here is an effort to develop new ideas." This framework is implicit in the very process that, working on this workbook, by definition, aims at increasing cognitive flexibility and, possibly, the ability to solve problems creatively. The second step consists of defining the problem. Respondents' identification of which assignment to use in the workbook is one of the most important aspects of this step. This process must serve as a stimulus for developing a sequential view, according to constructions derived from the 16 styles based on the elementary pragmatic model. Thus, it must be a strongly perceived problem, arousing deep interest, with strong motivation to solve it. In short, the problem must be a real one, able to set in motion the "tape of the mind" that continuously runs in our heads.

The first assignment of this workbook invites respondents to find a problem whose solution is important to them. This invitation forces respondents to find an important problem that presently is occupying and preoccupying their awareness, attention, and energy. The more specific the focus of the attention and awareness, the easier it might be to mobilize a solution to the specific problem. This step, which seems vital, is to invite respondents to enter into a process that will allow them to generalize from one solution to one specific problem to solutions of other problems. After overcoming the first step in a search for a problem to solve, respondents enter a phase where they proceed along a sequence of frames corresponding to the 16 styles in the elementary pragmatic model, as shown in detail below.

After finishing the sequential series of assignments dedicated to problem finding and solution, there is a section where it is possible to complete free assignments, without necessarily following the original sequence. The functions that seem most mentally demanding can be practiced. They are also more useful for constructive thinking. When respondents become expert in the use of the framework of 16 styles, they are invited to make an assessment of the entire workbook (very useful, useful, not very useful, useless).

Finally, there is a supervisory mode that is independent from the respondent mode. This supervisory mode serves to analyze how respondents have reacted to the 16 steps of the workbook. In this way, it is possible to evaluate how whoever has completed the workbook has answered at every step of the sequence. Thus, it is possible to have documentation, through printing, of the answers given by each respondent. This mode can be accessed using a special password at the beginning of the respondent mode. Essentially, this second mode serves as a feedback function over the respondents' answers.

We now embark on a brief description of the 16 steps of the sequence of the workbook assignments, where we administer 16 functions of the elementary pragmatic model as 16 single modules according to three approaches: (1) individual, (2) relational, and (3) problem solving.

For F0, a single module is proposed: respondents should empty their minds completely. There are no individual, relational, or problem-solving modules.

For F1, the proposal for the *individual approach* is to focus on a nearby object (e.g., the computer mouse, a pen, etc.) until it becomes sharply outlined against a blurred background. For the *relational approach*, respondents are told to think about something that is common to their own and their partner's mental worlds. As to *problem solving*, respondents are asked to solve the problem using elements common to their own and their partner's worlds.

For F2, the *individual approach* proposes that respondents should concentrate on a part or function of their body that nobody else except they know about.

For the *relational approach*, respondents have to think about something that can only exist in their own mental world. *Problem solving* involves solving their problem with their own highly personal mental organization, without taking into account any other person or external factor.

For F3, respondents in the *individual approach* are asked to concentrate on a part or function of their body that is also accessible to others' experience. For the *relational approach*, they are to think about something that belongs to their own world (even if it also belongs to their partner's mental world). As to *problem solving*, they are asked to solve their problem adopting the attitude that they must decide on the solution according to their own personal mental organization (even if this organization may coincide with the partner's).

For F4, the *individual approach* proposes concentration on an object that does not belong and that could never belong to the respondent. For the *relational approach*, respondents have to think about something that belongs exclusively to their partner's mental world. As to *problem solving*, they are asked to solve their partner's problem exclusively by using their own highly personal mental organization if one refers to the partner's highly personal cognitive makeup.

For F5, the *individual approach* proposes concentration on an object belonging to somebody else. For the *relational approach*, respondents are to think of elements that exist in their partner's mental world. For the *problem-solving* task, they are to solve their problem by identifying with their partner's mental world.

For F6, the *individual approach* asks respondents what might come to mind if they avoid thinking about the thing that is foremost in their mind at that moment. The *relational approach* asks them to think about elements that exist in their own and their partner's worlds but that they do not talk about. As to *problem solving*, respondents are asked to think about how not to solve their problem, by approaching it exclusively from their own or from their partner's point of view without finding any common point of agreement. Or, they can think about two antithetical types of solution and balance the two so that no concrete solution can be found.

For F7, the *individual approach* proposes concentration on two objects that should then be linked through identifying their common, connecting points and differences. In the *relational approach*, respondents are asked to think about specific elements of their own world and specific elements of their partner's world and to link them through identifying their common points and differences. As to *problem solving*, respondents are asked to find a solution that may include their own world and their partner's world.

For F8, the *individual approach* proposes that respondents should empty their minds and then quote the first thought that comes to mind. This exercise should be repeated five times to give this function a greater weight than the others. For the *relational approach* (if the partner is present), respondents are asked to repeat the previous exercise, writing down alternately their partner's thoughts and their own (this approach, too, should be repeated five times). For the *relational approach* (if the partner is absent), respondents are asked to empty their minds and then write down the first thought in reference to their partner that comes to mind. As to *problem solving*, they are asked to empty their minds and think of the first solution that comes to mind, even the most absurd (this exercise should be repeated ten times).

For F9, the *individual approach* proposes that respondents should place a thought at the center of their minds (a dominant thought at that moment or else any thought, or a thought that can be drawn from F8) and then modify it paradoxically (deform it, distort it, grossly expand a single part of it, etc.). For the *relational approach*, respondents are asked to think of something (a thought, an object, a behavioral act) that is common to them and their partner and then modify it paradoxically (deform it, distort it, grossly expand a single part of it, etc.). As to *problem solving*, respondents are asked to imagine a possible solution that could be agreed on by their partner and to exaggerate it paradoxically (deform it, distort it, grossly expand a single part of it, etc.).

For F10, the *individual approach* asks respondents to think of the way they can perceive the world, build up their thoughts, and act on the world in that moment. After this step, they are asked to turn the thought upside down, to invert it and think of the reverse, the opposite. For the *relational approach* they are asked to think of their partner's world and turn it upside down, thinking of the reverse. Finally, as to *problem solving* they are asked to think of a possible solution and then find its opposite (the antisolution).

For F11, for the *individual approach* respondents are asked to think of something in their own world that is so important that they would give their life for it. In the *relational approach* they are asked to think of what they could do if they had absolute, dictatorial powers over their partner. Finally, in *problem solving*, they are asked how they would proceed to solve the problem if they had absolute powers.

For F12, the *individual approach* asks respondents to concentrate on an object that does not belong to them and never could and to transform it paradoxically (to exaggerate it, deform it, distort it, grossly expand a single part of it, etc.). For the *relational approach* they are asked to think of something that would apparently favor the partner but in reality favors themselves. As to *problem solving*, they are asked to think of a solution that would apparently favor the partner but in reality favors themselves.

For F13, the *individual approach* asks respondents to think of an object that belongs to somebody else and to transform it paradoxically (to exaggerate it, deform it, distort it, grossly expand a single part of it, etc.). For the *relational approach* they are asked to think of something that belongs to their partner's world and to transform it paradoxically (to exaggerate it, deform it, distort it, grossly expand a single part of it, etc.). As to *problem solving*, they are asked to think of the solution that could be adopted by their partner and to transform it paradoxically (to exaggerate it, deform it, distort it, grossly expand a single part of it, etc.).

For F14, the *individual approach* asks respondents to think of phrases with internal contradictions (like realistic fantasy, controlled delirium, productive backsliding, reasonable folly, oriented disinhibition). For the *relational approach* they are asked to think of a situation that could involve them and their partner and to transform it into a metaphor (e.g., a wife who had various affairs with other men was able to tell her husband that she was like a butterfly that flew from flower to flower). As to *problem solving*, they are asked to transform the problem into a metaphor of the problem.

Finally, for F15, no guidelines are given. The respondents' minds can range freely: they can think and write whatever they like.

Evaluating the *Mental Flexibility* Workbook

Our workbook has been evaluated thus far through consumer satisfaction (well-functioning individuals) and the clinical outcome in the functioning of psychiatric patients, as reported in representative case studies to follow.

This workbook's consumer satisfaction was evaluated by: (1) medical students that were attending a first-year psychology class—men and women of 19 years of age from the academic years 1996, 1997, and (2) graduate students attending a course on Theories and Techniques for the Development of Creativity, with a mean age of 30 years, enrolled in the years 1996, 1997, 1998, for a total of 535 respondents. The age range for all respondents was from 19 to 39.

Problems reported by the students after completing this workbook can be grouped into five areas:

- problems concerning study and work, 30.28%
- relationship problems, 24.67%
- existential psychological problems, 21.50%
- everyday life problems, 15.33%
- leisure time problems, 8.22%

The *Mental Flexibility* workbook was completed by all respondents in the sample. The final workbook assessment was made on a four-point scale, included as a last task at the end of the workbook. The consumer satisfaction was positive in the great majority of cases. The final evaluation of the workbook usefulness was anonymous because reading and printing the answers was entirely independent from the grades obtained in the classroom course. The final evaluation consisted of: (1) very useful, 7%; (2) useful, 79%; (3) not very useful, 7%; and (4) useless, 7%.

For each step of the workbook, that is, each of the 16 functions, there was also an attempt by each respondent to grade the difficulty of each passage (very difficult, difficult, not difficult, not difficult at all). It was found that the greatest difficulties were encountered with F10, corresponding to antithetical thinking

Table 7–1
Workbook Assessment

Parameters	Group 1		Group 2	
Values	N	%	N	%
Excellent	128	23.93	202	37.76
Good	220	41.12	200	37.38
Fair	156	29.16	104	19.44
Poor	31	5.79	29	5.42
Total	535	100.00	535	100.00

(i.e., turning the problem upside down) and F14, corresponding to metaphorical thinking (transforming the problem into a metaphor of the problem).

The qualitative evaluation of the respondents' answers, although standardized, is based on subjective judgments by male-female couples of judges, usually working outside the university setting. One member of each couple was a psychologist, while the other was either a medical doctor or a psychiatry resident. Both judges were extremely familiar with the workbook, rendering their personal opinion about the respondents' answers on a four-point scale (excellent, good, fair, and poor), expressed for each workbook on the basis of four parameters: (1) presence of originality; (2) coherence of the answers; (3) assessment of the thinking process; and (4) completeness of the program.

As shown in Table 7–1, about 60% to 70% of the workbooks were judged by these assessors to deserve excellent or good evaluation. This final evaluation confirms that the workbooks were completed adequately and correctly, respecting the parameters set at the beginning for assessment.

In the few cases that presented some difficulty, we observed that these few exceptions occurred during the first execution of the workbook, while in later executions these rare difficulties disappeared. We can also reasonably suggest, on the basis of our own experience, that repetition of this workbook makes its execution progressively easier. Indeed, a dozen professionals, who completed this workbook more than once, reported facilitation with repetitions.

THE *MOODINESS* WORKBOOK

The idea of developing a workbook for improving knowledge of states of mind was first derived from the computer, writing down thoughts by hand at set intervals during 24 hours, according to nine mental constructions, which then became ten (thanks to L'Abate's contribution). The results presented in the first research with this workbook (De Giacomo, 1995) are described below. (This workbook is available on the internet at *http://www.mentalhealthhelp.com*.) Of a total of 69 patients, 34 experimented with the method and 31 constituted the control group. There were four dropouts from the experimental group. This workbook is based on the principle that the mind is like a continually running tape, carrying out an unending series of mental constructions. These mental constructions are linked to pleasant, unpleasant, or neutral states of being. When the mind ceases to function well (e.g., in depression) the tape tends to stop running and, as a result, the mental construction tends to remain the same. The aim of this workbook is to get the tape and its mental constructions running again, and running harmoniously. Unlike the 16 functions described previously, which originate from a precise theoretical model, a second group of topics proceeds from an experiential basis.

This workbook originates from the possibility that our minds work like a series of mental constructions that succeed one another (either due to continuous interior motion or to external factors). In this regard, our mental functioning is metaphorically similar to a continuously running tape on which mental constructions, as well as the emotions and feelings linked to those constructions, are recorded. By "constructions" is meant our mental productions as we perceive them and as we reflect about them (De Giacomo & De Giacomo, 1997).

Below we describe this workbook in detail, with brief descriptions of each assignment. Here are the ten assignments and what they mean.

1. Constructing a great tragedy: the mind is thinking, with great intensity, of tragic, sad, anguishing, desperate events; it seems as though there is no way out: severe losses, major disappointments, heavy remorse, serious mistakes we have made, frightful experiences, and the like.

2. Constructing a moderate tragedy: unlike in the great tragedy, the intensity is lower; the darkness is not absolute, there is at least some dim light, one can bear it, although only barely. The themes are the same—losses, errors, awful experiences, humiliation—although less intense.

3. Constructing a minor tragedy: unlike in the great and in the moderate tragedies, the level of intensity is very low. It is quite tolerable: losses, errors, humiliation, and so forth, only attain a very low intensity.

4. Constructing a very amusing comedy: the mind thinks of very amusing things: nice situations that make us laugh and put us in a very good mood.

5. Constructing a moderately amusing comedy: unlike in the case of a very amusing comedy, here the mind thinks of fairly amusing, although not too amusing events, which certainly make us feel good, but do not make us roar with laughter.

6. Constructing a slightly amusing comedy: unlike in the very amusing and the moderately amusing constructions, the mind thinks of things that are just a little bit pleasant, just a little amusing, slightly gratifying, which make us smile just a little.

7. Operational construction: this means that the mind is engaged in carrying out a certain task, like when one thinks, "Now I'm going to do this, now I've got to do that." For instance: "Now I am typing on a computer, now I'm going out to buy some bread, etc."

8. Triumph construction: this is when we feel we are so very clever, so proud of ourselves, we are riding the high horse, we feel we are invincible—triumph of our ego.

9. Constructing indifferent recollections of the past: this is when we recall something unimportant which translates neither into tragedies nor into comedies: we are just dealing with plain recollections.

10. Dreams for the future: this means daydreaming, fantasies, aspirations, and hopes for the future, about what we would like to happen in our future lives to make us feel happy.

Here again, like with the 16 functions of the workbook on mental flexibility described earlier, one can recognize that each so-called construction, just like each function, corresponds to a way of organizing "reality" as perceived by each of us. Administration of the Beck Depression Inventory and Zung's Depression Test to depressed patients, before and after workbook administration, yielded statistically significant results. There was a decrease in mean depression scores on both instruments in comparison to the scores of a control group that did not receive this treatment (De Giacomo, Tarquinio, Sperindeo, Storelli, Panaro, & Caniglia, 1999).

Jordan and L'Abate (1999) have presented a single case study using the same workbook and obtaining qualitatively significant results after six months of treatment using both face-to-face psychotherapy and completion of all the assignments in this workbook.

REPRESENTATIVE CASE STUDIES

After testing the computer workbooks on so-called normal respondents, mostly medical students, these workbooks were extended to psychotherapy for couples, families, or individuals. We did not make any diagnostic selection because the cases we followed combined pharmacological treatment with psychotherapy. They are virtually all severe cases from a psychiatric viewpoint. The 20 cases that underwent this treatment can be subdivided into the following diagnostic categories: ten cases of schizophrenic disturbances, eight cases of major depression, and two cases of obsessive-compulsive disturbances.

Referral of patients to the therapist who was experimenting with workbooks occurred at the end of the course of traditional talk-based, face-to-face psychotherapy. Otherwise, cases were referred if, during the course of treatment, the referring physician had observed that a "stalemate" condition was taking place and no progress was evident.

Both computer workbooks, *Mental Flexibility* and *Moodiness*, directed respondents to express their thoughts and give a picture of their relational life. This process would probably be difficult to communicate in other contexts, including psychotherapy. Usually, we preferred to start with the *Moodiness* workbook and then proceed to *Mental Flexibility*. The reason for this sequence lies in the tendency in the former to reveal individual ways of thinking, then suggesting new ways to modify them. The *Mental Flexibility* workbook, on the other hand, starts right away with a problem and presents all its various solutions, a process that seems more successful in a sequential administration of the two workbooks.

We report the most complex cases subjected to this treatment in which a certain degree of chronic psychopathological disease could be discerned.

Case No.1

This case consisted of a of 30-year-old woman who suffered from an obsessive disturbance. She was greatly opposed to her parents and family. She was so opposed to treatment that although she had had serious problems for more than ten years, her family had not succeeded in persuading her to seek professional help. Above all, they were unable to persuade her to take any kind of treatment, not even pharmacological. Indeed, some years previously, after having only seen a specialist once, she had then refused to go back for checkups and would not take prescribed medications.

Over a period of ten years, her problems had grown to such an extent that she no longer had any contact with the external world. She had abandoned her studies, did not work, had no friends, and spent all her time in the house. Her parents were clearly exasperated at being forced to submit to their daughter's various rituals.

On the first visit, this woman had been brought in against her will. She was, therefore, unwilling to undergo any kind of therapy. The psychiatrist, one of the authors, having observed this refusal, decided that it would be wise to start with the computer workbook to increase mental flexibility, giving as the reason that this approach was needed to improve the quality of life. This was no psychotherapy, which she would have refused right away out of hand.

Not only the identified patient (IP) but also her parents took part in carrying out the assignments in the workbook. The problem that they most wanted to solve and that they unanimously wrote down was: "How to get out of the tunnel that they had themselves built up, and which was making all the family suffer." As the whole family had chosen to carry out the completion of all the assignments, they all had to follow the relational approach, which requires active involvement from all participants and commitment to complete all written homework assignments. At home, the daughter was given the task of putting the simplest solution into practice, while all the others would write their reactions to this task separately. At the next session, to everybody's surprise, the IP decided to take part and to go on carrying out the computer workbook.

For F1, in the relational approach, where one must "think of something that is common to your and your partner's mental worlds" (*partner* stands for one or more people considered to be the main points of reference in a relationship) the obsessive ritual involving all family members emerged, whereby the IP would sit on her mother's knee and ask both her parents the same questions, requiring exactly the same answers; the whole ritual lasted about an hour.

In responding to the prompts for the same function but in the part concerning the approach to the problem, how to solve it in agreement with their daughter, the parents were stimulated to give many practical solutions. The daughter wrote the possible solutions on the computer and seemed fairly receptive, after her first opposition to any form of computer-assisted treatment.

In F2, when the IP had to write what existed exclusively in her own world, her strong opposition to everybody and everything emerged. When she had to write what she thought "belongs exclusively to your family's mental world" the IP wrote out a brief summary of her parents' philosophy of life. An interesting point to note was what she began to write at home after an office session about "How would you solve the problem if you identified yourself with your family?" (F5).

Going over the written assignment of F5, it became clear to the therapist that the IP had understood her parents' need for her to become independent as quickly as possible, even though, through her symptoms, her relationship with her parents remained complicated and intertwined.

In F6, where she was asked to think and then write down "elements that exist in your and your parents' worlds but that nobody talks about," the IP wrote about her brother's divorce, an experience they were all caught up in and which made them all suffer.

In F8, where she was asked to "empty your mind and think of the first solution that comes to mind, even the most absurd" and then write it down, the IP had an idea: when she had "bad thoughts" she should iron clothes (a task she dislikes). This solution of hers was used as a home prescription. The IP had some difficulty in using paradoxical thinking, perhaps due to her limited intellectual level. However, she had no problem at all with F10, where she was asked to think the opposite, the reverse of what one normally thinks, probably because she used this kind of thinking all the time in her determined opposition to everybody.

In F12, where everyone had to "think of a solution that apparently favors the other person but in reality favors yourself" they wrote about all the behavior they had adopted in the previous years. This behavior apparently projected them toward the other person but in reality served only to perpetuate the problem, guaranteeing a minimum degree of survival for each member of the family. An example was that of acquiescing to the daughter's insistence not to go to a psychiatrist, which in reality also worried the parents because they were afraid they would have to expose themselves too far and would be subjected to aggressive reactions. Her parents were afraid they would have to disclose and expose themselves at an uncomfortable level. They also worried that they would be subjected to possibly aggressive reactions from their offspring.

Carrying out this workbook enabled the family to overcome the rigid attitudes that had prevented the IP from undertaking any form of therapy, and to learn new ways of thinking projected toward a solution. Moreover, because the assignments were presented as processes for developing thinking abilities for normal people, it was possible to overcome the initial refusal of therapy. Six sessions were required, in which the IP finished the entire workbook and agreed to go on with traditional, face-to-face, talk-based psychotherapy.

This case is significant because the improvements could not have been due to medications, since the IP was not taking any at the time. On the other hand, the workbook made it possible to overcome the initial opposition even to a clinical interview or traditional psychotherapy and to get the IP to try to solve her problems.

Case No.2

This 28-year-old university graduate in a scientific field was referred for family psychotherapy after trying to commit suicide twice. In the most recent months his closed attitude to any type of communication had gotten worse and was diagnosed as a psychotic disorder. His family included the parents, the IP, who is the elder son, and a daughter three years younger, studying in a health profession. The decision to ask the whole family to complete the computer workbook was made because all the family had difficulty in talking about the recent months in family psychotherapy sessions.

Interaction between the therapist and the family brought to light that everybody's problem was "how to bring out his hidden personality," referring to the IP. The family was very active, particularly the IP, who had tended to stay rather detached and uninvolved during past psychotherapy sessions. The task of writing on the computer involved what every member of the family thought in regard to the assignments administered to the IP.

In F2, asking them to "Think and then write down exclusively what exists in your own mental world," the IP was thus obliged to write down his thoughts. The important information he related was that he was convinced his genitals were small. This thought had caused him to stop going out and to avoid the main roads in the town: "Where those who know me can see from my pants that my genital organs are too small." In the same function, in regard to the problem-solving approach, where he was asked, "How would you solve your problem if you had to decide on the solution with your own personal mental organization, without taking into account other people or external factors?" the patient wrote that he needed a urological consultation to check whether there really was a problem, although he had never had the courage to talk about it. Of course, when he brought us the results of this consultation in a closed letter, there was nothing there to support his conviction.

In F4 when asked to "Think and write about something that belongs exclusively to your family's mental world," he wrote about the pervasive apprehension and anxiety in his family about even the smallest events in everyday life. It was interesting to note, that, when he got to F6—"Think of elements that exist in your world and your family's but that nobody talks about"—the IP talked about his sister's anorexia, which had been resolved about a year before but that nobody had ever talked about. While nobody had the courage to talk about this experience that had made all of them suffer, the IP in particular had a major hand in helping his sister overcome her anorexia problem.

In F7, for the problem-solving approach where he was asked to "Find a solution to the problem that involves your world and your partner's" they all continued, both in the psychotherapy session and at home, to write out a multitude of possible solutions, including the strategies used in the family's previous critical period to cope with the sister's anorexia. In analyzing the homework assignments, the IP's great ability to help his sister was observed, while his thinking became more organized. His thinking became particularly active in the divergent thinking assignment, when he had to think up and write down even the most absurd solutions to the problem.

Two years later, during follow-up, the IP told one of the authors that the effort required by these assignments had unblocked his psychopathological condition and straight away improved his "worries." We know that he is now teaching in his scientific field at a high school and has since come back to our department to follow a postgraduate course on creativity. In this case, too, we are convinced that the results obtained were determined by the workbook to increase *Mental Flexibility* and not by other forms of treatment.

Case No.3

Our third case was a 40-year-old, extremely intelligent man who had been treated by a psychiatrist for major depression. He had improved, by his report, reaching virtually normal levels of satisfaction. However, although it was no longer necessary for him to take antidepressive medication he had developed an addiction to medication that prevented him from being able to stop it. He realized that the doses he was taking were so low that they could not be responsible for any improvements in his behavior.

The computer workbook was proposed because this patient would not accept verbal sessions. In the past years he had a rather negative experience with psychotherapy. It was decided that he should carry it out on an individual basis, bearing in mind his age and the problem of breaking away from his family. Treatment began with the *Moodiness* workbook, from which an underlying depression in all his thoughts emerged, even if the patient initially denied this possibility. Writing down his thoughts made him realize how he tended to build up in his mind only thoughts based on slight or moderate tragedies. When he had to turn these thoughts upside down into comedy, this turn made him more willing to accept the idea of change and a certain self-criticism and self-irony in his behavior. Becoming aware of his way of building up thoughts negatively led him to an "enlightening," like a peak "ah-ha" experience, that pushed him to think seriously about changing his life.

When the patient progressed to the *Mental Flexibility* workbook, after adequate interaction with the therapist, the problem was found to be "Difficult relationship with women." The patient had never succeeded in building up a lasting relationship with a woman, owing to a series of prejudices against women and his way of looking at relationships between couples.

In F1, where he was asked to "Think about something that is common to your mental world and your partner's mental world," the patient wrote that he could not break away from his parents and family, despite having a very conflictual relationship with his father.

In F2, where he had to "Think about something that exists exclusively in your own mental world," he wrote about his work, that he had no particular problems with, since his job involved individual tasks or work with the computer. Good resources emerged in this field, but he could not manage to use them outside the work field in intimate relationships.

In F3, for the relational approach—"Think about something that belongs to your world (even if it belongs to your partner's mental world)"—the patient wrote about his lack of relations with others, because he had always avoided social relationships as he felt inferior to other people. The fact that he had no friends meant that he seldom got out of the house except when at work. On the rare occasions when he had to go away for a few days, he suffered such anxiety crises that he had to come home early.

In F6, where asked to "Think about elements that exist in your world and your partner's but that nobody talks about," owing to his lack of dialogue in recent years, he reported that he spent most of his day thinking about the world of women, without ever getting to know one. In this way, he built mental constructions that did not correspond to objective reality.

In the more creative functions, where greater flexibility is required, and divergent thinking is necessary, the patient had some initial difficulty but eventually he became unblocked. In F9, where he was asked to think up solutions, exaggerating them and making them paradoxical, he succeeded in making his mind work and gaining a more humorous outlook on his problems.

F10 then brought about a real change, where he was asked to "Think about the way you perceive the world at this moment, how you build up your thoughts and act on the world. Then turn it upside down, invert your thoughts, think the reverse, the opposite, and think up a possible solution and then think up the opposite (the 'antisolution')." Although this was apparently an easy question, the patient spent such a great deal of time writing down his answers that the answer was prescribed to him as a homework assignment.

His homework assignment showed that he was starting to abandon his stereotypical way of thinking. This improvement was then confirmed in the ways in which he had adopted and used paradoxical thought and metaphor.

A year later, when the second author saw him again for a follow-up, he reported that he had left home and that he had developed a relationship with a woman that had lasted a few months, although he was still not sure that she was the soulmate of his life. The results seemed quite satisfactory, as the workbooks certainly triggered a change in his way of thinking.

Case No.4

A university student 24 years of age was assigned the computer treatment because he refused to start psychotherapy, even though he agreed to take new generation antidepressive and antipsychotic medications that should have acted on negative symptoms but had failed to do so in his case. Face-to-face sessions were carried out in the presence of his parents. He not only lived at home, but he was so entangled with his family that he had not been able to succeed in becoming entirely independent.

The father, nearly 60 years old, was head of a middle-level educational concern, where the mother also worked in a technical capacity. This information turned out to be important. During the course of the sessions, it appeared that at home, the mother played a subordinate role to her husband and her two children. Indeed, her primary occupation was as a housewife entirely at the service of the three male members of the household. The brother, two years older, a university student studying away from home, was the only one who had a more independent life from the family. He was a model student with a good social life.

The IP had a schizophrenic disturbance. When treatment was started, he had no floridly delirious or hallucinatory symptoms. Even though he was taking new antipsychotic medication, his negative symptoms did not disappear. He spent most of his time in bed, rarely went out, had no friends, and did not follow the university coursework in his chosen field. In the *Mental Flexibility* workbook, which was carried out by the whole family, they defined the problem as: "How to help him get out of the house."

In F1, where he was asked to think and write about something that was common to the whole family, the mystique built up around the importance of an advanced university degree emerged. For the father in particular, the most important problem was really his son's studies. His recovery was only secondary to studies and the attainment of a degree.

In F4, in the relational approach, where asked to think and write down something that belonged exclusively to the family's mental world, the IP tried to list all the characteristics of the other family members. This task was difficult because he was usually not inclined to reflect on the other family members' characteristics. There were very few differences among them because they were so entangled with each other. The task that began in a session was prescribed as homework: "How to solve your problem if you identify yourself with a member of your family."

This function obliged the IP to emerge from his closed world and look for concrete solutions as to how to break away from his parents. What he had written at home turned out to be a long list of abstract ideas. In F6, "How not to solve your problem by approaching it exclusively from your own point of view or your partner's without ever finding any common point of agreement," the IP was obliged to reflect on solutions adopted in the past. These solutions had never resulted in any change. They were more like promissory notes that he could never manage to keep. For instance, during the past few months he had told his parents that the best solution would be to commute to the university. This trip would take only a couple of hours. However, in the end he just remained in bed all morning and was never able to get out of bed and out of the house.

His efforts to find new solutions to put into practice were confirmed in F8, where he had to find alternative solutions (somebody outside the family should get him out of bed in the morning, when his parents were already at work). This idea was then put into practice. When we came to F10, where the subject in the relationship is contrary, the parents recognized this style as being the one most used by their son. At the end of the session the parents were asked to write down during the coming week all the situations where they noticed their son's use of this style. Apart from writing down what happened, they were to "abandon the field" to avoid useless symmetry in their behavior with their son's.

In the last parts of the workbook, the patient showed a change. While working together on the *Moodiness* workbook, the parents wrote down thoughts of great tragedies when the IP suggested abandoning his studies. The crucial point was that of transferring their goal from his study problems to how to encourage him to get out of the house.

At the end of the sessions, while the family seemed satisfied with the results, because the IP had passed an exam a few days before, the therapists did not feel they had obtained great changes. Only six months later, when he phoned for a checkup, did we learn that the IP had changed universities, moving away from home, and thus, at last, had become relatively independent. Again in this case, other experiences could not have caused the change as he had not undergone psychotherapy in the same period and no important events had occurred in his or his family's life.

THE *RELATIONSHIP STYLES* WORKBOOK

Lastly, the elementary pragmatic model has been used to prepare a workbook entitled *Relationship Styles* (available on the Internet at *http://www. mentalhealthhelp.com*). In this workbook, the 16 styles making up the model have been translated into the following 16 adjectives:

a. Empty/absent; b. Participant/sharing; c. Solitary/reserved; d. Tenacious/egocentric; e. Docile/surrendering; f. Altruist/involved; g. Mysterious/ambiguous; h. Collaborative/mediator; i. Abstract/unpredictable; j. Sharing/innovative; k. Rebel/antagonist; l. Dominant/dictatorial; m. Double-faced/false altruist; n. Unpredictable/altruist; o. Inconclusive/disorganized; p. Confused/chaotic.

This workbook is organized in the following manner. Respondents are invited to define one by one the 16 styles, making sure what they mean exactly. Once these styles are understood thoroughly, they have to apply them to themselves, by arranging them in a rank order corresponding to what each respondent believes he or she is really like. This rank order starts with the style that corresponds to the way the respondent sees himself, or herself the most, proceeding toward styles that do not apply to the self in any way. Once respondents have completed this part of the first assignment, they may ask their partners, parents, or some other important person/people, to describe them on the basis of the 16 adjectives listed above. This process will allow a comparison between the respondent's viewpoint about the self and views of those who know the respondent well. From this comparison and from the differences that emerge from it, one might acquire a better awareness of self.

This workbook suggests a number of procedures that respondents can develop either freely or following certain patterns proposed by the assignments. This process might help gain a clearer understanding of the way respondents perceive the world, build up their thoughts, and act on the world according to the feedback received from important others.

This workbook has been adopted in seven cases, within the context of a family therapy course taught by the first author. Impressionistically, there was a clear improvement in the organization of the way of communicating in all seven cases. That improvement might be related to a better understanding of what is meant by interpersonal relationships. Although not yet used in the treatment of relational disturbances, we hope that this workbook can profitably be used not only in relational but also in individual psychotherapy.

From the follow-up data that we have collected thus far, the results obtained seem positive enough to pursue further research with this workbook.

CONCLUSION

The results of the cases treated with these workbooks seem satisfactory, even though we need more time to provide statistically significant data. The cases were chosen at random from among those patients who were unwilling to start individual or family psychotherapy. In these cases the psychiatrist referred them for treatment with computer workbooks. This could have constituted a disadvantage from a research viewpoint because these were the least motivated cases. In fact, their initial determined opposition to change further validates the usefulness of workbooks as additional or alternative approaches to psychiatric treatment.

We observed that in respondents with a tendency to autistic closure to the world, when the problem is identified as "How to bring out the hidden personality of . . ." some affective and cognitive mechanisms are activated that favor interaction and communication. Solutions using these workbooks are found even in single respondents or families who seem uncommunicative or very reticent in relating to a professional. In families who ought to be in psychotherapy, but who are too guilt-ridden to accept this form of treatment, carrying out computer-generated assignments seems to activate a certain sense of involvement and a later commitment to undergo psychotherapy.

Moreover, in all cases, we found that F6 in the elementary pragmatic model, corresponding to the *Mental Flexibility* workbook request to write down "the thing that everybody in the family knows about but nobody talks about," seems to activate communication and a cognitive organization directed toward the solution of the problem in the respondent (and any other participant). In view of these results, we now use routinely the prescription of workbooks during the course of traditional, talk-based psychotherapy. These workbooks enlarge the range of clinical and even pathologically severe cases that can be treated, adding a third alternative to face-to-face verbal psychotherapy and medication.

REFERENCES

Cassidy, J., & Shaver, P. R. (Eds.). (1999). *Handbook of attachment: Theory, research and clinical applications.* New York: Guilford.

De Giacomo, P. (1993). *Finite systems and infinite interactions: The logic of human interactions and its application to psychotherapy.* Norfolk, CT: Bramble Books.

De Giacomo, P. (1994). A method to develop creativity. A round table presentation on new models and techniques (Presenter). American Family Therapy Academy. Sixteenth Annual Meeting, Santa Fe, NM.

De Giacomo, P. (1995). Creativity-based methods for developing intervention techniques in short term interactive psychotherapy. Seventh World Family Therapy Congress, Guadalajara, Mexico.

De Giacomo, P. (1996). Creative techniques used by the Bari Short-Term Interactive Psychotherapy group, as they are used with several Axis One Disorders (dissociative disorders, anxiety, depression, and schizophrenia). Seminar at Philips Graduate Institute in collaboration with UCLA Department of Psychiatry, Los Angeles.

De Giacomo, P. (1999). *Mente e creatività: Il modello pragmatico elementare quale strumento per sviluppare la creatività in campo medico, psicologico, manageriale, artistico e di ricerca.* Milano: Franco Angeli.

De Giacomo, P., & De Giacomo, W. (1997). *Psicoterapia: Un metodo basato sul un modello relatiozionale della mente.* Fasano di Brindisi: Schena.

De Giacomo, P., L'Abate, L., & De Giacomo, A. (1997). Integrating models of human interactions: Three models, one reality? *Italian Journal of Psychiatry and Behavioral Science, 7,* 17–23.

De Giacomo, P., Storelli, M., De Giacomo, A., & Vaira, F. (1998). Il "Nastro della mente." Un intervento intervento integrativo nel trattamento psicofarmacologico dei disturbi mentali. *Atti VIII Congresso della Società Italiana di Psichiatria Biologica*, Napoli.

De Giacomo, P., Tarquinio, C., Sperindeo, A., Storelli, M., Panaro, V., & Caniglia, A. (1999). Le "frasi bussola." *Atti XLI Congresso Nazionale*, S.I.P. (pp. 586–589). Bari, Italy: CIC, Edizioni Internazionali.

Gardner, R., Jr. (1997). Book review: Three abstracts/extracts on single bit information exchange (SBIE) & the elementary pragmatic model (EPM). *ASCAP Newsletter, 10*, 7–13.

Jordan, K. B., & L'Abate, L. (1999). The tape of the mind workbook: A single case study. *Journal of Family Psychotherapy, 10*, 13–25.

L'Abate, L. (1994). Book review: De Giacomo's *Finite Systems and Infinite Interactions: The Logic of Human Interactions and Its Application to Psychotherapy. American Journal of Family Therapy, 22*, 88–93.

L'Abate, L. (1997). *The self in the family: A classification of personality, psychopathology, and criminality.* New York: Wiley.

L'Abate, L. (1998). Discovery of the family: From the inside to the outside. *American Journal of Family Therapy, 26*, 265–280.

Price, J. (1997). Defining relationships. *ASCAP Newsletter, 10*, 7–13.

CHAPTER 8

Marital Adjustment and Programmed Distance Writing with Seminarian Couples

Oliver McMahan and Luciano L'Abate

Few would argue that a graduate professional school experience places stress on the marriages of seminarians. These stressors evolve as a result of a two-income household, child care, shortage of quality time together, and the unavoidable personal growth changes that accompany new learning experiences. For some of these couples, answers to deal with the stressors are to nurture social support systems, including friends and the church, decrease spending, extend educational programs, or seek professional mental health help. Some seminarians are not aware of or deny the impact of these stressors. Others refuse to seek out professional help when needed. Others are located in areas where mental health services are not available. Ministers in general may not be familiar with or open to psychological, psychiatric, or other interventions such as individual, verbal, and face-to-face counseling for themselves or for referrals, when they act as consultants to their congregations. Despite a history of resistance to care, ministers, seminarians, and their spouses could benefit personally and professionally by utilizing counseling and mental health–related services (Domino, 1990; Keddy, Edrberg, & Sammon, 1990; Lyles, 1992; Misumi, 1993), especially in view of their future role as mental health consultants to their congregations.

Societal expectations on the seminarian and spouse have traditionally been that the couple serve as role models for others. Seminarians and spouses are part of the larger expectation that ministers and spouses in general maintain near-perfect marriages. Parishioners look at them as models of marital satisfaction. Experts have also claimed that marital satisfaction or dyadic adjustment is associated with ministerial effectiveness (London & Wiseman, 1993). As Trull and Carter (1993) indicated, "When a minister has a satisfying relationship with spouse and children then that person will be more effective in ministry and more fulfilled as a person" (73–74). A significant variable found by Stone (1990) in ministerial marital ability has been dyadic adjustment.

In light of the perception of society and parishioners and the anticipated professional demand for marital skill and dyadic adjustment ability, seminary students find themselves addressing issues of dyadic adjustment with their spouses not only as a matter of personal and marital living but also as part of professional expectations that success in dyadic, spousal adjustment is related to ministerial effectiveness. A problem arises when ministers and spouses have needs but do not seek out professional help (Misumi, 1993). Additionally, mental health services may not be available due to geographic location or perceived lack of time or money.

One intervention that does not demand constant face-to-face encounter with a therapist and avoids the problems of accessibility to service resources is PDW. Couples who are unwilling to face a therapist can be helped to review relevant individual and couple issues in the privacy of their homes through PDW. If a busy couple is not able to see a therapist, is not able to afford professional counseling, or has little access to a mental health care professional, PDW is affordable. It can be mailed back and forth between a couple and a therapist at their mutual convenience, or can take place through the Internet, through e-mail. This study investigated PDW as an intervention for seminary couples.

THE NEED FOR CLERGY CARE IN LIGHT OF RESISTANCE

A review of the literature has indicated a need for care even though clergy couples have been resistant to interventions (Hopkins, 1991; Muse & Chase, 1993). One aspect of the problem is the overall lack of clergy closeness with other individuals. Muse and Chase (1993) found that 70% of the clergy they surveyed "did not have someone they considered to be a close friend" (146). Warner and Carter (1984) reported that 56% of pastors' wives "had no close friends in the church" (125). Besides a hesitancy about becoming involved in close, supportive relationships, ministers and spouses are resistant to being perceived by their congregation as having trouble in their marriages and being less than ideal role models of marital fidelity and solidarity. The result is a struggling clergy marriage which is left hanging with little or no support. As reported by Blackmon (1990), "Congregations often idealize their ministers, projecting qualities onto pastors which they may in fact not actually possess. Such projection militates against forming a realistic and supportive relationship between pastor and congregation" (5).

In addition to a deficit in seeking help within the congregation, clergy are resistant to seek help among colleagues. Kunst (1993) reported that "Since ministers rely on their colleagues for recommendations when they seek other jobs or advancement, they are unlikely to discuss professional or personal problems with denominational or ecumenical organizations" (210). In a clinical report of 65 cases of male clergy involved in extramarital affairs, Steinke (1989) cited narcissism as a prevailing problem not only causing the affair but creating a resistance to care. He noted that clergy in the clinical sample "became incensed and impatient with others who insisted on counseling or a leave of absence from their posts. Counseling was resisted or resented. . . . [T]hese same clergy had great difficulty in self-evaluation" (61).

Problems affecting marital quality may be even more intense for pastors and spouses as compared to nonpastors. Warner and Carter (1984) found that pastors and their spouses "had significantly more loneliness and diminished marital adjustment in comparison with males and females in non-pastoral roles . . . in the same church" (125). Benda and DiBlasio (1992), in a multivariate study model, identified four relevant factors affecting marital adjustment. The first three were in the area of marriage and family, that is, "(a) perceived stress from work and family, (b) number of children from age 5 and younger, (c) perceived stress from family" (367).

Implications of Resistance to Care

The resistance of clergy to professional help for themselves is especially evident in the area of marital relationships and fidelity. In an evaluation of infidelity among male Protestant clergy, Thoburn and Balswick (1994) indicated that in ministerial marriages, clergy themselves typically experience an alarming set of factors, including "mistrust," "rejection," "shame," and "pornography" (286–288). One pastor felt that "ministers have a special degree of 'forbidden fruit' temptation simply because expectations of purity of thought and action by themselves are much higher" (289). Marital dissatisfaction was the second most contributing factor to marital unfaithfulness as reported by 41% of the 300 participants in their study (289). Thoburn (1991) suggested that the greater the emotional distance between clergy couples the greater was the likelihood of infidelity. All too often, according to Thoburn and Balswick (1994), pastors, rather than seeking counsel and help, fail to open themselves up to treatment. A pastor in need of counseling will seek to "hide his real self or compensate for perceived inferiorities, when he becomes trapped in his congregation's expectations that he be more than he is" (294).

HISTORICAL OVERVIEW

Using DW within the context of a therapeutic relationship is not new. In every decade since the 1940s, writing has been suggested as a tool in psychotherapeutic interventions. In 1942 Gordon Allport included personal writing in psychological science. In the 1950s, Landsman (1951), Messinger (1952), and Farber (1953) advocated the integration of writing in clinical practice. In 1965, Ellis clearly advocated writing in therapy in the form of assigned homework between sessions. In the 1970s Watzlawick, Weakland, and Fisch (1974) formulated the postulates of second-order change, advocating conversion from verbal to written modalities as a significant component in the cognitive patterns of second-order change. Shelton and Ackerman (1974) continued the progress on the use of writing in the form of regular homework assignments as part of therapy. Creativity in written therapy in the form of poetry writing was part of the repertoire of Harrower (1972). In the 1980s the use of DW expanded even further in prevention, through the work of Pennebaker and his collaborators (reviewed in Chapters 2, 3, and 4) and through psychotherapy. For instance, the use of poetry was suggested but it is still questionable whether it was helpful or just another well-intentioned fad (Brand, 1987; Fuchel, 1985; Mazza, 1981; Rothenberg, 1987; Silverman, 1986). L'Abate (1986) produced three workbooks that were isomorphic with interactive, multirelational models of depression (see Chapter 1), negotiation, and intimacy. Interactive DW between clients and significant others was proposed by Farley and Farley (1987). Short story writing (Graves, 1984), letter writing (Diets, 1988; Lindahl, 1988), and journal writing (Faria & Belohlavek, 1984) were being used in the 1980s at new levels of formalization and sophistication not used before in writing as therapy.

In the 1990s the use of writing continued (L'Abate, 1990, 1992). Lemberg (1994) expanded writing to a journaling technique used by couples, noting that couples felt a "greater sense of active participation in therapy" (65) as a result of writing. Leucht and Tan (1996) affirmed several reasons for the use of written homework between sessions, citing increased number of times clients directly address problems, "increasing a client's sense that he or she is not completely dependent on the therapist to produce change" (258) and the application of skills learned in therapy to other life tasks. Riordan (1996), in an approach called "scriptotherapy," reviewed a variety of formats for written therapy, including, "structured writing," "counseling by correspondence" (226), and written therapy in group work. Nau (1997) advocated the writing of letters by therapists as well as clients as part of therapy. He further developed writing in the use of problem solving in family systems, as well as grief and loss counseling. He even instructed a client to write to an amputated leg. Again, there is no indication that any of these suggestions were ever coupled with evidence to suggest their therapeutic usefulness.

Prescriptiveness

DW as an intervention need not be kept isolated from the treatment process. It can become a vital part of treatment planning. As such, DW needs to be seen as relating to all the various parts of the process of intervention, that is, assessment, verbal, face-to-face treatment, homework assignments, and post-treatment assessment. Treatment adherence is the issue concerned with the consistency and integration of the various parts of the treatment process. Treatment adherence is necessary for treatment effectiveness. Houge, Liddle, and Rowe (1996) reviewed several studies regarding treatment adherence, advocating research to find ways to link "treatment specification and manualization, comparative clinical efficacy, and therapeutic accountability" (341). A number of studies (Burns & Nolen-Hoeksema, 1992; Conoley, Padula, Payton, & Daniels, 1994; Neimeyer & Feixas, 1990; Startup & Edmonds, 1994) focused on the specific area of homework adherence, affirming that homework adherence is vital for positive treatment outcome. In line with this affirmation, DW, especially PDW, is a way to document, measure, and monitor treatment adherence and homework adherence.

In what L'Abate (1992: 36–37) called "prescriptive tests," these tests, as exemplified later by the PIRS, as well as many others (as described in Appendix C in Chapter 1), may become a viable way to guarantee the necessary links among assessment, treatment, and treatment adherence. Consistency of content among assessment instruments, therapeutic interventions, and post-therapy follow-ups are maximized and coordinated through the use of prescriptive tests. They link a specific workbook with a specific test score (Beck's or Hamilton's Depression Scales), a specific test profile (MMPI-2), or referral question (co-dependency, impulsivity, procrastination, etc.). Traditionally, most tests were constructed to understand behavior, not to prescribe treatment. They were intended to be simply and solely descriptive, or at best predictive, but never prescriptive. Once an array of treatment workbooks covers a wide range of clinical, semiclinical, or quasi-clinical conditions, it is possible to match a workbook with either a single test, a scale in a multiphasic test, or referral questions with individuals, couples, and families (Chapter 1).

Prescription for behavioral change is also enhanced by PDW because this medium links relationship skills, developed in face-to-face therapy sessions, with structuring skills, required at home to generalize from and complete the therapeutic process. PDW also allows the therapist to utilize a nomothetic approach, that is, DW or PDW for specific, idiographic treatment. PDW further increases the effectiveness and efficiency of predictiveness by encompassing both immediate and specific needs of a specific client with variable and uncontrollable content, and structuring homework assignments with fixed, known, and predictable content. Prescription is enhanced by PDW as an intervention because the goals of therapy are more explicitly monitored and measured (L'Abate, 1990, 1992, 1994a, 1994b, 1997).

In conclusion, the literature indicates a need for interventions for ministers, seminarians, and their spouses as an addition or an alternative to traditional talk therapy. Whether in actual ministry or in preparation for ministry while at a seminary, clergy and spouses are resistant to therapy. In light of the continuing need for them to receive some help, the resistance to therapy must be overcome.

PDW may be an effective intervention that, when applied to ministerial couples, may help them overcome resistance to therapy that might meet their needs.

METHOD

Respondents for this study were seminarians and spouses in a mid-size seminary with an on-campus enrollment of 200 located in the southeastern United States. All seminarian couples attending the main campus of the seminary were solicited for the study. Couples who elected to participate in the study were required to complete all the assessment instruments on campus in a standard classroom. There was no time limit for the completion of the assessment instruments. The assessment instruments were given in a pre-test and then repeated in two post-tests. Couples were permitted to take homework assignments administered over the span of six to eight weeks. Each seminarian participating received free of charge one-hour semester credit from the seminary.

Assessment

Six instruments were used to evaluate the outcome of PDW. Five of these instruments were used to derive demographic and personality information about seminarians and spouses. The five instruments were the Social Information Form (SIF), the Basic Adlerian Scales for Interpersonal Success—Adult Form (BASIS-A), the Neuroticism Extraversion Openness Five-Factor Inventory (FFI), the PIRS, and the Self-Other Profile Chart (SOPC). The Dyadic Adjustment Scale (DAS) was used to measure the gain effect of the PDW intervention (Spanier, 1976). The DAS continues to be used in religious studies, as represented in a study by Snow and Compton (1996). They found that "religion in a person's life" (979) was a significant predictor of both satisfaction and communication patterns as measured by the DAS.

The intervention for this study consisted of two five-part series of PDW assignments. The design for the study allowed for comparison between treatments and no-writing control groups. The first treatment was a five-part workbook based on the BASIS-A (PDW-BASIS-A). Adlerian lifestyle themes formed the substance of the content of these assignments in PDW-BASIS-A. There are five dimensions measured by the BASIS-A: Belonging-Social Interest (BSI), Going Along (GA), Taking Charge (TC), Wanting Recognition (WR), and Being Cautious (BC). The first and last assignments covered general lifestyle theme topics. The second through fourth assignments were based on the BASIS-A results for each respondent, asking them to review their profile from the BASIS-A, which was provided for them, and then respond integrating their profile in their responses.

Homework assignments for the other treatment group (PDW-PIRS) were based on the PIRS scores of participants. The PDW-PIRS consists of 20 homework assignments developed by L'Abate and his collaborators (1992). PDW-

Table 8–1
Design Orders Distributed to Participant Couples

Order Number	Distribution
1	SIF, BASIS-A, PIRS, FFI, DAS, SOPC
2	SIF, PIRS, FFI, BASIS-A, DAS, SOPC
3	SIF, FFI, BASIS-A, PIRS, DAS, SOPC
4	SIF, PIRS, BASIS-A, FFI, DAS, SOPC
5	SIF, BASIS-A, FFI, PIRS, DAS, SOPC
6	SIF, FFI, PIRS, BASIS-A, DAS, SOPC

PIRS assignments focus on 20 dimensions of conflictful areas culled from the extant literature on marital relationships. PIRS scores reveal discrepancy range scores between spouses. The PIRS's dimensions matched isomorphically the 20 assignments of the workbook. From the PIRS profile it is possible to match assignments according to the highest discrepancy scores obtained by each couple. The second through fourth assignments were assigned to couples based on their largest discrepancy scores. For instance, if the Emotional Expressiveness dimension had the largest discrepancy score, the couple would be administered the matching homework assignment on "Emotional Expressiveness." If the second highest discrepancy score was on Affection, the matching homework assignment would be administered second, and so on. The administration of assignments is isomorphic and idiographic with the discrepancy scores on the PIRS that are specific for that couple and for that couple alone.

In this study a pre/post-test two-group design was used. Completing the entire study were 30 married ministerial student couples. Couples were administered a pretest battery of five self-report instruments and a demographic questionnaire before PDW treatments were given. The SIF was given at the same time as the pre-test inventories. Estimated times for taking the instruments during the first assessment were: SIF (20 minutes), BASIS-A (20 minutes), PIRS (40 minutes), FFI (20 minutes), SOPC (10 minutes), and DAS (20 minutes) for a total of 2 hours and 10 minutes during the pre-test. The only time participants were administered all of the instruments was during the first assessment pre-test. In two subsequent assessment post-tests, they were only required to complete the DAS.

The order of the first assessment pre-test was divided into six different order designs. The SIF was always first, the DAS was always next to last, and the SOPC was always last in each order design. The other three instruments varied in order between the SIF and DAS. The alteration order is given in Table 8–1.

Three assessment times were conducted. Seminarians scheduled assessment times with the secretary of the study's author. Seminarians and spouses could

Table 8–2
Study Design

Group	Pre-Test	Treatment 1	Post-Test 1	Treatment 2	Post-Test 2
1	Pre-Tests	PDW-BASIS-A	DAS	Control	DAS
2	Pre-Tests	Control	DAS	PDW-PIRS	DAS

Note: Pre-test battery is the same for Groups 1 and 2.

take the inventories at different times. The ability to schedule their own times and come at different times was offered to facilitate scheduling of seminarians and spouses. Most seminarians and spouses worked and had different schedules. Students returned the assessment instrument battery from the classroom where they were taken to the office of the study's author immediately upon completion.

Order designs were assigned at random to each individual in the study. Spouses did not necessarily receive the same order.

PDW Interventions

The PDW-BASIS-A was given to one group during the first half of the study, between the pre-test and the first post-test. The PDW-PIRS was given to the other group during the second half of the study, between the first and second post-tests. The two treatments (PDW-BASIS-A and PDW-PIRS) were assigned on the basis of a randomized table. Couples received the same treatment, but different couples were assigned to different groups randomly. The treatment design is shown in Table 8–2.

Pre-test assessment scores were used for administration of PDW assignments. As described earlier, the administration of PDW-BASIS-A and PDW-PIRS depended on pre-test assessment scores. Homework materials were returned at the time that respondents took the first and second post-tests. The PDW-BASIS-A group returned their homework at the time that the first post-test was taken. The PDW-PIRS group was the control and had no homework to turn in between the pre-test and first post-test. The PDW-PIRS group returned their homework at the time that the second post-test was taken. The PDW-BASIS-A group was the control and had no homework to turn in between the first and second post-tests. Data were kept confidential for each couple. Couples were assigned a number that identified their names, gender of each partner, group membership in design order, and homework group membership, thus making the whole process confidential.

The essential research questions of this study asked, "Does PDW based on the BASIS-A or the PIRS make a difference in the dyadic adjustment mean scores of seminarians and their spouses?" The anticipated result was a significant

Table 8–3
MANCOVA Analysis of Writing Groups

Variables	Type III Sum of Squares	df	Mean Square	F	Sig.
DC (1)	81.41	1	81.41	2.15	0.15
AF (1)	1.14	1	1.14	0.32	0.57
DS (1)	235.74	1	235.74	15.17	0.00
DCoh (1)	44.34	1	44.34	1.44	0.24
DA (1)	1.35	1	1.35	7.62	0.01
DC (2)	8.81	1	8.81	0.91	0.34
AF (2)	3.28	1	3.28	0.72	0.40
DS (2)	7.43	1	7.43	0.96	0.33
DCoh (2)	55.54	1	55.54	5.95	0.02
DA (2)	196.72	1	196.72	5.03	0.03
DC (3)	55.29	1	55.29	1.91	0.17
AF (3)	0.55	1	0.55	0.15	0.17
DS (3)	159.47	1	159.47	9.17	0.00
DCoh (3)	0.63	1	0.63	0.03	0.88
DA (3)	515.43	1	515.43	2.94	0.09

Note: n = 60; First and Second Post-Test Gain Scores and GOT as Dependent Variables; Writing
Group as Fixed Factor; (1) = First Post-Test; (2) = Second Post-Test; (3) = Gain over Time;
DC = Dyadic Consensus; AF = Affectional Expression; DS = Dyadic Satisfaction; DCoh =
Dyadic Cohesion; DA = Dyadic Adjustment; $p < 0.05$.

difference between dyadic adjustment mean gain scores of PDW-BASIS-A and
PDW-PIRS as compared to each other and control groups with no PDW.

Analysis of Results

An analysis of the gain scores for both PDW groups addressed the essential
research question. MANOVA test results between both writing groups are presented on Table 8–3. The overall gain scores from independent samples t-test
analysis are presented in Table 8–4. The only positive intervention effect that
was significant was in the PDW-PIRS group, registering a 0.406 gain ($p < 0.05$)
in Dyadic Adjustment (DA). Most of the intervention effects, as will be reflected
in the following analyses, were negative. The MANOVA (Table 8–3) of gain
score comparisons indicated significance for five gain score variables, the first
post-test Dyadic Satisfaction (DS) gain scores [DS-1] (sig. = 0.0, $p < 0.05$),
the first post-test DAS overall gain scores [DA-1] (sig. = 0.01, $p < 0.05$), the
second post-test Dyadic Cohesion (DCoh) gain scores [DCoh-2] (sig. = 0.02,
$p < 0.05$), the second post-test DA overall gain scores [DA-2] (sig. = 0.03, p
< 0.05) and the gain over time DS gain scores [DS3] (sig. = 0, $p < 0.05$).

The independent samples t-test gain scores analysis (Table 8–4) indicated

Table 8-4
Gain Score Analysis of Means

BASIS-A Group

	First Post-Test/Intervention						Second Post-Test/Control					Gain over Time			
	Pre-Test	Post-Test /1	Gain	SD	t	Sig.	Post-Test/2	Gain	SD	t	Sig.	Gain	SD	t	Sig.
DC	52.54	50.11	-2.43	5.96	-1.47	0.15	51.64	1.89	2.83	0.96	0.34	-0.89	5.60	-1.38	0.17
AF	8.82	9.29	0.46	1.79	0.57	0.53	9.54	0.25	2.25	-0.85	0.40	0.71	1.92	-0.31	0.76
DS	41.61	40.82	-0.79	3.57	-3.89	0.00	41.46	0.64	2.44	0.98	0.33	-0.14	2.88	-3.03	0.00
DCoh	16.21	16.93	0.71	6.15	-1.20	0.24	17.86	0.93	3.91	2.44	0.02	1.64	4.73	0.16	0.88
DAS	120.50	116.72	-3.79	14.39	-2.76	0.01	120.80	4.04	5.78	2.24	0.03	0.25	14.09	-1.72	0.09

PIRS Group

	First Post-Test/Control						Second Post-Test/Intervention				
	Pre-Test	Post-Test/1	Gain	SD	t	Sig.	Post-Test/2	Gain	SD	t	Sig.
DC	50.72	50.63	-0.01	6.34	1.47	0.15	51.75	1.13	3.33	0.96	0.34
AF	8.81	9.00	0.19	1.96	0.57	0.53	9.72	0.72	2.02	-0.85	0.40
DS	38.50	41.69	3.19	4.24	-3.89	0.00	41.63	0.01	3.06	0.98	0.33
DCoh	15.19	17.63	2.44	4.98	-1.20	0.24	16.63	-1.00	2.06	2.44	0.02
DAS	113.20	118.90	5.72	12.29	-2.76	0.01	119.30	0.41	6.63	2.24	0.03

Note: n = 60; df = 58; Independent Samples t-Test of Both PDW Groups; DC = Dyadic Consensus; AF = Affectional Expression; DS = Dyadic Satisfaction; DCoh = Dyadic Cohesion; DA = Dyadic Adjustment; $p < 0.05$.

primarily negative, initial reactions to intervention. In three of the intervention variables, there was a significant negative effect. In the PDW-BASIS-A intervention there was a 0.78 effect ($p < 0.01$) for DS and a -3.79 effect ($p < 0.01$) for DAS. At the same time there was a 3.19 gain in the control ($p < 0.01$) for DS and a 5.72 gain in the control ($p < 0.01$) for DAS. In the PDW-PIRS intervention there was an effect of -1.00 ($p < 0.05$) for DCoh while in the control there was a -0.93 gain ($p < 0.05$). Also, there was a positive gain in the PW-PIRS intervention group in DA of -0.406 ($p < 0.05$), with a greater gain in the control, 4.04 ($p < 0.05$). Negative effects as a result of writing have been among the discoveries in DW research (Donnely & Murray, 1991; Esterling, L'Abate, Murray, & Pennebaker, 1999; Murray & Segal, 1994; Pennebaker, Colder, & Sharp, 1990; Riordan, 1996; Spera, Buhrfeind, & Pennebaker, 1994).

A Gain Over Time (GOT) measurement was possible because of the second measurement of gain for the PDW-BASIS-A group when the second post-test was taken. GOT is represented in Table 8–4. The only significant intervention effect over time in the independent samples t-test for all respondents was in the DS variable, registering a -0.14 ($p < 0.01$) effect over time (Table 8–4). There were significant differences between the PDW-BASIS-A and PDW-PIRS groups in intervention gain scores effects in independent samples t-test of all scores (Table 8–4). The significant result shown in the independent samples t-tests was a positive gain for DA in the PDW-PIRS group (0.41, $p < 0.05$) and a negative intervention effect for DA in the PDW-BASIS-A group ($-3.79, p < 0.01$). The net difference between the two scores was 4.2. The MANOVA (Table 8–3) verified the significance of interaction for the DA variable in both the first and second post-tests ($p < 0.05$).

MANCOVA of GOT scores overall is shown in Table 8–5. Pre-test scores served as covariants for the first post-test MANCOVA. The pre-test and first post-test served as the covariants in the second post-test MANCOVA. Cells for the GOT groups were too small to use a MANCOVA. There were significant results in Table 8–5 in the adjusted gain scores for the DS variable between the PDW-BASIS-A group (0, $p < 0.01$) and the control group (2.52, $p < 0.01$) for a difference of 2.52, the DA variable between the PDW-BASIS-A group (-2.17, $p < 0.05$) and the control group (4.31, $p < 0.05$) for a difference of 6.48, and the DCoh variable between the PDW-PIRS group (-1.06, $p < 0.01$) and the control group (1, $p < 0.01$) for a difference of 2.06. In each case the intervention had a sizable negative effect variables to pass Levene's Test of Equality of Error Variances.

MANCOVA analysis failed to yield significant results because the adjusted gain scores failed significance in the Levene's Tests of Equality of Error Variances (Table 8–6). The comparison of covariant results for writing groups for the DA variable indicated a significant negative intervention effect for the PDW-BASIS-A group compared to a significant positive intervention effect for the PDW-PIRS group. However, the results failed Levene's Tests of Equality of

Table 8–5
MANCOVA Gain Score Analysis

| | BASIS-A Group | | | | | | | |
| | First Post-Test Intervention | | | | Second Post-Test Control | | | |
	Adj. Gain	Mean Square	F	Sig.	Adj. Gain	Mean Square	F	Sig.
DC	−2.44	73.38	2.67	0.11	1.35	0.64	0.10	0.75
AF	0.40	0.36	0.14	0.71	0.50	0.00	0.00	0.99
DS	0.00	84.45	7.82	0.01	0.28	0.00	0.00	0.97
DCoh	0.89	25.27	2.07	0.16	1.00	45.68	6.70	0.01
DA	−2.17	548.41	5.14	0.03	3.48	71.86	1.90	0.17

| | PIRS Group | | | | | | | |
| | Control | | | | Intervention | | | |
	Adj. Gain	Mean Square	F	Sig.	Adj. Gain	Mean Square	F	Sig.
DC	0.00	73.38	2.67	0.11	1.60	0.64	0.10	0.75
AF	0.24	0.36	0.14	0.71	0.54	0.00	0.00	0.99
DS	2.52	84.45	7.82	0.01	0.25	0.00	0.00	0.97
DCoh	2.28	25.27	2.07	0.16	−1.06	45.68	6.70	0.01
DA	4.31	548.41	5.14	0.03	0.89	71.86	1.91	0.17

| Levene's Tests of Equality of Error Variances | | | | | | | | |
| | First Post-Test | | | | Second Post-Test | | | |
	F	df1	df2	Sig.	F	df1	df2	Sig.
DC	0.09	1	58	0.77	1.84	1	58	0.18
AF	0.06	1	58	0.81	0.45	1	58	0.50
DS	0.56	1	58	0.46	1.54	1	58	0.22
DCoh	5.60	1	58	0.02	0.05	1	58	0.83
DA	0.08	1	58	0.78	3.15	1	58	0.08

Note: BASIS-A Group n = 28, df = 27; PIRS Group n = 32, df = 31; $p < 0.05$.

Error Variances. What the negative intervention effect indicates, as compared to the positive control change score, may be difficult to determine. However, as mentioned earlier, similar evidence has been found in other research. The apparent positive gain scores for the PDW-PIRS group may in fact be a milder form of negative reaction when the intervention groups are compared to the controls in subsequent hypotheses. Control groups experienced significantly more positive gain than either intervention group.

There were significant intervention effects differences between the PDW-

BASIS-A group and the control group in the independent samples t-test (Table 8–4). The independent samples t-test analysis indicated intervention effects in the PDW-BASIS-A group in the DS (-0.79, $p < 0.01$) and DA (-3.79, $p < 0.01$) variables as compared to the control group for the same variables, DS (3.19, $p < 0.01$) and DA (5.72, $p < 0.01$). The significant net differences in intervention effect gain scores between the PDW-BASIS-A group and the control group were 3.98 for DS and 9.51 for DA. The MANOVA (Table 8–3) verified the significance of interaction for the DS and DA variables in the first post-test ($p < 0.01$). The definite trend was toward a greater positive change in control as compared to a negative intervention effect for the PW-BASIS-A group. MANCOVA analysis failed to yield significant results because the adjusted gain scores failed significance in the Levene's Tests of Equality of Error Variances (Table 8–5).

There were significant intervention effect differences in the PDW-PIRS group compared to the control group in the independent samples t-test (Table 8–4). The independent samples t-test analysis indicated intervention effects in the PDW-PIRS group in the DCoh (-1, $p < 0.05$) and DA (0.41, $p < 0.05$) variables as compared to the control group for the same variables, DCoh (0.93, $p < 0.05$) and DA (4.04, $p < 0.05$).

The significant net differences in gain scores between the PDW-PIRS group and the control group were 1.93 for DCoh and 3.63 for DA. The MANOVA (Table 8–3) verified the significance of interaction for the DCoh and DA variables in the second post-test ($p < 0.05$). As with the PDW-BASIS-A group, there was a much greater gainful change in the control group as compared to intervention effects in the PDW-PIRS group. The MANCOVA analysis failed to yield significant results because the adjusted gain scores failed significance in the Levene's Tests of Equality of Error Variances (Table 8–5).

Analysis of Results According to Gender

Gain scores were further analyzed by gender in independent sample t-test (Table 8–6), MANOVA, and MANCOVA analysis (Table 8–7). Regarding MANCOVA on gain scores for both post-tests, in the first post-test the pre-test scores were the covariants and in the second post-test the pre-test and first post-test served as the covariants. The independent samples t-test analysis of gain scores split by gender is in Table 8–6. Gender analysis indicated several significant results. The pattern of low or negative effects were the same for each gender. However, there were more significant measurements for husbands. For them, the PDW-BASIS-A intervention had a negative effect of -0.57 ($p < 0.01$) for DS while the control had a 3.5 ($p < 0.01$) gain. With the same intervention there was also a -2.57 effect ($p < 0.05$) for DAS while the control had a 7.31 gain ($p < 0.05$). Also, for the husbands the PDW-PIRS intervention had a negative effect of -0.875 ($p < 0.05$) while the control had a gain of 4.79

Table 8-6
Gain Score Analysis According to Gender

BASIS-A Group (Males)

	First Post-Test Intervention				Second Post-Test Control				Gain over Time			
	Gain	SD	t	Sig.	Gain	SD	t	Sig.	Gain	SD	t	Sig.
DC	-1.91	5.74	-0.68	0.50	2.29	2.92	0.81	0.43	-1.36	5.34	-0.68	0.53
AF	0.79	1.84	0.45	0.66	0.14	2.91	-0.66	0.52	0.93	2.06	-0.31	0.76
DS	-1.00	2.93	-2.55	0.02	0.86	2.57	-0.28	0.78	-0.14	2.51	-2.42	0.02
DCoh	1.64	6.00	-0.21	0.84	0.00	2.08	1.81	0.08	1.64	5.54	0.52	0.61
DAS	-5.00	15.94	-1.61	0.12	3.28	4.14	0.77	0.45	-1.71	16.05	-1.38	0.18

PIRS Group (Males)

	Control				Intervention			
	Gain	SD	t	Sig.	Gain	SD	t	Sig.
DC	-1.25	7.53	-0.68	0.50	1.25	3.92	0.81	0.43
AF	0.44	2.34	0.45	0.66	0.81	2.66	-0.66	0.52
DS	2.88	4.96	-2.55	0.02	1.13	2.58	-0.28	0.78
DCoh	2.06	4.96	-0.21	0.84	-1.50	2.42	1.81	0.08
DAS	4.13	15.09	-1.61	0.12	1.69	6.68	0.77	0.45

BASIS-A Group (Females)

	Intervention				Control				Gain over Time			
	Gain	SD	t	Sig.	Gain	SD	t	Sig.	Gain	SD	t	Sig.
DC	-1.93	6.34	-1.47	0.15	1.50	2.79	0.52	0.63	-0.43	6.00	-1.27	0.22
AF	0.14	1.79	0.34	0.74	0.36	1.45	-0.56	0.58	0.54	1.83	-0.10	0.93
DS	-0.57	4.22	-2.88	0.01	0.43	2.38	1.64	0.11	-0.14	3.35	-1.80	0.08
DCoh	-0.21	6.39	-1.44	0.16	1.86	5.04	1.78	0.09	1.64	3.89	-0.41	0.68
DAS	-2.57	13.15	-2.44	0.02	4.79	7.15	2.27	0.03	2.21	12.15	-0.98	0.33

PIRS Group (Females)

	Control				Intervention			
	Gain	SD	t	Sig.	Gain	SD	t	Sig.
DC	1.06	4.81	-1.47	0.15	1.00	2.73	0.50	0.63
AF	-0.01	1.53	0.34	0.74	0.63	1.15	-0.56	0.58
DS	3.55	3.50	-2.88	0.01	-1.25	3.11	1.64	0.11
DCoh	2.81	5.13	-1.44	0.16	-050	1.55	1.78	0.09
DAS	7.31	8.87	-2.44	0.01	-0.88	6.54	2.27	0.03

Note: Both Males and Females n = 30, df = 28; BASIS-A Group n = 14; PIRS Group n = 16; Independent Samples t-Test Between PDW Groups Split by Gender; DC = Dyadic Consensus; AF = Affectional Expression; DS = Dyadic Satisfaction; DCoh = Dyadic Cohesion; DA = Dyadic Adjustment; $p < 0.05$.

Table 8–7

MANCOVA Gain Score Analysis by PDW Groups and Gender

Variables	Type III Sum of Squares	df	Mean Square	F	Sig.
DC (1)	5.62	1	5.62	0.20	0.66
AF (1)	0.00	1	0.00	0.01	0.91
DS (1)	0.00	1	0.00	0.00	0.98
Dcoh (1)	24.19	1	24.19	1.99	0.17
DA (1)	35.89	1	35.89	0.33	0.57
DC (2)	0.16	1	0.16	0.02	0.88
AF (2)	0.53	1	0.53	0.14	0.71
DS (2)	15.35	1	15.35	2.39	0.13
DCoh (2)	0.00	1	0.00	0.00	0.99
DA (2)	47.72	1	47.72	1.25	0.27

Note: n = 60; Gain Score Analysis of Adjusted Mean Gain Scores Between Both PDW Groups and Gender; MANCOVA of Post-Test Scores with Pre-Test as Covariant in First Post-Test and Pre-Test and First Post-Test as Covariants in Second Post-Test; (1) = First Post-Test; (2) = Second Post-Test; DC = Dyadic Consensus; AF = Affectional Expression; DS = Dyadic Satisfaction; DCoh = Dyadic Cohesion; DA = Dyadic Adjustment; $p < 0.05$.

($p < 0.05$). For the wives, the PDW-BASIS-A intervention had a -1.00 effect ($p < 0.05$) while the control had a gain of 2.88 ($p < 0.05$).

The consistent pattern of negative intervention effect and positive control effect suggests the disruptive nature of PDW. The implications for interventions may include the introduction of a pattern that disrupts marital satisfaction because of confrontation with personal and marital issues. The negative effect appears to be evident regardless of gender. There was also a significant negative effect for husbands in the GOT measure for the DS variable. The intervention effect over time was -0.143 ($p < 0.05$). MANOVA by gender found no significant interactions between the group and gender comparisons ($p < 0.05$).

Discussion of Findings and Original Hypotheses

The original hypotheses for this study compared gain scores for ministers and spouses for two PDW interventions. One intervention was based on Adlerian lifestyle personality themes and the other was based on relationship dimensions. There were significant results supporting comparison of gain scores between Adlerian-based and relationship-based PDW. The comparison indicated a slightly more negative treatment effect for Adlerian-based PDW as compared to relationship-oriented PDW. However, the most significant finding of this study was that when the gains for both relationship- and Adlerian-based PDW were compared to control scores with no homework, gains were positive for the control group and negative for the intervention groups. These results are the opposite of what was predicted at the outset but were not surprising. PDW does have a significant impact on seminarians and spouses. Analysis of negative intervention effects is important to determine the nature of seminarians' and spouses' responses to PDW as opposed to no intervention and to consider the implications for therapeutic interventions.

PDW in all these areas should be beneficial for dyadic adjustment, especially if the homework is tailored according to the assessment. Prescription of homework, according to assessment, retaining the same theoretical assumptions for the intervention as for the assessment instrument would enhance therapy. Perhaps the prescription-based nature of both PDW sets used in this study is the reason that the reaction to intervention was consistently negative. This negative response to the intervention was not anticipated, especially to the degree of consistency with which it occurred. However, the negative intervention effect does not necessarily imply a reduction in intervention impact. Interventions can be confrontive and stress-producing. Many therapists, for instance, inform their clients from the first session that "Things may go worse before they go better." Individuals may not like the issues that PDW assignments expose. The initial emotional impact may be negative. Negative reactions to written interventions are not uncommon. In a study involving undergraduate students, Murray Lamnin, & Carver (1989) measured emotions immediately before and after writing interventions. Significant upsurges of negative emotions were reported after each DW session. Murray and Segal (1994) discovered the same increase in negative emotions when respondents were asked to write about traumatic experiences for 20 minutes. Esterling, Antoni, Fletcher, Margulies, and Schneiderman (1994), after analyzing writing intervention studies in which negative emotion was regularly displayed by treatment groups, suggested that in face-to-face therapy the therapist has the opportunity to ameliorate negative emotions while DW interventions just record the effect. Results from this study with seminary couples, therefore, affirm an initial negative response to interventions using the PDW format. The question is whether eliciting negative reactions is necessarily antitherapeutic.

A negative initial reaction to intervention may be more likely with PDW as compared to face-to-face therapy. Respondents may be improving by opening up emotionally. However, the initial experience is negative. Could negative reactions be more therapeutic? Rather than emotionally appeasing areas that are in need of exposure, confrontation, or disinhibition, DW invites respondents to deal with these negatively charged issues. Privacy, writing without interruption, or bias from another person in a face-to-face encounter may invite respondents to deal with unpleasant issues and emotions heretofore avoided or denied. Verification of the negative effect of PDW intervention is important information for therapists who may choose it as an intervention.

Knowing that PDW as an intervention does make a difference, the written format could be effectively used with clergy and their spouses. The review of literature indicated that dealing with negative emotions before the public contributed significantly to pastoral apprehension toward counseling. This study suggested that PDW is a format that may invite respondents to display negative emotions. Whether the issues are confrontive, traumatic, or distasteful, ministers may be more apt to deal with them in the privacy of their homes. PDW may be more effective at getting at the negative issues that are part of clergy life and marriage than face-to-face formats. This study suggested that PDW may draw out negative emotions from respondents.

Limitations of This Study

This study was limited by the number of seminarians and spouses who did not complete their homework assignments. The statistical analysis, particularly of intervention gain scores, may have yielded more significant information with a greater number of respondents. There were a number of geographic and scheduling conflicts for students and spouses, limiting their ability to participate. Perhaps a different study design may have facilitated more participation.

This study was also limited by the dynamics involving sensitivity to therapy by seminarians and spouses. Participants could be resistant to participation in the study because of sensitivity issues including self-examination, already present marital issues, and perceived role model expectations related to peers and church membership.

The study was also limited by the logistics of graduate school students, many of whom commuted. Many spouses were employed as well as the seminarians. Finding time to participate in the midst of a graduate study load, full-time jobs, dual employment, and managing a household may have been difficult. Significant portions of the study were located on the main campus of the seminary, thus making it difficult for spouses as well as students to commute and find time for the study.

CONCLUSION AND RECOMMENDATIONS FOR FUTURE RESEARCH

There are a number of suggestions about the direction of future research indicated by this study. The nature of emotional responses over time may indicate further direction for the use and effectiveness of PDW as an intervention. While it is important to be aware of the probability that elicited initial emotions may be negative, what are the effects over time? There may be a positive trend after seemingly negative initial reactions. However, the study was limited by design and completion rates, not allowing further analysis.

Further research into the value of prescribed interventions should continue investigating the kinds of benefits PDW can provide. For example, the literature indicated that Adlerian lifestyle personality and social interest are well suited for marital therapy and pastoral settings. Prescribing Adlerian PDW with more attention to specific factors may yield more exacting results. The PIRS-based PDW indicated that interventions specific to same-theory assessments produce significant effects. Tracking PIRS variables and gains in specific factors may further guide development of PDW.

REFERENCES

Benda, B. B., & DiBlasio, F. A. (1992). Clergy marriages: A multivariate model of marital adjustment. *Journal of Psychology and Theology, 20,* 367–375.

Blackmon, R. (1990). Family concerns for the minister. *Theology News and Notes, 37,* 4–6.

Brand, A. G. (1987). Writing as counseling. *Elementary School Guidance & Counseling, 21,* 266–275.

Burns, D. A., & Nolen-Hoeksema, S. (1992). Therapeutic empathy and recovery from depression in cognitive-behavioral therapy: A structural equation model. *Journal of Consulting and Clinical Psychology, 60,* 441–449.

Conoley, C. W., Padula, M. A., Payton, D. S., & Daniels, J. A. (1994). Predictors of client implementation of counselor recommendations: Match with problem, difficulty level, and building on client strengths. *Journal of Counseling Psychology, 41,* 3–7.

Diets, B. (1988). *Life after loss: A personal guide to dealing with death, divorce, job change, and relocation.* Tucson, AZ: Fisher Books.

Domino, G. (1990). Clergy's knowledge of psychopathology. *Journal of Psychology and Theology, 18,* 32–29.

Donnely, D. A., & Murray, E. J. (1991). Cognitive and emotional changes in written essays and therapy interviews. *Journal of Social and Clinical Psychology, 10,* 334–350.

Ellis, A. (1965). Some use of printed, written and recorded words in psychotherapy. In L. Pearson (Ed.), *The use of written communications in psychotherapy* (pp. 21–29). Springfield, IL: Thomas.

Esterling, B. A., Antoni, M. H., Fletcher, M. A., Margulies, S., & Schneiderman, N. (1994). Emotional disclosure through writing or speaking modulates latent Epstein-Barr virus antibody titers. *Journal of Consulting and Clinical Psychology, 62,* 130–140.

Esterling, B. A., Antoni, M. H., Kumar, M., & Schneiderman, N. (1990). Emotional repression, stress disclosure responses, and the Epstein-Barr viral capsid antigen titers. *Psychosomatic Medicine, 52,* 397–410.

Esterling, B. A., L'Abate, L., Murray, E. J., & Pennebaker, J. W. (1999). Empirical foundations for writing in prevention and psychotherapy: Mental and physical health outcomes. *Clinical Psychology Review, 19,* 79–96.

Farber, D. J. (1953). Written communication in psychotherapy. *Psychiatry, 16,* 365–374.

Faria, G., & Belohlavek, N. (1984). Treating female survivors of childhood incest. *Social Casework: The Journal of Contemporary Social Work, 65,* 465–471.

Farley, J. W., & Farley, S. L. (1987). Interactive writing and gifted children: Communication through literacy. *Journal for the Education of the Gifted, 10,* 99–106.

Fuchel, J. C. (1985). Writing poetry can enhance the psychotherapeutic process: Observations and examples. *The Arts in Psychotherapy, 12,* 89–93.

Graves, P. L. (1984). Life event and art. *International Review of Psychoanalysis, 11*, 355–365.

Harrower, M. (1972). *The therapy of poetry*. Springfield, IL: Thomas.

Hopkins, N. M. (1991). Congregational intervention when the pastor has committed sexual misconduct. *Pastoral Psychology, 39*, 247–255.

Houge, A., Liddle, H. A., & Rowe, C. (1996). Treatment adherence process research in family therapy: A rationale and some practical guidelines. *Psychotherapy, 33*, 332–345.

Keddy, P. J., Edrberg, P., & Sammon, S. D. (1990). The psychological assessment of Catholic clergy and religious referred for residential treatment. *Pastoral Psychology, 38*, 147–159.

Kunst, J. L. (1993). A system malfunction: Role conflict and the minister. *Journal of Psychology and Christianity, 12*, 205–213.

L'Abate, L. (1986). *Systematic family therapy*. New York: Brunner/Mazel.

L'Abate, L. (1990). *Building family competence: Primary and secondary prevention strategies*. Newbury Park, CA: Sage.

L'Abate, L. (1992). *Programmed writing: A self-administered approach for intervention with individuals, couples and families*. Belmont, CA: Brooks/Cole.

L'Abate, L. (1994a). *A theory of personality development*. New York: Wiley.

L'Abate, L. (1994b). *Family evaluation, A psychological approach*. Thousand Oaks, CA: Sage.

L'Abate, L. (1997). *The self in the family: A classification of personality, criminality, and psychopathology*. New York: Wiley.

Landsman, T. (1951). The therapeutic uses of written materials. *American Psychologist, 5*, 347.

Lemberg, R. (1994). Couples journaling technique: A brief report. *The Family Journal: Counseling and Therapy for Couples and Families, 2*, 64–65.

Leucht, C. A., & Tan, S. Y. (1996). "Homework" and psychotherapy: Making between-session assignments more effective. *Journal of Psychology and Christianity, 15*, 258–269.

Lindahl, M. W. (1988). Letters to Tammy: A technique useful in the treatment of a sexually abused child. *Child Abuse and Neglect, 12*, 417–420.

London, H. B., Jr., & Wiseman, N. B. (1993). *Pastors at risk, help for pastors, hope for the church*. Wheaton, IL: Victor Books.

Lyles, M. R. (1992). Mental health perceptions of black pastors: Implications for psychotherapy with black patients. *Journal of Psychology and Christianity, 11*, 368–377.

Mazza, N. (1981). The use of poetry in treating the troubled adolescent. *Adolescence, 16*, 403–408.

Messinger, E. (1952). Auto-elaboration: An adjuvant technique in practices of psychotherapy. *Disorders of the Nervous System, 13*, 339–344.

Misumi, D. M. (1993). Asian-American Christian attitudes towards counseling. *Journal of Psychology and Christianity, 12*, 214–224.

Murray, E. J., Lamnin, A. D., & Carver, C. S. (1989). Emotional expression in written essays and psychotherapy. *Journal of Social and Clinical Psychology, 8*, 414–429.

Murray, E. J., & Segal D. L. (1994). Emotional processing in vocal and written expression of feelings about traumatic experiences. *Journal of Traumatic Stress, 7*, 391–405.

Muse, S., & Chase, E. (1993). Healing the wounded healers: "Soul" food for clergy. *Journal of Psychology and Christianity, 12*, 141–150.

Nau, D. S. (1997). Andy writes to his amputated leg: Utilizing letter writing as an interventive technique in brief therapy. *Journal of Family Psychotherapy, 8*, 1–12.

Neimeyer, R. A., & Feixas, G. (1990). The role of homework and skill acquisition in the outcome of group cognitive therapy for depression. *Behavior Therapy, 21*, 281–292.

Pennebaker, J. W., Colder, M., & Sharp, L. K. (1990). Accelerating the coping process. *Journal of Personality and Social Psychology, 58*, 528–537.

Riordan, R. J. (1996). Scriptotherapy: Therapeutic writing as a counseling adjunct. *Journal of Counseling and Development, 74*, 263–269.

Rothenberg, A. (1987). Self-destruction, self-creation, and psychotherapy. *American Journal of Social Psychiatry, 7*, 69–77.

Sell, K. L., & Goldsmith, W. M. (1988). Concerns about professional counseling: An exploration of five factors and the role of Christian orthodoxy. *Journal of Psychology and Christianity, 7*, 5–21.

Setterlund, M. B., & Niendenthal, P. M. (1993). Who am I? Why am I here?: Self-esteem, self-clarity, and prototype matching. *Journal of Personality and Social Psychology, 65*, 769–780.

Shadel, W. G., & Cervone, D. (1993). The Big Five versus nobody? *American Psychologist, 48*, 1301–1302.

Shafer, R. B., & Keith, P. M. (1991). Self-esteem agreement in the marital relationship. *Journal of Social Psychology, 132*, 5–9.

Sharpley, C. F., & Cross, D. G. (1982) A psychometric evaluation of the Spanier Dyadic Adjustment Scale. *Journal of Marriage and the Family, 8*, 739–747.

Shelton, J. L., & Ackerman, J. M. (1974). *Homework in counseling and psychotherapy: Examples of systematic assignments for therapeutic use by mental health professions.* Springfield, IL: Thomas.

Shelton, J. L., & Levy, R. L. (1981). *Behavioral assignments and treatment compliance.* Champaign, IL: Research.

Silverman, H. L. (1986). Poetry therapy. *The Arts in Psychotherapy, 13*, 343–345.

Snow, T. S., & Compton, W. C. (1996). Marital satisfaction and communication in fundamentalist Protestant marriages. *Psychological Reports, 78*, 979–985.

Spanier, G. B. (1976). Measuring dyadic adjustment: New scales for assessing the quality of marriage and similar dyads. *Journal of Marriage and the Family, 2*, 15–25.

Spera, S. P., Buhrfeind, E. D., & Pennebaker, J. W. (1994). Expressive writing and coping with job loss. *Academy of Management Journal, 37*, 722–733.

Startup, M., & Edmonds, J. (1994). Compliance with homework assignments in cognitive-behavioral psychotherapy for depression: Relations to outcome and methods of enhancement. *Cognitive Therapy and Research, 18*, 567–579.

Steinke, P. L. (1989). Clergy affairs. *Journal of Psychology and Christianity, 2*, 13–26.

Stone, H. (1990). Seminary drop outs: A study of predictability. *Journal of Psychology and Theology, 18*, 270–278.

Thoburn, J. W. (1991). *Predictive factors regarding extra-marital sexual activity among male Protestant clergy.* Unpublished dissertation, Fuller Theological Seminary, Pasadena, CA.

Thoburn, J. W., & Balswick, J. O. (1994). An evaluation of infidelity among male Protestant clergy. *Pastoral Psychology, 42*, (4), 285–294.

Trull, J. E., & Carter, J. E. (1993). *Ministerial ethics: Being a good minister in a not-so-good world.* Nashville, TN: Broadman.

Warner, J., & Carter, J. D. (1984). Loneliness, marital adjustment and burnout in pastoral and lay persons. *Journal of Psychology and Theology, 12,* 125–131.

Watzlawick, P., Weakland, J. H. & Fisch, R. (1974). *Change: Principles of problem formation and problem resolution.* New York: Norton.

CHAPTER 9

Workbooks and Psychotherapy with Incarcerated Felons: Research in Progress

Rudy Reed, Oliver McMahan, and Luciano L'Abate

The purpose of this chapter is to illustrate how talk psychotherapy can be combined with workbooks to produce synergistic effects in trying to rehabilitate incarcerated felons. A brief rationale for the use of PDW to improve the thinking processes of these individuals is given. A preliminary pilot study by Everett Gorman suggested the feasibility of combining face-to-face psychotherapy with written homework assignments with incarcerated felons. An illustration of a rehabilitation program conducted by the first author under the direct support of the second author, and the ultimate responsibility of the third author, is described. Even though there is still not a control group and long-term effects have not yet been evaluated, this program is illustrative of how workbooks can be combined with talk therapy to obtain synergistic results. Only time will tell. Two detailed case studies have already been published, one with long-term negative results (L'Abate, 1992), the other with somewhat positive and promising results (L'Abate, 1999a).

TALK PSYCHOTHERAPIES WITH ACTING-OUT CHARACTER DISORDERS

The outcome of traditional psychotherapies with acting-out character disorders in individuals including criminals, psychopaths, sociopaths, and persons characterized by externalization, anger, hostility, aggression, and impulsivity has been overwhelmingly pessimistic, if not negative (Millon, Simonsen, Birket-

Smith, & Davis, 1998; Palmer, 1992; Raine, 1993; Roth, 1987; Simon, 1998; Tafrate, 1995; Tardiff, 1997; Watkins, 1983). These reviews indicate that talk therapies, as traditionally conceived and conducted, are certainly at best, not promising, and, at worst, certainly not cost-effective. Given the extremely large number of incarcerated individuals plus former felons outside jails and penitentiaries, it behooves the mental health professions to find new, innovative, and cost-effective ways and means of intervening with these individuals, without the expenditure of time and energy that has taken place in the past using talk therapies with few if any positive results. When the same literature is reviewed from the viewpoint of fresh and innovative interventions, beyond usual platitudes and generalities, one finds a paucity of innovative ideas and possibilities, let alone positive results.

With this rather pessimistic outlook about the treatment of criminals and felons in the background, it is important not to raise false hopes or to make unwarranted claims. As Simon (1998) concluded at the end of her review concerning treatment of offenders,

effective treatments should be developed and evaluated and made available to offenders motivated to undergo the difficult process of change, regardless of the sentence imposed. There are many offenders, in and out of prison, who would like the opportunity to change and are unable to do it alone. These offenders should have the best treatment available; it is hoped that both they and society will benefit. (152)

In the spirit of her conclusion, we want to consider cost-effective treatments that will fit into the nature of criminality rather than in the nature of functioning individuals (L'Abate, 1993, 1994, 1997). One cost-effective approach is PDW as represented by workbooks.

PROGRAMMED DISTANCE WRITING AND CEREBRAL DOMINANCE IN ACTING-OUT INDIVIDUALS

If criminal behavior represents the failure to engage the left hemisphere and use it for constructive reasoning and behavior (Henry & Moffitt, 1997; Raine, 1993; Rygaard, 1998; Siever, 1998), putting this behavior under the dominance of the right hemisphere instead, we should be looking for ways to engage the parts of the brain that are either not used effectively or that are used for nefarious, negative, and hurtful outcomes (Ornstein, 1997). In the case of most acting-out individuals talk is used to con, cheat, and manipulate, not to think. Hence, the issue is one of expanding and improving thinking processes under the relative dominance of the left hemisphere, directing those processes toward constructive goals and behaviors (L'Abate, 1993, 1997). However, as long as talk is the predominant and preferred medium of intervention, which may well be based mostly on the right hemisphere (Ornstein, 1997), as discussed already in

Chapter 1, it is extremely doubtful whether any substantial improvement in the treatment of aggressive and criminal behavior will take place (L'Abate, 1999b).

A rather unlikely comparison does come from research on training primates to talk, with historically limited if any results. These animals are not equipped either with vocal cords nor with auditory-oral neural connections present in human beings. A distinct advance was made when instead of training them in their "weak" area of ear-mouth coordination, they were trained in their area of strength, eye-hands connection and coordination. The implications of primate research apply to many incarcerated individuals, even though some may dislike the analogy with primates. Yet, the Performance IQ > Verbal IQ remains but one of the most enduring characteristics of aggressive individuals (Henry & Moffitt, 1997; Siever, 1998). Eye-hand coordination seems superior to ear-mouth coordination, as would be the opposite of functioning individuals, where the former would be equal or lower than the latter. As Raine (1993: 115) concluded: "In spite of . . . criticisms, left hemisphere dysfunction in criminals does receive substantial support from more traditional neuropsychological data." This generalization leads to the view of "reduced lateralization for linguistic functions" (Raine, 1993: 117–121), that, however, might be limited to "blue-collar" violent criminals. It might not hold water with "white-collar" crime, like embezzlement, fraud, and the like. White-collar crime requires behaviors like planning, deceit, and time-related manipulations without direct physical aggression. Whether this asymmetry in cerebral functions may be due to organic damage is a possibility that cannot as yet be discarded (Rygaard, 1998).

Consequently, if this differentiation is valid, that is, if talk seems more related to right hemisphere than thinking, while the latter seems more related to the left hemisphere than talk (Ornstein, 1997), then one would conclude that talk is definitely the most inappropriate and inefficient medium to use with criminals. This conclusion is supported by most negative results of psychotherapy shown with criminal populations cited above. Even if DW and especially PDW were to fail, they would not involve the time and energy required by talk. Furthermore, they may engage parts of the brain that are not used effectively by many criminals.

A proviso, however, is necessary here. If cerebral dominance is also specific to feelings, with positive ones more related to the left hemisphere and "negative" ones more related to the right hemisphere, as suggested by Ornstein (1997), then one needs to ask the same question asked in Chapter 1: "What kind of writing?" If one were to follow Pennebaker's model (Chapters 2, 3, and 4), then it is possible that writing directed toward past traumas, tribulations, trials, sadnesses, and overall painful and unpleasant events might be more related to the right hemisphere. If these feelings are avoided and expressed mainly in aggression and anger instead (L'Abate, 1993, 1994, 1997), then it would stand to reason that writing might be a relatively safer way to access unpleasant feelings, thus undercutting their expression through anger and aggression. Furthermore, PDW directed toward a more positive expression of anger might need to be preceded by the written approach and expression of painful past experiences, a process that, stereotypically, seems difficult for men in general and for aggressive individuals in particular.

If the foregoing reasoning is even partially correct, it would suggest that talk therapies with offenders are directed toward an area of weakness rather than one of strength. As long as thinking and talk are used to cheat, con, and manipulate, there is almost no room left for thinking about the consequences of anger, violence, and aggression. One needs to introduce thinking before acting, an intrusion that is difficult to obtain through talk. Of course, as one complete case study of PDW with an incarcerated felon strongly suggests (L'Abate, 1992), writing can be used for exactly the same self-defeating purposes as talking. One needs to be very careful and sensitive to characteristics like exaggerated obsequiousness, uncharacteristic avoidance of angry outbursts, uncritical and unquestioning conformity to the professional's demands, and extreme compliments made to the professional, among other signs. We still have a lot to learn about how PDW can be used to help incarcerated felons. This chapter is just one small step in that direction.

THE PRELIMINARY EXPERIENCE OF EVERETT GORMAN

Gorman was the first to use the social training workbook with ten incarcerated felons in a Canadian penitentiary, outside the experience of the third author. A needs survey conducted by the Psychology Department's summer intern (Jocelyne Lock) found that the most prominent criminogenic factor in the inmate population was Personal/Emotional Development. Out of 16 criminogenic factors, the two most frequently identified were Aggression/Hostility and Impulsivity/Risk-taking. On the basis of these findings, an impulse control program was developed by Gorman. This program was based strictly on the verbal medium and produced a dropout rate of 50%. Since most inmates were highly impulsive and acted out their aggression and hostility during the group sessions, a need to change the delivery system was implemented. An extensive review of the literature dealing with impulsive behavior suggested that *programmed writing* (L'Abate, 1992) might be a more appropriate method of treating impulsive individuals in a correctional setting.

The revised impulse control program was based on the following aims and goals:

1. To provide participants with the theoretical and practical knowledge to change their impulsive behavior.

2. To provide participants with awareness of the etiology and effects of impulsive behavior on thoughts and actions.

3. To improve participants' social and interpersonal problem-solving skills.

Table 9–1
Results of Psychotherapy and Social Training in a Canadian Penitentiary

	Impulsivity Scores	
Subject #	Pre-Test	Post-Test
1	48	42
2	50	42
3	51	38
4	76	45
5	52	39
6	68	10
7	74	42
8	81	62
9	87	52
10	55	20

To meet the stated goals all the assignments of the social training workbook were completed by all ten respondents according to the procedures suggested by L'Abate (1992). Gorman administered the Basic Personality Inventory before and after a ten-session course of therapy, once a week for ten weeks. From this inventory, he used the Impulse Control Scale to measure whether any changes had taken place as a result of treatment. During each face-to-face session, he reviewed verbally the felons' answers to each assignment, with a subsequent discussion of whatever each offender might have learned by completing each assignment. His preliminary results, shown in Table 9–1, suggest that impulse control scores of the Basic Personality Inventory decreased significantly from each other with a paired t-value of 4.89 and a $p <. 005$ (df $= 9$).

One limitation of this preliminary experience consisted of a nonrandom selection of respondents. Its value, however, lies in its going one step beyond the anecdotal, and suggesting the possibility of further work using the same social training workbook in other correctional settings. Of course, in addition to the absence of a control group, Gorman, since retired from that institution, recognized the importance of detailed personality profiles and long-term follow-up. On the basis of this experience, therefore, a second project with incarcerated felons was started.

RESEARCH IN PROGRESS: REHABILITATION PROGRAM USING PROGRAMMED DISTANCE WRITING

Research is being conducted on incarcerated inmates using PDW in a pilot study. The study is being conducted in a country justice center in the southeastern United States. This center houses approximately 180 inmates, male and female. Male inmates are currently the respondents in this study. As research continues, female inmates will also receive the written intervention. The research

Table 9–2

Results of Psychotherapy and Social Training in a Southeastern U.S. Penitentiary

Variable	Mean Scores		Mean Gain Scores	t-Score	SD	2-tail p
	Pre-Test	Post-Test				
Anger Inventory	58.85	31.93	−26.74	−6.08	16.03	0.000
Reaction Inventory	214.41	156.52	−57.87	−2.76	19.54	0.016
Aggressiveness Scale	86.33	71.66	−14.72	−2.77	19.51	0.019
Irrational Beliefs Scale	68.85	57.33	−11.42	−3.96	10.47	0.000
Automatic Thoughts Questionnaire	87.64	53.23	−34.41	−7.37	16.92	0.000

Note: n = 13 (df = 12, $p < 0.01$).

is being conducted as part of the counseling program that is an extension of graduate counseling training for a local religious seminary. These services are provided free of charge.

Felons in the study received a pre- and post-assessment battery. The battery included the Anger Inventory (Schutte & Malouff, 1995), Reaction Inventory (Evans & Strangeland, 1971), Aggression Questionnaire (Buss & Perry, 1992), Irrational Belief Scale (Malouff, Valdenegro, & Schutte, 1987), and Automatic Thoughts Questionnaire (Hollon & Kendall, 1980).

As an intervention to supplement face-to-face talk therapy, inmates were given PDW using assignments from L'Abate's social training workbook (1992). This workbook includes assignments from a variety of themes, including goals and wants, mistakes, control, emotions and feelings, thinking, and other subjects. Each assignment is designed to take approximately 45 to 90 minutes to complete. Thirty inmates began the program and 13 completed it after a nine-month period of intervention.

Pre-and post-assessments from preliminary data were analyzed with a paired samples test (see Table 9–2). This analysis indicated that the PDW intervention along with face-to-face talk therapy made a significant ($p < 0.01$) positive difference in anger, irrational belief, and automatic thought measures. Reduced gain scores indicated a positive result. The data for reactivity and aggressiveness also indicated acceptable significance ($p < 0.05$) and positive results through reduced gain score levels.

Anecdotally, felons reported less depression and greater ability to control anger. They also reported increased cognitive responsiveness. They reported that after completing written homework assignments along with face-to-face therapy, they were more apt to think rather than feel and react violently first. The following are two case studies of inmates using PDW. They represent the two extremes among the first ten felons who completed this program.

Case Study No. 1: Alpha

The first case, called Alpha, was a male in his late 30s. His gain scores were among the most positive of the group. He had some of the greatest reductions in levels of anger, aggression, reactivity, and irrational beliefs in comparison to the other inmates measured in pre- and post-tests. He was unmarried but had been living with the same woman for over ten years. Neither had any children. Alpha was incarcerated for repeated violations of driving under the influence of alcohol and aggressive acts of violence.

Alpha has had problems with anger and depression. He had taken Prozac for depression but was not on medications during the time of this study. He reported that when he started drinking he lost control of his temper and would fight with whomever was around him. Sometimes without overt stimuli he became agitated and would aggressively strike out at others. He had struggled with aggression for most of his life. He was at the point of breaking up with his girlfriend when he decided to come for counseling. Since receiving counseling, his relationship with his girlfriend has improved.

Alpha's initial mood was usually depressed to some degree and irritable. His behavior was cooperative during counseling. His appearance was appropriate. He reported several situations in his cell block that made him tense and angry. He came to counseling voluntarily and appeared willing to change. Willingness on the part of the inmate is of the utmost importance when counseling. It does not take long to determine whether an inmate is willing to learn or just wants to consume time, as yet another distraction from tedious prison life.

As with most inmates, the object in this study was to help them think before reacting. Alpha was started on the social training workbook, in which Alpha wrote responses as homework. Then, during face-to-face sessions, Alpha would read aloud questions with the answers that he had written. Also, as part of this intervention, Alpha would keep a daily log of thoughts, do personal journaling, and read assigned passages from the Scriptures.

With Alpha, cognitive interventions, such as positive self-talk and reframing, were reinforced with homework assignments. As a result, Alpha reported an improvement in confidence and his mood seemed more positive. He reported that he felt more in control of his life. He asserted that he was more focused. He appeared self-motivated, sincere, and willing to work toward change. The time that he invested in doing the assignments indicated a substantive measure of follow-through regarding his seeming willingness and intentions.

Case Study No. 2: Omega

The second case was an inmate called Omega. Omega was among the least responsive in pre- and post-test measures. Her scores indicated some of the lowest levels of reduction in anger, reactivity, and irrational beliefs compared to the results of other respondents. Across the spectrum of inventories used in this study with Omega, she showed no reduction in any of the levels of reactivity, anger, or aggression. She had a slight reduction in irrational belief and some improvement in the automatic thought measure.

Omega was a 30-year-old female. She was not married and was not in a present relationship. She had no children. She had a history of aggression, drug addiction (cocaine), and was currently incarcerated for a shoplifting offense. She used prostitution to gain money for drugs. She was overweight and extroverted. Her primary employment was restaurant work. She received emotional support from some family members, especially a sister.

Omega voluntarily requested counseling to work on controlling her anger. She also wanted to work on other issues relating to drug use and shoplifting. Her initial mood during sessions was irritable. Her appearance was normal and her speech was reactive. Initially, she appeared to only be in counseling to see if she could get special favors, such as an early timeout and a reduced sentence. At mid-point during the course of treatment, she asked the counselor to send a letter of referral to two judges stating that she was active in counseling. The counselor did not comply. She appeared to have little proper motivation for change. She struggled with homework assignments, with a low completion rate. Her motivation for therapy appeared low, as shown by her poor homework completion rate. She attended intervention sessions with the goal of receiving from the therapist a positive recommendation for early release from incarceration.

Conclusion

The current study is limited by the absence of a control group and no long-term follow-up. Nevertheless, results have been encouraging and the research is continuing, expanding to new inmates and female prisoners. Inmates did report progress in their ability to control anger and think through reactions before acting-out. Furthermore, preliminary post-intervention assessment suggests progress in categories of anger, reactivity, aggressiveness, irrational beliefs, and automatic thoughts.

ADVANTAGES OF WORKBOOKS WITH CRIMINALS

We need to look for cost-effective methods that, even if and when they fail, will not take time and energy from professional and para-professional personnel.

This medium may well be PDW, as epitomized by workbooks, as already discussed in Chapter 1 and supported with preliminary evidence from Chapter 5. Their advantages and disadvantages may be amplified with a criminal population. However, in this regard, there is an interesting, strictly anecdotal, pattern found in many criminals: they seemingly do not like to write in general, especially using pens or pencils. This avoidance may support the possibility that criminals do not like to think, might not know how to think, and do not want to think. However, for reasons that are still unfathomed, they do like to write using computers! Even though one may not find supporting evidence for the validity of this pattern, the fact remains that computers do have a potential for the rehabilitation of criminals that cannot be matched by talk-based psychotherapies (Magaletta, Fagan, & Ax, 1998). Therefore, workbooks may well serve as software for computer-assisted interventions that may help incarcerated felons approach areas of thinking that have been avoided in the past, for whatever reasons.

Appendix C in Chapter 1 shows which workbooks are available for acting-out character disorders, where externalization (impulsivity, blaming external targets, anger, aggression, avoidance of responsibility for one's actions, criminal acting-out) is the main reason for their being incarcerated. Just as one cannot build a skyscraper with bare hands, but only with a variety of personnel and materials, criminal rehabilitation requires a variety of workbooks, as well as many other types of intervention. If one workbook does not work with one felon, it may work with another. This conclusion brings us to the issue of individual differences in incarcerated populations. As Slaton, Kern, and Curlette (in press) found, there are at least three different clusters of criminal profiles. One cluster includes inmates who would reject any intervention. The second cluster includes inmates who would be unable to use psychological interventions because of their psychiatric impairments. However, a third cluster, representing one-third of the prison population in their sample, presented characteristics that made them seem amenable to psychological interventions. Even if just one-third of the existing prison populations could be helped through cost-effective methods like PDW, it would represent an enormous saving of lives and energy.

CONCLUSION

Given two different treatments with equal results, workbooks and psychotherapy, one would choose first the most economical one or use both contemporaneously. By the same token, workbooks (i.e., PDW) might be used as a first sieve in a rehabilitative program with incarcerated inmates. Of course, any course of rehabilitation should take place under controlled conditions, pre/post-test evaluation, control groups, and long-term follow-up. We shall continue to implement these conditions in the ongoing research.

REFERENCES

Buss, A. H., & Perry, M. (1992). The aggression questionnaire. *Personality Processes and Individual Differences, 63*, 452–459.

Butz, M., & Austin, S. (1993). Management of the adult impulsive client: Identification, timing, and methods of treatment. In W. G. McCown, J. L. Johnson, & M. B. Shure (Eds.), *The impulsive client: Theory, research, and treatment* (pp. 223–244). Washington, DC: American Psychological Association.

Evans, D. R., & Strangeland, M. (1971). Development of the Reaction Inventory to measure anger. *Psychological Reports, 29*, 412–414.

Henry, B., & Moffitt, T. E. (1997). Neuropsychological and neuroimaging studies of juvenile delinquents and adult criminal behavior. In D. M. Stoff, J. Breiling, & J. D. Maser (Eds.), *Handbook of antisocial behavior* (pp. 280–288). New York: Wiley.

Hollon, S. D., & Kendall, P. C. (1980). Cognitive self-statements in depression: Development of an automatic thoughts questionnaire. *Cognitive Therapy and Research, 4*, 249–383.

L'Abate, L. (1992). *Programmed writing: A self-administered approach for interventions with individuals, couples and families.* Pacific Grove, CA: Brooks/Cole.

L'Abate, L. (1993). A family theory of impulsivity. In W. G. McCown, J. L. Johnson, & M. B. Shure (Eds.), *The impulsive client: Theory, research, and treatment* (pp. 93–117). Washington, DC: American Psychological Association.

L'Abate, L. (1994). *A theory of personality development.* New York: Wiley.

L'Abate, L. (1997). *The self in the family: Classification of personality, criminality, and psychopathology.* New York: Wiley.

L'Abate, L. (1999a). Programmed distance writing in therapy with acting-out adolescents. In C. Schaefer (Ed.), *Innovative psychotherapy techniques in child and adolescent therapy* (pp. 108–157). New York: Wiley.

L'Abate, L. (1999b). Taking the bull by the horns: Beyond talk in psychological interventions. *The Family Journal: Counseling and Psychotherapy with Couples and Families, 7*, 206–220.

Magaletta, P. R., Fagan, T. J., & Ax, R. K. (1998). Advancing psychology services through telehealth in the Federal Bureau of Prisons. *Professional Psychology: Research and Practice, 29*, 543–548.

Malouff, J. M., Valdenegro, J., & Schutte, N. S. (1987). Further validation of a measure of irrational belief. *Journal of Rational-Emotive and Cognitive-Behavior Therapy, 5*, 189–193.

Millon, T., Simonsen, E., Birket-Smith, M., & Davis, R. D. (Eds.) (1998). *Psychopathy: Antisocial, criminal, and violent behavior.* New York: Guilford.

Ornstein, R. (1997). *The right mind: Making sense of the hemispheres.* New York: Harcourt & Brace.

Palmer, T. (1992). *The re-emergence of correctional intervention.* Newbury Park, CA: Sage.

Raine, A. (1993). *The psychopathology of crime: Criminal behavior as a clinical disorder.* San Diego, CA: Academic.

Roth, L. H. (Ed.). (1987). *Clinical treatment of the violent person.* New York: Guilford.

Rygaard, N. P. (1998). Psychopathic children: Indicators of organic dysfunction. In T.

Millon, E., Simonsen, E. M. Birket-Smith, & R. D. Davis (Eds.), *Psychopathy: Antisocial, criminal, and violent behavior* (pp. 247–259). New York: Guilford.

Schutte, N. S., & Malouf, J. M. (1995). *Sourcebook of adult assessment strategies*. New York: Plenum.

Siever, L. J. (1998). Neurobiology in psychopathy. In T. Millon, E. Simonsen, E. M. Birket-Smith, & R. D. Davis (Eds.), *Psychopathy: Antisocial, criminal, and violent behavior* (pp. 231–246). New York: Guilford.

Simon, L. (1998). Do offender treatments work? *Applied & Preventive Psychology*, 7, 137–159.

Slaton, W. J., Kern, R., & Curlette, W. L. (in press). Lifestyles profiles and anger expression among inmates in a metropolitan detention center. *Journal of Individual Psychology*.

Tafrate, R. C. (1995). Evaluation of treatment strategies for adult anger disorders. In H. Kassinove (Ed.), *Anger disorders: Definition, diagnosis, and treatment* (pp. 109–129). New York: Guilford.

Tardiff, K. (1997). Evaluation and treatment of violent patients. In D. M. Stoff, J. Breiling, & J. D. Maser (Eds.), *Handbook of antisocial behavior* (pp. 445–453). New York: Wiley.

Watkins, J. T. (1983). Treatment of disorders of impulse control. In C. E. Walker (Ed.), *Handbook of clinical psychology* (pp. 590–632). Homewood, IL: Dow Jones–Irwin.

PART IV

Teaching Psychotherapy Through Writing

CHAPTER 10

Teaching Psychotherapy Through Workbooks

Karin B. Jordan

The purpose of this chapter is to illustrate how PDW workbooks can be used as an additional form of teaching psychotherapy. By adding writing to classroom lectures, the discovery of knowledge is hastened, in a process called participant learning. This process exists inside and outside the classroom. PDW workbooks dealing with psychotherapy issues (i.e., theories, therapy stages, techniques) compel students to do more than just read and receive information. They are put in a position of needing to produce and use critical thinking, and to gain a sense of discovery and understanding.

Until now, teaching psychotherapy has been, and in a great many circles still is, dominated by traditional classroom instruction. Successful teaching, however, need not occur only in the classroom, but can also occur outside the classroom by students completing homework assignments and behavior tasks in between class meetings, allowing the instructor to assess the students' motivation and competence to become powerful learners who are able to draw information, ideas, and wisdom from in and out of the classroom learning experiences. Traditionally, students are expected to move from primarily classroom lecture and discussion to clinical, hands-on experience in a smooth process of increasing involvement. PDW can be used in this process by asking students to explore their thoughts and feelings about different aspects of therapy prior to beginning the clinical experience. Through structured writing assignments outside class, and in Internet chatrooms and discussion groups with peers and instructors, followed by discussion in class, this goal can be accomplished, a process that probably would not ordinarily occur until the clinical experience started.

A study conducted by Sharan and Shaulov (1988) revealed that student learning is accelerated with larger learning gain when students engage in group activities versus traditional classroom lectures. Gagñe (1967) goes as far as saying that it is the learner's activity that will result in the actual learning. It is therefore the instructor's responsibility to use more than classroom lectures that put the student in a passive mode, finding new learning strategies in and out of the classroom, increasing the probability of overall student learning.

PDW is an interactive strategy designed to help students increase their power of learning. PDW assignments, which are structured, self-administered, self-instructional, and systematically written, are given as regular homework and completed by each individual student. Individual answers are then discussed by classmates via the Internet and later reviewed with the help of the instructor. Generalization, lack of understanding, distortion, and other error thinking are pointed out by the instructor, and explored and worked on in the classroom or through additional homework assignments. Unlike traditional classroom lecture, dialogical conversation with peers and instructors about each assignment creates an opportunity to learn from many voices. Learning occurs by listening to others, being open-minded, and reevaluating one's knowledge. Dialogical learning presupposes that some guidelines have been provided by the instructor to ensure a certain sense of respect between learners, and to avoid a feeling of superiority in one or the other learners. Ground rules should be set by both students and instructors, and should include the following details:

1. Each student should spend an approximately equal amount of time on the assignments each week as she or he spends in the classroom.

2. Each student should put a moderate to intense amount of energy into completing each assignment.

3. Assignments should be completed on time, and posted on the Internet for discussion group dialogue.

4. All students should participate in the discussions, both on-line and in class.

5. Specific ground rules for sharing and discussing assignments should be agreed on by students before the first discussion, to provide a safe learning environment. The instructor can help establish these rules as needed, and should encourage the review of these rules periodically, making adjustments as needed.

Through these and other ground rules, each student is given an opportunity to contribute to the learning process of themselves and others. Knowledge is then constructed through written assignments and mediated though discourse with others, as opposed to merely existing within one's own head.

Combining PDW assignments and then discussing the assignment responses with others in group discussions becomes an alternative way of learning, and as such it changes the students' involvement in their own learning process. Multiple learning opportunities inside and outside the classroom, through PDW and in discussions with classmates and instructors, are a valuable educational technique in which students are responsible for their own learning. Today's students are typically informed consumers who want to go beyond traditional classroom lectures to be challenged and engaged. In the author's experience, students who participate in such activities come to class with an increased level of attention and expectation and an appreciation for their own and their peers' growth. The major implication for using PDW assignments along with discussions is that students become active, self-motivated, empowered learners.

CASE EXAMPLE: USING THE INITIAL CLINICAL SKILLS PROGRAMMED DISTANCE WRITING WORKBOOK

This workbook was developed to enhance the learning experience of students in a graduate-level counseling course. The class was taught in four weeks, with six hours of class meetings twice weekly, versus the traditional one semester or one quarter. The instructor used a traditional text's (Murphy & Dillion, 1997) introduction to basic clinical skills for class lecture and discussion. This textbook is accompanied by a videotape that demonstrates clinical skills addressed in each chapter. Videotapes of students' clinical work are used as mid-term (to demonstrate clinical skills practiced and discussed in and out of class) and final exams (to demonstrate all clinical skills covered in the course, both in class and between class activities), along with multiple-choice question-and-answers, which cover assigned readings, classroom discussions, and Internet dialogue among students. Course assignments were: (1) a mock initial intake interview in the on-campus training facility followed up by a one-page reaction paper; (2) journaling after each class meeting and each PDW lesson and dialogue; (3) live observation of two therapy sessions conducted by a more advanced student in the on-campus training facility (a live observation form, focusing on issues such as theoretical orientation, clinical skills used [i.e., joining, reframing, reflecting], and techniques used [i.e., empty chair, genogram] is completed for each session observed, followed by a two-page reaction paper); (4) PDW assignments to be completed after class meeting and followed up by Internet discussion among students; (5) discussion room participation after each completed PDW lesson (students post their responses and respond to peer answers, identifying themselves by name, allowing the instructor to see that each student participates; all postings remain on the site until the end of the semester). Assignments were used to encourage outside-of-class learning through the accompanying use of the initial clinical skill workbook and dialogue with peers and instructors. Individual answers were first discussed among students via the Internet and later reviewed with the instructor. Concerns, worries, error thinking, and omissions were pointed out by the instructor and worked on in the classroom through additional focused discussion, role-plays, and video clips (such as *A Different*

Kind of Caring: Family Therapy with Carl Whitaker and *Escape From Depressoland: Brief Therapy of Depression* by Bill O'Hanlon, etc.). The PDW assignments were used as part of the evaluation process and were incorporated in the final grade. Assignments were assessed based on having completed the assignment on time, and having done some careful self-exploration (which was evidenced in the writing) as well as active participation in discussions and openness to corrective feedback from instructors and peers.

Students were required to complete one of the PDW assignments from the initial clinical skills workbook at home prior to each class meeting. They were informed that the assignments were structured, self-administered, self-instructional, and systematically written, to assist them in staying focused during the week. Students also were told that they were to complete each assignment alone and that their answers would be discussed among classmates and later reviewed with the help of the instructor. Assignments were to be used as a springboard for class discussion and other activities. Additionally, students were instructed to post their responses to each PDW assignment in the chatroom, contributing to the on-line discussion.

Students previously unfamiliar with PDW assignments seemed open to the concept and the ability to be actively involved in their learning process. Doing the assignments on the computer and participating in chatroom discussions resulted in anxiety for some students, who had no, or only very limited, computer knowledge. Computer training sessions helped students overcome most of their anxieties. The PDW initial skills training workbook consisted of eight assignments: (1) A View of Psychotherapy, (2) Questions Therapists in Training Often Ask, (3) Therapist Fears and Client Fears, (4) Intake Interviews, (5) Joining and Information Gathering, (6) Resistance or Reluctance, (7) Transference and Countertransference, and (8) Termination.

Assignment I: A View of Psychotherapy

This assignment focuses on the student coming up with a definition for psychotherapy, identifying limitations of psychotherapy, and thoughts and beliefs about the following statements: "Poor interpersonal relationships produce pathology"; "Are early interpersonal experiences important?"; "Do cultural and social environments impact the cause and maintenance of clients' difficulties?"

Student responses when defining psychotherapy varied from focusing on the individual and/or the environment, to specifically the interaction of the individual with others. Limits of psychotherapy were broadly defined from cultural sanction, to genetic endowment, to mental illness, to childhood experience and their current, self-created environment. Student responses to the next three statements (see above) varied broadly. Chatroom discussions brought about lively debate between students.

Individual student responses, as well as chatroom responses between students, were used as springboards in the class meeting. Students' values, beliefs, generalizations, and error thinking were pointed out and worked on face to face through class discussions, role-plays, and videos.

Assignment II: Questions Therapists in Training Often Ask

This assignment consists of over 40 short essay questions such as: "How will you introduce yourself to your client(s)?" "How will you introduce the initial paperwork to your client?" "How will you explain client rights and responsibilities regarding confidentiality to your clients?" "How will you deal with a client who doesn't like you?" "How will you talk with your client about sex?" "How will you deal with your client's silence?" "How will you deal with supervision difficulties?"

Students responded to each of these questions and reported in their chatroom discussions that they had previously never thought about such issues as "clients not liking them" and what would be the best way of dealing with these situations. Some of the students had previous therapy experience and provided helpful feedback to their peers. The question of touching clients, receiving gifts from clients, and giving one's home phone number to clients were discussed in depth in class. The code of ethics was used to search for some guidance and direction. Additional case examples helped clarify these issues for students. Students also recognized that some of these questions would be answered differently by different clinicians and that there are a lot of "gray areas" in the mental health field.

Assignment III: Therapist Fears and Client Fears

This assignment focuses on such topics as the therapist's fear of making the client worse; not knowing what to say or do; getting emotional; and having too rigid or too loose boundaries. The other topics addressed in this assignment focus on client fears and include such topics as "Will the therapist like me?" "Will the therapist think I'm bad?" "Will the therapist be honest?" "Will I become dependent on the therapist?"

Student responses clearly indicate that they had thought through some of the therapist fears prior to completing the assignments, including the fear of clients presenting with issues unfamiliar to the student (e.g., abuse issues, divorce, parenting issues, etc.). Chatroom discussions revealed students' surprise that others had the same fears as they had but had previously not felt comfortable addressing with peers. In-class discussion created an opportunity to explore ways to deal effectively with these fears and how to access peer support.

Individual responses and group discussion on client fears revealed the students' surprise about the parallel process that therapists and clients experience. Class discussions and instructor feedback were used to explore client fears and the therapist/client parallel process. Experimental exercises and role-plays were also used to enrich the learning experience.

Assignment IV: Intake Interview

This assignment focused on how to get started in the first session. Instructions to be followed by the individual student include: "Explain your role as a therapist to the client"; "Explain your theoretical orientation to the client"; "Explain your qualifications to the client"; "Explain how you will gather information"; "Explain how you will clarify the client's goal for therapy."

Students, in their individual responses as well as the chatroom discussions, reported difficulties identifying their theoretical orientation and describing their qualifications. Picking a theoretical orientation seemed overwhelming to the students. They reported feeling concerned about choosing a theoretical orientation that did not truly reflect who they are as therapists. Instructor feedback on how to identify one's theoretical orientation, and that the actual identification of one's theoretical orientation is a development process, seemed to help students.

Student difficulties in identifying how to present themselves as qualified therapists to their clients when they have limited or no experience was explored initially in the chatroom, and later in the classroom through role-plays and corrective feedback from the instructor.

Assignment V: Joining and Information Gathering

This assignment gives examples of clients entering therapy and has students identify how to get started with the client, for example, how to initiate the joining and information gathering process when dealing with a very verbal client, a very quiet client, or a resistant, court-ordered client. Students were also asked to determine if there is a different way of initiating the joining and information gathering process when dealing with clients of different ages, ethnicities, and genders.

Students' individual responses revealed general ideas of how to work with adults. Students reported little to no differences regarding client gender, but did indicate that the client's presenting problem (e.g., abuse issues versus communication problems) calls for different handling when joining and gathering information. The issue of ethnicity brought very broad responses from students. Three minority students, and two students with clinical experience, stimulated a challenging discussion in the chatroom on this topic. The discussion seemed to challenge the students' thinking and beliefs. In class, three guest speakers of different ethnicities shared their experiences as people of color who provided and/or received therapy. These presentations, and the discussions, enriched the students' learning experience. Students who had previously identified some clinical experience stimulated discussions on how to work with very verbal and very quiet clients. Creative strategies and paradoxical interventions were discussed in the chatroom. Students with no previous therapy experience requested an opportunity to be shown how to deal with these situations. Classroom activities were structured in response to these requests. Role-plays provided an opportunity to try out different strategies for working with these clients.

Assignment VI: Resistance or Reluctance

This assignment specifically focuses on such tasks as "Identify disarming behavior when working with resistant/reluctant clients"; "Identify ways you can reframe client resistance or reluctant behavior to make it a more workable situation"; "How will you deal with a resistant or reluctant client?"; "How will you know that your client's resistance or reluctance created counter-resistance on your part?" These and other questions were completed by students for this assignment. The majority of the students' individual responses, as well as chatroom discussions, revealed no difficulties with this topic. Students reported feeling able to deal with a client's resistance or reluctance without being impacted. The topic of counter-resistance on the students' part seemed more challenging. In the chatroom discussions, some students identified specific topics (e.g., substance abuse, divorce) which were their own family of origin issues that they had worked on in therapy. They indicated that they potentially still had some unresolved issues. Other students reported having gained valuable insight from the chatroom discussions, but felt uncomfortable about disclosing some of their personal issues in class or in the chatroom. They indicated that they were comfortable with either journaling or seeking therapy for their issues. In-class discussion of case examples and role-plays were used to challenge some of these beliefs and gave students an ability to challenge some of their original individual responses.

Assignment VII: Transference and Countertransference

This assignment asked students to identify both terms, give examples of transference and countertransference, and identify the challenges therapists are faced with when dealing with transference and countertransference. These and other questions were first individually answered by students and then responses were discussed via the chatroom. This assignment seemed to be of little challenge, and quite clear to students, which was confirmed during class discussions and activities.

Assignment VIII: Termination

This assignment focuses on both the client and therapist issues related to termination. Some of the questions asked in this assignment are: "Should termination be therapist- or client-initiated? Or both?"; "How do you know that it's time to terminate with a client?"; "If the client is ready, but the therapist is not, what is the therapist's responsibility?"; "Why does the therapist need to maintain the therapeutic stance during termination?" These and other questions such as "How do you feel about saying good-bye?" were answered by the assignment. Many students reported difficulties saying good-bye to their client unless they had resolved all of the client's issues. Students also reported that saying good-bye would be a loss that others do not understand, especially if the client or HMO decides when termination should occur versus a mutual decision to terminate made by both the client and therapist. Chatroom discussions revealed different comfort levels with the larger topic of ending relationships. Some students revealed family termination experiences, which they believe interfere with proper termination with their clients. Classroom discussion focused on how therapists need to deal with their own unresolved issues and how termination is an important part in the process of therapy. Termination rituals were introduced in the classroom. The importance of preparing the client and the therapist for termination was covered, as were the ethical responsibilities involved. Client abandonment was shown to be an important potential issue that should not be ignored.

Follow-up

Follow-up evaluation regarding the usefulness of PDW assignments when teaching psychotherapy revealed student satisfaction with this teaching strategy. Students reported that PDW assignments between class meetings kept them focused from meeting to meeting. Writing their responses resulted in students identifying learning that they previously had not been consciously aware of. The chatroom served as a way to be challenged and supported at the same time. Students reported that they felt they had been actively involved in the learning process and that PDW, although it is time-consuming and requires students to be self-motivated, was an asset to classroom instruction. They expressed appreciation for having student responses saved electronically and available for review and revision. Six- and twelve-month follow-ups revealed that students perceived PDW assignments as a way to enhance their classroom learning, but also as a transitioning tool for their practical clinical experience.

PROGRAMMED DISTANCE WRITING AS SECONDARY ACADEMIC ASSESSMENT TOOL

Used in graduate school, PDW assignments that deal with psychotherapy issues can fulfill a variety of functions. First, requiring students who study psychotherapy to work between class meetings allows the instructor to assess the students' motivation, competency, and knowledge. For instance, students with certain difficulties might be able to hide in the classroom where lectures predominate and where multiple-choice tests are used to assess the students' learning. In a lawsuit cited in Cusher (1994), a university was held accountable, even post-graduation, regarding the training (or lack of training) they provided for students. Responsibility to use teaching strategies that promote and assess student learning rests with the instructor. PDW assignments enable the instructor to make a more practical evaluation of students' motivation to learn and their ability to produce and to perform. The instructor can prescribe PDW assignments and evaluate individual student responses, as well as observe student group discussion of these assignments, to determine whether students truly are serious about learning.

Second, PDW assignments enable instructors to have a more comprehensive evaluation process of students' knowledge base. Multiple-choice and essay mid-term and final evaluations generally are limited in determining students' knowledge. This infrequent testing is inadequate to determine whether students have truly attained a certain level of knowledge. Discerning how much thinking and how much consistent effort students put into their assignments is a more comprehensive way to assess the students. Additionally, the completion of PDW assignments in the area of psychotherapy being studied may become another way to evaluate the students' knowledge and made part of the evaluation process and the final grade. If a student's performance is poor in class, the PDW assignments can be a written document that supports the instructor's grade. In an era of litigation and accountabilities, where students are informed consumers, instructors need to be able to verify through documentation that a student does not perform at a satisfactory level. PDW assignments can become this needed documentation.

For example, a graduate student who performed poorly on her mid-term and final evaluation protested about her grade, stating, "I have been working very hard during the semester and my grades on the mid-term and final are not reflective of my ability. The tests were not fair. I deserve an 'A' in this course." PDW assignments used in this course revealed that the student had only infrequently completed the assignments and her competence level was consistently poor. The student and instructor reviewed all PDW assignments and the student's responses to peers. The student was able to admit to inadequate participation and performance in comparison to peers. The student then decided to retake the course.

STUDENT LEARNING

PDW assignments can fulfill a variety of student learning needs. For example, graduate-level students are required to assume responsibility for their education. Commitment to complete PDW workbook assignments may encourage more student responsibility and less passivity. As a result, students may eventually become less and less reliant on the instructor. PDW assignments for graduate students increase students' active involvement in their education, allowing them to take responsibility for their learning, rather than relying on the instructor.

Written homework assignments can expedite and deepen the learning process. PDW assignments can also serve as a transition tool from classroom lecture to practical clinical experience.

Second, PDW assignments in psychotherapy can be adjuvant to classroom instruction, becoming a supplementary and complementary form of learning that overlaps little with conventional classroom instruction. In addition to addressing areas that have not been addressed in the classroom, it might also serve as a more enriching learning tool for the visual versus the auditorial learner. Quality instruction means providing learning opportunities that are sensitive to the visual and auditorial learner. One of the most practical implications of PDW assignments when teaching psychotherapy is sensitivity to the learner. PDW may also be a more comfortable medium for students who cannot express themselves well orally. So PDW workbook assignments are one way to reach the visual learner and give the student who has difficulty expressing himself or herself orally an opportunity to show what he or she thinks and knows.

Third, the multiple aspects of peer feedback enhance student learning. Mikhail Bakhtin (1981) illuminates this learning process through a concept he calls "dialogism," which is the process in which the student and his or her peers are learning through Internet communication. In this view, learning should not occur in the student alone, but alongside dialoguing with peers. In fact, one way to enhance learning is to develop PDW workbooks for multiple courses and encourage dialogue about lesson responses among peers. The idea of PDW workbooks is to enhance student learning in a new way of fostering critical thinking. Multiple voices become a valuable perspective in the learning process, where PDW, dialogue, and learning are perceived as inseparable. These expressive modes of writing (PDW) and dialogue (between peers and instructors) set up a reflective learning process called participant learning. Participant learning exists both inside and outside the classroom, where students are both givers and receivers through the recursive teaching method.

The advantage of PDW for students is that they gain a sense of self-mastery and control of specific topics on psychotherapy addressed in the assigned lesson when they work between class meetings. The student spends one hour each week on an assignment. After the assignment is completed, small groups of students in a particular class will discuss their responses, and later the student responses will be discussed in class. The instructor will review each student's responses and provide corrective feedback. Additionally, the student learns to think through and reflect on reading assignments, class lecture, and class discussion. Also, since PDW workbook assignments are used as homework assignments, there is the additional benefit of keeping the student centered during the week. PDW assignments, then, complement the instructional material and the instructor's teaching style. The personal, stylistic contributions of the instructor are not reproducible, even though they are a significant determinant of learning experience for students. Quality instruction is important and needs to be assessed more closely to provide models of know-how and guidance to beginning instructors. To accommodate diverse learning styles, instructors need to use all the modern instructional tools and techniques available. PDW is a tool that in the hands of a knowledgeable and responsible instructor can be used to enhance students' learning.

Additionally, PDW assignments strengthen students' cognitive skills and internal dialogue, a reflective skill. Writing is a way of creating meaning for the spoken word by ordering and reordering information (de Gramont, 1990). Writing, then, is a cognitive activity that requires thinking, maybe more so than talking does. This would indicate that PDW workbook assignments dealing with psychotherapy topics should produce as much learning for students, if not more, than classroom instruction. This finding seems to be confirmed by increasing numbers of Internet psychotherapy courses offered across the country, without any direct (person-to-person) instructor contact, but only written instruction about assignments and regular writing assignments.

PDW workbook assignments on the topic of psychotherapy might also be a new technique for graduate and undergraduate Internet courses offered by colleges and universities which could expedite the discovery of new insights, perspectives, and information, and thus, the creation of new learning. The potential for mass delivery of psychotherapy courses is immense when using computer technology and PDW workbook assignments, since PDW assignments are self-instructional and self-administered, allowing students to work independently through each lesson. Instructors, monitoring students' progress and process, provide corrective feedback to students through the Internet. Also, chatrooms provide opportunities for peer discussion. When the PDW workbook assignments have been completed, and feedback by peers and instructor feedback has been received to verify that students have an adequate knowledge base, students move on to the next assignment. Student responses to the PDW lessons, a tangible object as well as a process, serve as an artifact of the dialoguing between peers, and between students and instructors.

Finally, Jordan (1998), Jordan and L'Abate (1995, 1999), as well as many others suggest that writing is one of the major tools in developing critical thinking in adults. When PDW assignments on psychotherapy issues are used adjuvant to classroom instruction, critical thinking and cognition are fostered in students. An exciting aspect of using PDW to enhance cognition and the cognitive process is technology, which enhances this experience by having students discuss their responses in a chatroom, providing an opportunity for all students to dialogue about certain responses to certain questions on a particular lesson. For example, a nontraditional student who had previously avoided using the computer was forced to use the computer to complete PDW assignments for her class. She was at first very nervous and resistant. Through the support of her peers and instructor she started working on the computer. After a few glitches of thinking, she became more familiar and comfortable and engaged in the chatroom discussions. At the end of the semester she wrote in her Faculty Evaluation Questionnaire, "I was very nervous using the computer to do the [PDW] assignments but after I got over my initial fear I was glad that [instructor's name] made us do it. I learned so much from the assignments but more so from the chatroom discussions." This student benefited from this assignment on multiple levels. She learned basic ways of how to use a computer, she learned from the assignments, and through chatroom discussion received peer and instructor feedback.

THINGS TO REMEMBER WHEN USING PROGRAMMED DISTANCE WRITING TO TEACH PSYCHOTHERAPY

To summarize the foregoing considerations, the advantages of using PDW assignments when teaching psychotherapy are multiple. They serve as an assessment tool to evaluate student motivation, competency, and knowledge. They increase students' active involvement in their education, allowing them to take responsibility for their learning rather than rely solely on the instructor. Students benefit as technology such as on-line courses becomes increasingly available at colleges and universities across the country. On-line PDW assignments and peer discussion fit well into this information age that encourages learning without walls.

PDW assignments also help to structure the class agenda. Especially for the beginning instructor, they provide guidance and focus. As described above they are a way to assess student performance, especially in cases where students voice dissatisfaction with their grade to the instructor, file grievances, and/or threaten litigation. If PDW assignments reveal overall infrequent completion of assignments and poor competence level, the student request can be discarded. Using PDW assignments in teaching psychotherapy puts the responsibility for learning on the shoulders of the student and not solely on the instructor.

Still, in spite of these advantages, using PDW assignments when teaching psychotherapy has its limitations. For example, people with learning disabilities or physical disabilities might have difficulties with PDW assignments. Another disadvantage of these assignments is that they do not trigger poorly motivated students.

The use of PDW assignments when teaching psychotherapy may not be applicable to all instructors, and certainly not to all students. It is therefore the instructor's responsibility to remember that this is only one of the many different teaching strategies available and that more than one should be used, not making the serious mistake of assuming that one teaching strategy encourages learning in all students. Instructors therefore need to balance different teaching strategies, and when using PDW assignments need to consider the course appropriateness, student motivation, potential disabilities, multicultural issues (i.e., language barriers), and learning styles (i.e., visual versus auditorial learner). PDW assignments when teaching psychotherapy should never be administered pell-mell, without criteria for selecting or matching the instructor, course, and student needs.

PDW assignments are not a panacea for all instruction. They may not fit with the instructor style, or some instructors may feel (without any evidence) that PDW assignments may hinder them or distract them in their teaching. Some courses may be less amenable than others. Appreciating and using PDW assignments may have a great deal to do with the outcome of increased student learning. Clearly a great deal of evidence is still needed regarding PDW assignments' usefulness in teaching psychotherapy before widespread application can take place.

Using workbook assignments to teach psychotherapy adds a tool to the armamentarium of exciting instructional tools and techniques. This supplement to classroom instruction is still in its infancy, but the demand for more Internet coursework and ever more sophisticated computer technology rapidly changes this. To appreciate fully how this tool can enhance traditional teaching methods and cognition, student and instructor feedback will be needed, with the ultimate aim of integrating PDW workbook assignments into most psychotherapy teaching.

APPENDIX
INSTRUCTIONS TO WORKBOOK USERS

This programmed distance writing workbook (PDW-W) was developed to enhance the learning experience of graduate-level students as they study basic counseling skills. It should be used in conjunction with traditional classroom instruction. The workbook is designed to be used between class meetings. Students should be given one assignment at a time, to be completed independently. Responses can be (1) posted in an Internet discussion group so that students can engage in discussion about the assignment; or (2) printed out for small group discussion either before or during class. In either case, the instructor should review all student responses to each assignment and use that information as a guideline for in-class discussion, role-play, class lecture, and future homework assignments.

ASSIGNMENT 1: A VIEW OF PSYCHOTHERAPY

Name: _____ Date: _____

This assignment is designed to help students begin exploring their thoughts and views of psychotherapy.

1. Define the term "psychotherapy," using your own words.

2. Identify what you believe to be the limitations of psychotherapy. List and explain each limitation.

3. Write your thoughts and beliefs about the following.

    Poor interpersonal relationships produce pathology.

    Are early interpersonal experiences important?

Do cultural and social environments impact the cause and maintenance of clients' difficulties?

Comments:

ASSIGNMENT 2: QUESTIONS OFTEN ASKED BY THERAPISTS IN TRAINING

Name: _____ Date: _____

This assignment is designed to help students explore how they would respond to issues that are often a concern to beginning therapists. Please respond in short essay form to each of the following questions.

1. How will you introduce yourself to your client(s)?

2. How will you go about setting up your first appointment with your client(s)?

3. How will you deal with a client who "no-shows" for his/her first session?

4. How will you respond to a client who wants to tell you all about his/her issues on the telephone, prior to the first session?

5. How will you introduce the initial paperwork to your client?

6. How will you explain client rights and responsibilities regarding confidentiality to your clients?

7. How will you deal with a client who doesn't like you?

8. How will you deal with a client who wants to be your friend?

9. How will you deal with a client who is attracted to you?

10. How would you deal with your own infatuation with a client?

11. How will you deal with your own dislike of a client?

12. How will you deal with feeling overprotective of your client?

13. How will you talk with your client about sex?

14. How will you talk with your client about:

    Emotional Abuse?

    Physical Abuse?

    Sexual Abuse?

15. How will you talk with your client about substance abuse issues?

16. How will you talk with your client about gender issues?

17. How will you deal with your client if he or she is of a different ethnicity?

18. How will you deal with your client if he or she has different religious/spiritual values?

19. How will you deal with your client's silence?

20. How will you deal with your client's talkativeness?

21. How will you deal with a client who does not want to be in therapy?

22. How will you deal with a client who believes that you are part of the system (i.e., social services, the justice system, etc.), and that you will not help, but rather make life difficult for him/her?

23. How will you deal with a client who believes she or he does not need to be in therapy?

24. How will you deal with a client who expects you to "fix" him or her?

25. How will you address a client's concern that she or he is "crazy" and nobody can help her or him?

26. How will you deal with an adolescent who reports to you that she or he is:

    Sexually active?

    Had an abortion?

    Wants an abortion?

    Wants to run away?

    Is using drugs?

27. How will you deal with a client who is unable to identify his/her goal of therapy?

28. How will you help the client move from the joining to the working stage?

29. How will you know if it is time for your client to terminate?

30. How will you know if you are helping the client?

31. How will you know if you are ineffective with a client?

32. How will you know if a client feels comfortable working with you?

33. How will you know if a client feels unsafe?

34. How will you deal with supervision difficulties?

35. How will you deal with a supervisior who wants to be your friend?

36. How will you deal with a supervisor who is of different ethnicity than yours?

37. How will you deal with a supervisor who is:

    Younger than you are?

    The same age as you are?

    Older than you are?

38. How will you deal with a supervisor who is:

    The same gender as you are?

    The opposite gender?

39. How will you deal with_____? (Please complete and respond).

ASSIGNMENT 3: THOUGHTS AND FEARS AND CLIENT FEARS

Name: _____ Date: _____

This assignment is designed to assist students in exploring and dealing with fears that they might have. It also addresses client fears that students might not be aware of.

1. Therapist Fears. Please respond to the following statements:

    a) Will the client like me?

    b) Will I like the client?

    c) Will I know how to help the client?

    d) Will I make the client worse?

    e) Will I know what to say?

    f) Will I say too much?

    g) Will I be comfortable with silence in the session?

    h) Will I become too emotional with the client?

    i) Will I get frustrated with the client?

    j) Will I impose my values on the client?

    k) Will I get impatient with the client?

    l) Will I have overly rigid boundaries with the client?

    m) Will I have overly loose boundaries with the client?

    n) Will I feel attached to my client?

    o) Will I create a dependent client?

2. Client Fears. Please respond to the following statements, indicating what you could do or say to help the client.

    a) Will the therapist like me?

    b) Will I like the therapist?

    c) Will the therapist think I'm bad?

    d) Will the therapist be honest?

    e) Will the therapist be impatient with me?

f) Will I become dependent on the therapist?

g) Will the therapist be able to help me?

h) Will the therapist think that I'm "crazy"?

i) Will the therapist respect me?

j) Will the therapist value my opinion?

k) Will the therapist make me worse?

l) Will the therapist be able to handle my pain?

m) Will the therapist be knowledgeable?

n) Will the therapist become frustrated with me?

o) Will the therapist become impatient with me?

Comments:

ASSIGNMENT 4: INTAKE INTERVIEW

Name: _____ Date: _____

This assignment is designed to help students focus on how to get started in the first session.

1. Explain how you will schedule your first session with your client.

2. Explain how you will review all initial paperwork with your client (i.e., Personal Disclosure Form, Agency Disclosure Form, Financial Agreement, Problem Checklist).

3. Explain your role as a therapist to the client.

4. Explain your theoretical orientation to the client.

5. Explain your qualifications to the client.

6. Explain why you are video/audiotaping the therapy session.

7. Explain the purpose of supervision.

8. Explain how you will explore the client's expectations of therapy.

9. Explain how you will assess the client's previous therapy experiences.

   Pros:

   Cons:

10. Explain how you will gather information.

11. Explain how you will clarify the client's goal for therapy.

12. Explain how you will end the first session.

Comments:

ASSIGNMENT 5: JOINING AND INFORMATION GATHERING

Name: _____ Date: _____

This assignment is designed to help students explore how they will get started in the joining and information gathering process with divorced clientele.

1. How will you start the joining process with:

   a) A very verbal client

   b) A very quiet client

   c) A resistant, court-ordered client

   d) A male client

   e) A female client

   f) An ethinic minority client

   g) A child client

   h) A pre-adolescent client

   i) An adolescent client

2. How will you start the information gathering process with:

   a) A very verbal client

   b) A very quiet client

   c) A resistant, court-ordered client

   d) A male client

   e) A female client

   f) An ethnic minority client

   g) A child client

   h) A pre-adolescent client

   i) An adolescent client

Comments:

ASSIGNMENT 6: RESISTANCE OR RELUCTANCE

Name: _____ Date: _____

This assignment is designed to help students focus on how to deal with a client who is resistant and/or reluctant to enter into the process of therapy.

1. Identify disarming behavior when working with resistant/reluctant clients.

2. Identify ways you can reframe client resistant or reluctant behavior to make it a more workable situation.

3. How will you deal with a resistant or reluctant client?

4. How will you recruit a resistant or reluctant client to make use of the therapy process?

5. How will you know that your client's resistance or reluctance creates counter-resistance on your part?

6. Identify ways that might not work with a resistant or reluctant client.

7. Identify reasons why a client might be resistant or reluctant about therapy.

8. Identify therapist behavior that might lead to resistant or reluctant behavior.

Comments:

ASSIGNMENT 7: TRANSFERENCE AND COUNTERTRANSFERENCE

Name: _____ Date: _____

This assignment is designed to help students become more familiar with both transference and countertransference and raises their awareness of both in working with clients.

1. Define transference.

2. Give two examples of transference.

3. Define countertransference.

4. Give two examples of countertransference.

Comments:

ASSIGNMENT 8: TERMINATION

Name: _____ Date: _____

This assignment is designed to help students become familiar with the process of termination and client issues related to termination.

1. Should termination be therapist- or client-initiated? Or both?

2. How do you know that it is time to terminate with a client?

3. If the client is ready, but the therapist is not, what is the therapist's responsibility?

4. Why does the therapist need to maintain the therapeutic stance during termination?

5. How will you deal with termination when your client wants to terminate prematurely?

6. How will you deal with termination when therapy is time-limited?

7. When should termination be addressed if the therapy is time-limited?

8. How will you deal with such issues as:

    a) Clients giving you gifts?

    b) Clients who want to exchange addresses?

    c) Clients who invite you to their wedding?

    d) Clients who want to hug you?

9. How do you feel about saying good-bye?

10. What might hinder you from terminating effectively with a client?

Comments:

Please provide some feedback about the usefulness of these assignments

Please provide some feedback about how this workbook might be improved.

Thank You!

REFERENCES

Bakhtin, M. M. (1981). *The dialogic imagination*. Austin: University of Texas Press.

Cusher, G. (1994). Can universities be liable for incompetent grades? *APA Monitor, 25* (4), 7.

de Gramont, P. (1990). *Language and the distortion of meaning*. New York: New York University Press.

Gagñe, R. (1967). Instruction in the condition of learning. In Laurence Siegel (Ed.), *Instruction of some contemporary viewpoints*. New York: Harper and Row.

Jordan, K. (1998). Programmed writing and therapy with conflictual couples. *Journal of Family Psychotherapy, 9* (2), 27–39.

Jordan, K., & L'Abate, L. (1995). Programmed writing and psychotherapy with symbiotically enmeshed patients. *American Journal of Psychotherapy, 49*, 225–236.

Jordan, K. & L'Abate, L. (1999). The tape of the mind program: A single case study. *Journal of Family Psychotherapy, 10* (3), 13–25.

Murphy, B. C., & Dillon, C. (1997). *Interviewing in action: Process and practice*. Pacific Grove, CA: Brooks/Cole.

Sharan, S., & Shaulov, A. (1988). *Language and learning in the cooperative classroom*. New York: Springer-Verlag.

CHAPTER 11

Some Uses of Writing in Clinical Supervision

Richard J. Riordan, Gary L. Arthur, and Jeffrey Ashby

Much of the history of clinical supervision has revolved around defining its domain of activities and perfecting instruments or tools to assist with the ubiquitous tasks of feedback and evaluation. A variety of useful checklists have evolved that comprehensively establish priorities for the appropriate activities and attitudes of both counselors and their supervisors. One popular textbook in supervision (Bernard & Goodyear, 1996) includes six different instruments in its appendices measuring such attributes as working alliance, focus and styles of supervision, supervisor emphasis, and counselor behaviors.

Instruments such as these have been helpful because they have allowed us to more easily codify and evaluate behaviors that have been made so richly and abundantly available through the various behavioral and mechanical technologies such as Interpersonal Process Recall (Kagan, 1980). Supervision instruments have helped verbal feedback to be more precise and served as mental reminders or laundry lists of some priorities in the supervision process. They have increased efficiency and thoroughness, and have often reduced time-on-task supervisory rituals such as monitoring counselor core condition behaviors in early sessions. They have often freed the supervisor from teaching elementary counseling behaviors and allowed the supervisory alliance to concentrate on the integrative aspects that focus more on counselor and client personalities, styles, and outcome issues.

In this chapter we argue that personalized written communication has a special place in supervision, particularly in formative and summative feedback and evaluation activities. We in no way diminish verbal or other forms of feedback. However, we detect from the literature that writing and written forms of communication offer additional, if not unique, framing opportunities that may not be available in other forms of feedback. Therefore, in this chapter we first derive the theoretical rationale from the general counseling and therapy literature, apply it to supervisory activities, and offer some examples of written communications that can be used in supervision. We use the terms "counseling" and "therapy" interchangeably, although we understand the distinctions some readers may wish to make between the terms. Likewise, we use distance writing, therapeutic writing, and scriptotherapy somewhat interchangeably, with there being an equal possibility of some readers wanting to make some distinctions among this nomenclature.

THEORETICAL UNDERPINNINGS OF WRITING IN THERAPY

Distance writing as an adjunct to therapy has considerable history. In 1942, Gordon Allport was one of the first to outline the potential therapeutic value of writing in psychology (Allport, 1942). More recently, Riordan (1996) adopted the term "scriptotherapy" as he reviewed the research that was swiftly accumulating in support of therapeutic writing. This term corresponds well with another adjunct, bibliotherapy, and often these two techniques are used in a complementary fashion as in the case of "interactive bibliotherapy." One form of interactive bibliotherapy combines reading and writing and may use materials such as workbooks that invite a written response to stimulus material. And, of course, anyone who reads what the scriptotherapist has written is engaging in the process of bibliotherapy.

Writing as a differing form of communication between two people has been used in a variety of counseling specialties, such as couples counseling, to enhance therapeutic outcomes. Watzlawick, Beavin, and Jackson (1967) describe the way a breakdown of verbal communication between two people can lead to a reliance on analogic or nonverbal exchanges. This encrypted form of communication often results in misinterpretation, misunderstanding, and deterioration of the relationship, particularly where trust has been diminished. Scriptotherapy reestablishes digital language, forcing communication into an explicit written format that is less open to misinterpretation. Writing slows down the pace of communication, allowing the couple to reflect on their feelings, accurately express themselves, and, reciprocally, better understand the meanings of the other partner (Riordan & Soet, 2000).

Theoretical support for the therapeutic benefits of writing comes from many sources. For example, one psychosomatic theory of inhibition postulates that the effort required to repress traumatic and troubling thoughts and feelings produces short-term increases in autonomic nervous system activity (Buck, 1984; Pennebaker, 1990). This increase in activity takes its toll on the body's overall physical system and may increase the probability of stress-related disease. Writing offers an individual the opportunity to cognitively process and gain a sense of control over his or her experiences, which leads to a decrease in stress to the autonomic nervous system. This is consistent with the findings of Smyth (1998) and others, who conclude that writing about upsetting topics can have positive effects on health.

The benefits of therapeutic writing can also be understood using general learning theory, in which practice and physical activity are considered critical factors in knowledge and skill acquisition (L'Abate, 1992). The physical aspect of writing can assist clients in participating actively in practicing desired thinking skills, for example, which had been previously identified in therapy as important target acquisitions for the client. Finally, research in human communication and change has contributed to our understanding of the benefits of writing in therapy. Watzlawick, Weakland, and Fisch (1974) noted that rigid patterns of ineffective interaction can sometimes be altered by changing some aspect of the event. A shift from talking to writing can allow the interacting parties to reframe the situation, generating different perceptions, expectations, and ultimately behaviors.

While derived from a diversity of conceptual bases, therapeutic writing is pantheoretical as a technique and can be integrated into any counseling approach (Riordan, 1996). Each theory, however, may have slightly different tactical uses for it. For example, a client-centered therapist may use it to explore existential issues in search of insight. Adlerians may use scriptotherapy to help in identifying mistaken assumptions. Strategic practitioners may use the technique to assist in uncovering those system variables not visible in the session. A cognitive behaviorist may ask clients to practice what they have learned in their therapy by writing.

The differences between writing and talking as modalities of intervention in therapy, and by extension, in supervision, have drawn considerable attention in the literature in recent years (L'Abate, 1992). Fundamental differences between the two modalities can account for the variety of outcomes that may occur. Each modality is subject to different rules of communication. In face-to-face communication, for instance, nonverbal communication such as facial expressions, inappropriate smiles, and fluttering eyes can codify messages differently, add important nuances to the interaction, and frequently change the entire meaning of the utterances. A supervisor or therapist can listen for inflections, changes in pronunciation, stuttering, or nervous laughter. Verbal exchanges are more negotiable transactions. That is, if you say something wrong, you can immediately retract it, change it, apologize, or claim to be kidding. During a face-to-face encounter, you can clarify or cancel utterances immediately while listening and looking at the effect they are having on the clients. Writing has none of these features unless the writer—like fiction writers do—meticulously and graphically incorporates them onto the page. And even then, writing is not retractable and is usually one-way communication. However, it is these basic differences between face-to-face and written communication that qualify each as having its own unique appeal as a tool in therapy and supervision. Each modality has its special purposes which the therapist uses as efficiency or as other tactical purposes indicate. For a therapist or supervisor, then, writing may provide an alternate means of communication that can serve client or supervisee and therapist in selectively addressing issues in a different way or in ways that complement what is being done during session time.

In the past decade or so therapeutic writing in the form of distance correspondence has become popular in certain family approaches and has been strongly influenced by the narrative and solution-focused therapies (Nunnally & Lipchick, 1989; Wojcik & Iverson, 1989). For example, White and Epston (1990) in outlining the usefulness of writing in therapy argue that Western society is ocularcentric. This means that it often privileges the seen over the heard. Given such a cultural value, written communications by both client and therapist more dramatically formalize and legitimize the knowledge, authority, and experience of clients. In order to perceive change, or the possibility of change, clients can be enabled to plot the sequences of life events through time. Writing can thus facilitate the mapping of clients' experiences onto the temporal dimension. This frees them to author and reauthor their experiences at the same time that more constructive and mentally sound approaches to life are being incorporated through therapy. And finally, White and Epston suggest that writing frees clients' short-term memory, allowing for an expansion of the volume of information that can be processed.

APPLICATIONS TO SUPERVISION

Verbatim Transcriptions

One of the most frequently used methods for supervision in therapy besides watching an actual session is to go over a supervisee's work sample in the form of an audio or video recording. Much less used is a written transcription of the session. However, such a use of the written therapeutic word to analyze the work of the therapist can be a most powerful means of training and learning for the same reasons mentioned earlier regarding the concreteness and specificity of the written word. Although an enormous amount of time may be required to transcribe taped sessions, the technique is becoming more feasible with improved technology such as voice-to-print equipment. The actual work of transcribing can also be shared by clerical staff, the supervisor, and the supervisee.

Research is accumulating which suggests that the more intense the involvement in the actual work product of the supervisee the greater are the outcomes. Shanfield et al. (1993), for example, used video transcripts to rate on a three-level scale the involvement level of supervisors. Supervisors who ranked highest were most involved in helping understand the supervisee's concerns while only mid-level ratings were achieved by supervisors who were less disciplined in tracking the supervisee's concerns. Low ratings corresponded with supervisors who paid little attention to the supervisee's concerns.

Using written transcripts of the therapy session emphasizes both written and spoken feedback as an instructional format. This interactive approach builds a foundation for process supervision that can be easily modified for the more action-oriented middle and later stages of supervision. The method is most recommended for the beginning counselor-in-training during the initial developmental stage of a supervisor-supervisee relationship. It can be particularly helpful for anxious students who come to the practicum desiring structure. The transcription becomes a concrete visible aid in analyzing and structuring clear communications, delineating a client's problem, developing focusing skills, verbalizing goal statements, and establishing interventions.

Assuming that the counseling sessions have client permission and may be audiotaped, a code sheet is introduced with an explanation as to how the tape feedback process is to be conducted. The value of taped feedback is carefully documented to gain maximum participation and support from the beginning counselor. If this groundwork is left undone, some trainees may not elect to tape or submit their sessions. A sample transcription is reviewed without critique and is intended to help in supervisee anxiety reduction as well as allowing the student to thoroughly conceptualize the interaction. Critiques will differ as supervisees typically use different theories, strategies, and approaches and it is important to emphasize this. The supervisor introduces the process in incremental stages, beginning with the supervisee's self-evaluation of his or her first taped transcription. The supervisor and supervisee then review transcriptions separately and make a comparison of their observations during individual supervision. In a supportive atmosphere students will develop self-observation skills while pointing out their own omissions and areas for potential improvement. Frequently, they will pose questions for the supervisor, who can then highlight positive and helpful behaviors, teach new material, reinforce positive aspects of the counselor work, and maintain professional support. As the process is understood by the supervisees, the supervisor initiates more intense written feedback and instruction on the transcribed therapy sessions. Feedback can be geared to a number of counseling topics, such as problem assessment, mental status interviewing, case notes, treatment plan writing, intervention choices, relationship building, ethics, and opening and closing a session.

Each supervisee submits code sheets, which are a shorthand way of noting common interview behaviors of clients according to a paradigm suggested by a particular theoretical approach. Code sheets can be developed for any of the major theories, but do not have to be theory-bound and can be an amalgam of clinical language most often used in the students' curricular offerings. Supervisees are asked to provide one or more written content or process questions in addition to the notes they keep on the transcription itself. These questions for the supervisor provide insight into the way the supervisee is processing a case and evaluating client behavior, as well as giving clues regarding the supervisee's method of problem solving. The questions for the supervisor can be a reflection of the amount of motivation and involvement the counselor has in learning about the counseling process, amount of frustration or anxiety the counselor is experiencing, problem strategies available, and amount of time the student has devoted to listening and analyzing the tape.

The initial phase of a counseling session is often a struggle for the beginning counselor. Transcripts allow the counselor to clearly see and review introductory and exploratory statements and to develop alternative styles. Frequently, counselors comment that they cannot believe they repeat statements from session to session. Some recognize that they begin each session with "How were things this past week?" or "What kind of a week did you have?" Nothing is wrong with these statements; however, counselors begin to question whether the same response is always desirable. Some counselors have to experience this redundancy and actually see it on paper a number of times before change or creative work takes place. The transcript provides for easy self-analysis regarding a multitude of dynamic and process behaviors such as whether or not the client is doing the work, how interruptions are affecting the work, and the lack of an appropriate closure. In the transcript, the "pause" is now in the written word as opposed to the tape, and this allows these types of statements to stand out. Confidence is acquired when counselors detect the way they manage and control the therapy hour by gently guiding the process. The counselor can focus on issues such as the amount of therapy time devoted to social talk and how much is "therapy talk," that is, what is an appropriate amount of nontherapeutic discussion and what is resistance and how is it different from other tension? The pace of the counseling can surface topics such as silence, control, anxiety, and how to modulate with a client. What is the effect of a pace that is too fast or too slow? Supervisees begin to question why they do what they do by asking questions. They may ask how material from the previous session can be utilized to start the next session or how they can better phrase closure statements.

Rather than provide the reader with interactions from an entire therapy hour, Appendix A is an excerpt from a sample case in which the supervisor provides feedback to the supervisee via the transcript. This is an example of how the supervisor can express a critique in written form and provide counselor feedback. This can help with supervision tasks such as goal articulation, processing of previous session content, client role function, and defining therapy while serving as another component of the working alliance. The supervisor can challenge the counselor to identify what was done in the session to enhance the development and quality of the relationship, determine the effectiveness of the communication, and process what is perceived as client strengths. Beginning counselors frequently shift topics. When using an intake form, topic jumping is common. However, once therapy begins, the counselor may shift at different times and for different reasons. When shifting occurs and the counselor is unaware, unsure how to respond, lacks skills to expand the topic, is going to a deeper level, feels threatened by the request, and/or has a personal agenda, these shifts become excellent times for supervisor intervention and involvement. Most counselors are aware of these shifts and that intervening with skill building activities will solidify the supervisor-counselor relationship. Trust and confidence will grow to overcome other areas of discomfort.

Another initial stage role of the supervisor is to be supportive of the supervisee. The counselor needs to hear what he or she does well so that growing confidence is acquired in developing communication skills, recognizing dynamic and process variables, developing a theory orientation, and managing the session. Providing feedback without the interactive loop often will leave the supervisee questioning his or her ability and effectiveness. Bringing clarity to any omissions or unspoken words frequently leads to a deepening of the relationship between the supervisor and supervisee. The supervisor remains alert to the process of ideal counselor development, which is to create the atmosphere for learning and a receptivity for feedback whereby the supervisee will move toward autonomy and independence. To do this the supervisor needs to be empathic, reinforce trying out new behaviors, and make an effort not to focus all the attention on areas that need work. A critical comment lasts longer than several positive affirmations. Verbal affirmations feel good at the time but are very difficult to retrieve whereas the written word remains and can be read and reread several times.

Beginning and advanced supervisees have rated encouragement and support by supervisors to be especially important (Worthington, 1984). Worthington and Roehlke (1979) researched supervisor behaviors and noted those behaviors that reflect good supervisors for beginning counselors. They found that good supervisors were those who developed a pleasant supervisor-supervisee relationship, provided relatively structured supervision sessions, taught supervisees how to counsel, and encouraged supervisees to practice new behaviors.

Advantages and Disadvantages of Using Transcriptions

In using transcripts of live counseling sessions the supervisor and/or counselor-in-training may:

1. experience a sense of being heard in totality rather than in spot excerpts.
2. likely detect from early transcripts to later ones a change in skill attainment.
3. feel a reduced sense of supervision fear; it may be easier to look at the words than hear the words and be less time-consuming than searching through a tape.
4. not feel the separation that sometimes exists between supervisor and supervisee.
5. find a decrease in psychological distress through the actual writing process; writing closes the gap.
6. find it helpful in determining the effects of anxieties and feelings.
7. find the transcript a helpful tool in teaching corrective listening skills.
8. find it helpful in sharpening assessment skills, formulating problem statements and goals.
9. find the transcript provides complete and exact recall. The ability of the counselor

to recall important client events stated in the session and the accuracy of information suggests that less than 30% of material on transcripts is recalled or included in process notes (Wynne et al., 1994). Information does escape memory and is often omitted in chart writing immediately after the session.

10. find that it is a rich source in which to provide support. The written word, coupled with supervisory verbal reinforcement, further enhances skill development.

11. find the transcript a good source to point out to the supervisee his or her personal growth and receptivity to supervision.

12. aid the supervisee to better provide feedback to peers.

Examples of disadvantages in using transcriptions are that they can sometimes:

1. create resistance to trusting and openness. Glickauf-Hughes (1994) and Friedman and Kaslow (1986) indicate that resistance in the form of perceived threats of evaluation and performance anxiety, deficits in the supervisory relationship (trust, autonomy), and personal and developmental issues (formation of a personal identity) are abundant in supervision. Transcripts may intensify these issues by focusing on the external to the exclusion of the internal.

2. risk exposing aspects of the supervisee's personality that are meant to be private.

3. elicit fear of uncovering limitations.

Following are two case study examples of ways transcriptions contribute to enhanced therapist training.

Example 1

A supervisee was counseling a 21-year-old female college student who, at times during the session, had made hostile remarks toward the counselor. On more than one occasion the client became impatient and commented that the counselor was not listening to her. Later during the same session this client referred to the counselor as her "mother" when talking about the client's personal goals for improving her relationship with her parents. The counselor did not catch this slip during the session nor later when listening to the tape. It was only when she was transcribing the session and focusing on each of the spoken words that the reference to "mother" clearly pointed to the counselor. The counselor brought the transcript and tape to supervision for feedback and direction. The counselor indicated that it was hard to believe that she did not hear "mother" when first spoken because she had been focused on goal formation. With the assistance of the supervisor she explored the meaning of the reference and an appropriate response. The counselor examined her own attitude toward the client, reactions to being told she was not listening, and the significance of the material (mother) to the overall therapeutic goal.

Example 2

A counselor recognized by the sheer number of transcript pages that she needed to reduce the amount of time devoted to session warm-up in order to capture more therapy work time. This became evident to the counselor when several clients indicated that the therapy hour passed too rapidly. Also, clients, in a variety of ways, began expressing mild discontent with their progress, comments the counselor-in-training took personally as being signs of her ineffectiveness. In supervision the counselor indicated that her clients waited until late in the hour to share important therapy talk. The supervisor encouraged the counselor to analyze the concern using her transcripts. A natural question became how much time should be devoted to initial anxiety reduction versus time with therapy material. The first step was to review the client goal formation(s), followed by reviewing the case notes for key words or content relevant to the goals. The transcribed pages were divided into early, middle, and late sections, noting when significant content material began to appear. As the counselor reviewed the transcripts, it became evident that she was waiting for the client to bring up goal-relevant material. In waiting for client readiness, she felt she was conveying respect. A reasonable step was to analyze the interactions that took place between starting time and the time when relevant material emerged. She noted such material starting to emerge toward the latter part of the middle phase. The counselor determined for herself that this material should begin earlier in the hour if it was to be processed sufficiently. She wanted to know how to get it started earlier. The supervisor then taught her how to manage the counseling session efficiently while maintaining an atmosphere of respect toward client initiative.

In summary, transcriptions demand the total commitment of the supervisor. Carifio and Hess (1987) indicate that, in reviewing the supervision literature, there is a corresponding similarity between the way supervision and psychotherapy are conducted. They found the same guideposts or tenets to exist in both. Findings revealed that a good supervisor is one who exercises the appropriate levels of the core conditions, is knowledgeable, provides clear and explicit goals, is experienced, is supportive and noncritical, and uses direct and systematic feedback. Transcripts are a means to put into practice these good supervisory behaviors. According to Friedman and Kaslow (1986), if transcripts are utilized and reflect an external and reflective component, then the supervisor can maintain an alertness and sensitivity to the internal component of identity development.

Written Supervisory Evaluations of Audio- or Videotapes

Sometimes work samples, such as tape recordings of sessions with clients, are reviewed at a distance from the supervisee. This happens frequently when the intern has to send the sample because of distance, timing, or some other factor. These audio or video samples are useful, even if the two have reviewed the session together, because they can be meaningful as concrete summaries and records of the supervision. While considerable attention is paid to seeing that they have adequate site supervision, students who are doing their internship away from the geographic area of their university sometimes want or need additional supervision of their work products. In addition, written feedback of therapy sessions, whether the student is at a distance or not, is often beneficial as a concrete record of what the supervisee needs to work on. This kind of a summary of the work sample, such as an audiotaped therapy session, is also sometimes prepared by the supervisor after a student presents the tape in group supervision. This practice can winnow important points from what sometimes is an overwhelming barrage of observations and suggestions from the supervision group. Partially as a result of this, training in giving written feedback is an important part of many doctoral programs. The practice forces supervisors to be specific and focus their help in a way that gives a suggested map for the student to follow. They have to go on record as a role model for clear written communication regarding the way therapy needs to be conducted. Appendix B contains an example of a written feedback statement after the review of a student's tape in group supervision.

Written Summative Evaluations

Written summative evaluations are another example of distance writing. The summative evaluation is designed to communicate feedback over a longer period of time such as a semester, practicum, or year-long internship. This type of purposeful feedback provides a concrete synopsis of supervisee goal attainment. Late in the initial phase of counselor development, interns begin to wonder if they are making a difference or are effective in their work. This summary type of writing and feedback is critical to sustaining their counseling growth. Interns often take for granted what they have learned and focus on what they do not know only to experience anxieties about how much there is to learn. It is easy to lose sight of their own growth when client concerns are heavy. A written form by the supervisor is a record of this progress that includes highlighting areas for needed growth and continued learning.

The summative evaluation component parts may include documentation hours, client management, communication, counseling dynamics, counseling process, theory development, working alliance, and supervision work. Examples of documented hours may include the number of tapes presented, clinical hours, total hours, supervision hours, and site visitations. As the supervisor listens to tapes or reviews previous transcriptions, it is easier to illustrate changes and improvements. Appendix C is an example of a summative evaluation. While the supervisee reads the feedback and makes adjustments to the observations, he or she can sense the collaborative nature of the relationship between the supervisor and supervisee. The summative evaluation is a supervisor's written document demonstrating one aspect of the supervisor's role, that is, evaluation.

Interactive Journaling

Involving supervisees in the writing process through the interactive journal focuses on another area of development for the supervisee. The value of journaling has already been well discussed in the literature and seems to be used selectively, but widely, in clinical practice (Riordan & White, 1996). It clearly has a set of rules governing the feasibility of its use in clinical practice, and we are not suggesting its blanket use in all supervision instances. However, while we emphasize the use of journaling in a university situation in our flowing descriptions, application of the practice to private postgraduate supervision seems to have similar advantages and disadvantages.

Based on our supervisory experiences, we have found it quite helpful to start the process of journaling at the beginning of internship. We meet weekly with the students at the university as a group and, on a contracted basis, with individuals to do some co-supervision with the site supervisor throughout the term. At least 30 hours per week are spent on the internship site, so students do not always have time for as much contact with the university supervisor as their needs might suggest. So unlike practicum, where we always meet individually each week for an hour as well as with the group, there is potential for slippage, which we find much reduced through the use of an interactive journal.

Thus, the assistance that supervisor writing offers to supervisees can also be understood from the perspective of availability. That is, unlike the scheduled appointment with the supervisor or telephone or other informal consultation, the opportunity to journal is always available. Supervisees may use early morning or late evening to process experiences through writing. These are times when they might be appropriately hesitant to contact supervisors. The writing experience is not time-limited as most face-to-face encounters are. As a result, writers may express certain issues that required more time than is typically available in the supervisory session. Students have noted the advantage of documenting their experiences through journaling because the practicum/internship experience is "so intense, and so much happens in a week that is important but is replaced by other important things by the time supervision rolls around." Supervisees have acknowledged that journaling helps them attend to important issues, not just urgent ones.

Journaling also offers the writer the opportunity to revisit thoughts after some time away from the supervisory or therapy session. Journaling is unique in that it allows the writer to choose how much time might be necessary or helpful. The writer may be "done for now" but feel some pressure to begin again or revisit issues and is free to do so without waiting for the next supervisory meeting. Writing also offers the supervisee a venue through which ideas can be tested. Putting thoughts, reactions, and perceptions of experiences on paper provides writers with a record to which they can react later, and decide how or even whether they wish to express them. Writing may allow the supervisee the chance to reduce the emotional press around issues, as it seems to for clients (e.g., Smyth, 1998). Thus the journal provides space for supervisees to process reactions that might otherwise dominate a group seminar or an individual supervision session. Students have described how journaling helps them to avoid "being overwhelmed by issues, because there is someplace to take them, process them at [their] own pace, and decide whether to bring them back to supervision or not."

In our experience, a critical element of the interactive journal is the early shaping of the experience with the students. Many of the same rules apply in its use with clients. However, the differences between therapy and supervision influence the shaping that takes place early and throughout the supervision period.

In the early explanations of what is expected, we prefer to explain journaling as a means of communicating that may differ from verbal supervision. We emphasize that it is not meant to replace face-to-face, telephone, e-mail, or other forms of personal contact. We explain the principles of scriptotherapy and may give students a reprint of an overview (Riordan, 1996) of the practice. We cover confidentiality as it applies to our exchanges, and we downplay or suspend the importance of grammar and spelling as a trade-off for spontaneous and candid communication. We plead with them, however, to use a word processor if possible because of the sheer impossibility of decoding some handwriting. We ask their forgiveness in return for our handwritten responses to them, which we promise will be eminently legible.

The supervisor and supervisee exchange the journals at the group meeting. We collect the one written for the current week and return the one with our overwritten responses. Students always seem eager to see what we have written, and often comment privately after class or in the next journal about what we have written. The variability, however, is as great as students' personalities, and this is one of the special qualities of the experience. It is consistent with the literature reports of the use of journals (e.g., Riordan & White, 1996), which report that some students treat it perfunctorily while others use it as a cathartic way of integrating their experience or getting additional answers to their problem solving, such as by asking specific questions. Students may use the journal to clarify thoughts, gain perspective on thoughts and feelings, and record meaningful insights. Others use it as a way of disclosing fears or suspected neurotic issues that are problematic.

By way of example, one 23-year-old straight male student interning at an addiction center wrote that he was propositioned by a gay male during an intake assessment. He had not had that experience before and found it confusing and threatening. He struggled in the journal with what it meant to be attractive to other males in a sexual way. At first he tried to be humorous about the experience, noting that he wished women had been so forward with him before his recent engagement to his fiancée. Within the same week, however, another male intake displayed similar, although more subtle, attraction to him and the first male found a way to get a note in his mailbox suggesting a specific place and time they could meet. The exchanges from the instructor attempted to normalize the feelings the student was having, although recognizing the somewhat unusual, but not strange, occurrences taking place in such a short time. The student had good supervision from the site regarding policy issues and appropriate responses by staff in such instances. However, the student had difficulty accepting his initial feelings of flattery, followed by a horrid feeling that he would ever feel such a way at all. He wondered what part he had played in this and if he was giving off sexual signals when he simply felt he was engaging in practicing the core conditions he had been taught. He wrote:

My first assessment today was with another homosexual male. I set clear boundaries and had a strictly objective manner during the assessment. I also admitted this patient due to his suicide attempt earlier today. After taking him to admissions, I was told by different admissions personnel that "That patient wants you!" This began to bother me. I did not see as much humor or flattery involved in this incident. I began to ask staff if I acted or presented myself as homosexual!

This was discussed much more in supervision and the student who processed this in his journal was able to explore what he feared might be sexual identity problems at a time of his impending marriage. In evaluation, this student described his journaling as an important part of his growth and development through the term because it allowed him to explore issues that he would have been extremely reluctant to disclose in supervision without the "forced" opportunity to acknowledge and explore them through journaling.

Journal Feedback

Another critical element in interactive journaling in supervision is the type of feedback that is given. Students are usually extremely sensitive to what the supervisor writes in response to their journals. They have frequently mentioned how their own practice is shaped by what feedback they get from the journal. It is safe to say that the role modeling aspect is as much in effect during this exercise as it is anywhere else in the student's training. Thus, what is practiced in responding to student journals is likely to be scrutinized for its value by the students in their own use of journaling with clients.

As a rule of thumb, written feedback in the journal needs to be positive, supportive, and encouraging. While this rule generally applies to all supervision, the permanent and somewhat irretrievable nature of written communication suggests that most corrective feedback, which has possibilities of being misunderstood, misinterpreted, or threatening to the journaler, be reserved for more immediate supervisory conditions. In such instances, the transaction is more easily negotiated because it has more robust opportunities for such conditions as immediacy, nonverbal cues, and retrievability of exchange. This section presents a few examples of the types and categories of supervisory feedback made in journals.

Personal Functioning

Often, the students will write about what they are doing to take care of their own physical or psychological well-being and health. Journal feedback allows the supervisor to reinforce behavior that contributes to the counselor's well-being.

Student: Yesterday, I did some art therapy (making beads out of clay), took a yoga class, and also a long walk. After going to church this morning, I actually feel good for the first time since January 1. I gardened during the afternoon and saw the daffodils and sedum reemerging. It seems the more that I nurture others the more I must nurture myself. Why is this?

Supervisor: You see the importance of taking care of yourself in order to be a healthy therapist. How this nurturing gets taken care of has raised some personal questions. This is healthy gardening. You have to plant the seed (question) before it can grow. Good for you.

Request for Help

Supervisees will sometimes use the journal as a request for assistance. The following student was counseling a client who was always making friends with individuals who were psychologically unhealthy and abusive to him.

Student: I've met with R. twice and when the session is over, I feel overwhelmed with his masochism and cannot get a feel for how much he is contributing to these psychopathic relationships. So, for right now, I am listening and reflecting feeling, and pointing out similarities and discrepancies in the person's behavior that he is telling me about. He began the session by telling me how pleased he was with himself for being able to tailor his behavior to the schizophrenic friend so the friend would not get angry. I do not know if I have the resources to help him construct an ego structure. Help!

Supervisor: You're doing just fine! You have developed the working alliance. This client seems to trust you. This work may likely be long-term therapy. Patience for now seems to be working for you. Let's talk more about this in our group.

Personal Therapeutic Issues

Client issues often bring to the fore issues the supervisees are working on either on their own or in therapy.

Student: I went to my individual therapy at five o'clock. I did some work in the abyss (ironically, I read that Object Relations book on containing rage, terror, and despair). I had not discussed the book with my therapist, so I'll attribute the experience to synchronicity. After being in that place of nothingness and realizing that my parents didn't love me for myself but for who they wanted me to be, I feel much more peaceful about my existence. And it's not that they were bad parents; they thought that they were raising me in the way that they should.

Supervisor: We go through life looking for people who will love us for our self, don't we? But we only find approximations . . . then, WE make up for the rest.

Offering Empathy to Supervisees

Student: Tony D. no-showed today. I called to see what was going on and he said that he forgot and was watching cartoons and that he had a really busy week. Tony is an intellectualizer who has had some really big feelings around death and dying. So, he rescheduled for next week. I'm not sure if he is protecting himself or may be angry with me or maybe just plain forgot. I will, hopefully, have the chance to check that out next week.

Supervisor: No-shows was one of those topics we discussed in peer supervision. It is frustrating and can be discouraging when it seems the client investment is so minimal. It's hard not to take it personally.

Celebration

Frequently, students can make use of the journal to celebrate successes and, in general, good feelings and thoughts about themselves and what they are doing in the training program.

Student: I feel so good about my therapeutic relationships right now! I was able to be present in the group on Thursday to help with the facilitation of the emotions around the death of Derrick. I feel a deeper sense of acceptance and peace with life in general. I haven't told you this recently, but we are still waiting to see if my husband got the job in Detroit (we have been waiting three months now). But having this uncertainty dovetail with intern experience has been a big lesson in patience and letting go of the outcome. There are remnants of the control and agenda parts of my personality, but in general I feel like a different person. The main difference is to feel like I have the ability to be present in the moment instead of projecting into the future all the time. I feel very grateful for this life-changing experience.

Supervisor: That's wonderful!!! You have worked hard and earned it!

CONCLUSION

Clinical supervision and psychotherapy are very much alike in that they value and depend on clear, open communication. Moreover, each relies heavily on the spoken word to accomplish its tasks. However, the spoken word, for all its virtues, including such desirable traits as efficiency and rapidity of communication, has limitations that sometimes can be addressed through the use of writing. We have approached writing in this chapter as a means of embellishing and enhancing the tasks of supervision, not as a usual or suggested replacement for face-to-face verbal exchange in either therapy or supervision. Writing in supervision has the potential of facilitating and further strengthening the supervisory working alliance. With the increased communication that comes through writing, supervisors and supervisees may more easily come to a greater sense of shared goals, tasks, and a deeper bond so characteristic of a good working alliance (Efstation, Patton, & Kardash, 1990). As in therapy, the choice of when to use writing as a preferred adjunct in communication is dependent on many factors. Some factors relate to logistical matters such as wanting the permanency or concreteness of a written record. Other factors depend on a supervisory judgment of the need for additional avenues of alternative expression that can expand the venues through which learning can take place. Writing in clinical supervision can provide value-adding options sometimes not available or as useful in direct face-to-face contact. We have cited several examples where we believe writing can make a quality contribution to the process and product that clinical supervision is supposed to accomplish. The success in using writing in clinical supervision, however, will be highly dependent on the artfulness of its application by the supervisor.

APPENDIX A
INTERACTIVE WRITING IN TRANSCRIPT ANALYSIS

CASE: The purpose of this set of interactions was to clarify goal statements, provide feedback to the client, and develop the working alliance. Writing to the supervisee is intended to teach, support, and develop a collaborative relationship with the supervisee.

Client (Session 2): Ya, but how do you do that? I seem to convey everything about me without saying one word. I am an open book, blank pages. When I get anxious it shows on my face.

Counselor: That was coming out in the last session (oh, good). Let me give you some feedback from our last session. This will give us direction. You felt overwhelmed, alone, frustrated, and in a lot of pain, which you associated with your interpersonal issues. You shared the need to meet people and the fear of doing so (ya), withdrawing from friends and associates (ya), and how your intimate relationships were being affected like family (ya, and work). One goal can be interpersonal, such as to explore how you see and feel about yourself, how you see and feel about others, and the communication between you and others.

Supervisor: S-summary, Gs-goal setting. Good summary. Client interruptions signal that the client is involved. Articulation of goals provides clear direction. Very good response.

Client: Ok, that sounds good.

Counselor: In what way?

Supervisor: Concreteness (C). Requesting how the client heard your response maintains clear direction and communication. Good communication.

Client: Your suggestions seem tangible, hands on. I can focus and understand.

Counselor: Good. Anything about last session for you that was helpful?

Supervisor: (Ps) Probe and shift (new topic). The probe is good, it allows you to determine if the client is processing material between sessions and elicits client feedback.

Client: After the session and during the week I thought about how I had never told anyone any of that stuff. I felt so relieved and a calmness came over me I had not felt since my high school years. The pressure was off.

Counselor: Sharing sort of clarified things for you.

Supervisor: (Rm-response to meaning). Focus is on the client and the client can share more. Very good.

Client: I didn't know what to expect, no expectations. I just knew how I felt afterwards.

Counselor: Your intake form indicated that you had been in counseling before. How was counseling for you?

Supervisor: (S-shift and P-probe) The counselor did not reply to the client comments, rather, shifted to another topic. Analyse the shift.

Client: Yes, some time ago.

Counselor: Tell me about the therapy? What helped or didn't work for you?

Supervisor: (Oitt) Open invitation to talk. Which question do you want answered? Your question sets up expectations about counseling, good.

Client: I had a counselor who was very quiet and did not ask me many questions. She told me to speak but I didn't know what to say. I was afraid of her. She said I wasn't working hard enough in therapy. It was hard because I wanted to talk back and forth so I could understand. I heard only my own voice and I wanted to quit several times. I felt all alone in therapy. Actually I was not sure I should come this time. It might be the same, get nothing. I wanted help.

Counselor: So you wanted more feedback from your counselor.

Supervisor: (RM) The client's request is to know how therapy works (expectations). As you pointed out she desired and wanted feedback. Good clarification and understanding.

Client: I guess so, I wanted to understand and figure things out faster.

Supervisor: (define therapy). Here is an opportunity to draw from the client what she perceives as therapy. With the client's interpretation the counselor can structure and practice articulating how therapy is to work for the two of them. Supervision time can be a good time to work on the counselor's definition.

APPENDIX B
TAPE FEEDBACK

Cynthia,

You have worked hard at both learning and practicing your skills at your site. Following is a summary of observations and suggestions from your tape presented in group supervision.

Observations:

It is clear that you have established a good rapport with the client. You sounded at ease with him and you were able to both laugh together and disagree at times.

You used praise to reinforce his progress in interacting with his mother. You specifically reviewed his goals for the week with him, which helped keep them clear and him focused on the important issues with you.

During the session you made a number of concrete suggestions and encouraged him to consider them. When he rejects them you don't force them on him, which communicates respect for him. At the end of the session you gave him a specific and relevant assignment and made it clear you would follow up with him on it.

Suggestions:

He was brief yet energetic in his response to you; however, you still had to take the initiative in keeping the interaction moving. You managed this by asking a number of questions. As he answers, it might be useful to respond to part of his answer that includes any new or particularly relevant information. This can help facilitate more exploration in one particular area and can help him take more initiative and responsibility in the interaction.

The client expressed a significant amount of resistance in planning how he would confront his mother. It might have been useful to recognize that with him and invite him to comment on his resistance. Some exploration of this could leave him more open to accepting your intervention, or it might help you tailor the intervention in ways that meet less resistance.

Your session included a review of the goals set for him by the program. It would be useful to also explore whether he has other goals for himself right now. As a patient advocate you are in a unique position to find out what he wants. Discussion in this area may facilitate his personal investment in the work you are doing together.

Overall, you established a therapeutic relationship and got the client engaged in the interaction, while gathering information and beginning to set goals. Facilitating his exploration of relevant areas may help him take a more active role and move toward new self-awareness.

APPENDIX C
WRITTEN SUMMATIVE EVALUATION
(REDUCED SAMPLE)

Summative Evaluation
Mike Grove
Betty Farthing—Supervisor
Wood Counseling Services
Fall Quarter, 1997

Mike, you have been diligent in attending to the many facets of a practicum experience. I have enjoyed working with you and the privilege of reviewing your taped counseling sessions.

From a learning and practical perspective what has been of particular interest and significance to me is the importance you placed upon managing your supervision time by prioritizing those client cases in most need of consultation. You have done very well in case management and ferreting out the essential from nonessential client content. You have directed your energies to purposeful action. You have been willing to share your style with others and as a result been able to receive constructive suggestions for corrective actions.

My observations and feedback will be limited to those 20 audiotapes reviewed, 10 individual and 22 group supervision hours, and the site visitation to the Wood's Counseling Center. You have completed a total of 231 hours and a total of 69 clinical hours. You have:

a. submitted 20 audiotapes for supervision and reviewed those transcripts. One client has been long term so you are well into the process of counseling.

b. had a variety of counseling clients, mostly male. Issues have varied from career, cultural, academic, time management, test interpretation, panic disorder, trauma, depression, medication, communication, interpersonal, anger management, among others.

c. prepared client file notes. Your process notes have improved as you are becoming more efficient and aware of how the notes, session material, and treatment are to merge. You have been very conscientious about the paperwork.

d. prepared questions for the supervision. The nature of these questions has been about your style, communication, and at times assessment skills. This suggests to me that you are listening to the tapes and processing the interaction. I commend you, as every client deserves this type of treatment.

e. utilized behavior change strategies and techniques. The techniques are in keeping with your theory of Cognitive-Behavioral. I have heard cognitive reframing, homework, stress management, assertiveness, analogies, self-talk, and knowledge sharing.

f. had one site supervision visitation (November 5) with you, Betty Farthing, and myself.

g. conducted two (2) case presentations. Receptivity to peer feedback was very good and you were supportive and helpful in case presentations of other counselors.

h. initiated a number of release forms, and made contact with at least two professionals who were providing services to your client. Informed consent procedures were practiced.

i. conducted one mental status (tape), one treatment plan, and turned in a log of hours.

Communication: I have noted you:

a. utilized effective communication skills such as response to content, feeling, and meaning. Personalized communication is improving.

b. improved in the application of minimal encouragement to talk, open invitations to talk, 5 w's; and have improved in validating the client.

c. have been empathic. Client feedback, if this is coming across, might be your next step.

d. becoming less uncomfortable with pauses, silences, and not answering each question posed by the client. Improvement has been noted in your ability to determine if the question(s) is a question, a thought, a shift in client uneasiness (anxiety), defensiveness, or that your answer is a response to yourself.

e. gaining significant improvement in focusing-refocusing topics. Initially, client and counselor had shifts and now you have become more adept at staying focused. More important, you are integrating the content into the identified problem (themes). This is a major alteration in your style to relax, to hear and to allow your problem solving mind to engage.

f. reduction in the number of self-disclosures. Review appropriate self-disclosures.

g. beginning to use immediacy was observed during the feedback from your long-term client.

h. gaining confidence in assessing and responding to nonverbal communication.

Process: A significant strength of your counseling style is that you work the entire session. You have worked diligently at sustaining longer periods of work. In slowing your pace you make fewer shifts, and thus enlarge upon what the client has shared. I have noted:

a. strength in establishing the working alliance with a fairly rapid assessment.

b. as you move from one session to the next, fewer inappropriate shifts occur. You have maintained focus on one or two topics for a session, and thus are more adept at working material.

c. goal statements and goal assessment are a part of your strategy.

d. when the session begins you move in a timely fashion into the work to be accomplished.

e. the client feedback you give signifies you are doing your homework, listening to your tapes, and are preparing for the next session. You cannot overdo fundamental work as it strengthens your working alliance.

f. improvement in seeing and asking the obvious (client becomes silent). You are beginning to exhibit a steadier pace in the face of anxious moments during counseling interactions.

Theory: I have noted:

a. a behavioral-cognitive style where you teach through information giving or technique demonstrations such as self-talk, rational-irrational thought, etc.

b. you have devoted time and effort to session closures. Learning how to grasp the hour, client material, client involvement, and how to taper for an integrated closure has become a part of your overall strategy in development.

c. early in practicum you had a number of abrupt shifts. You have been open to discussing these shifts, yet a continued analysis of the "why" and the feel for the "why" of client or counselor shifts remains important.

d. you search for ways to increase your resources for client homework.

e. a need to learn your theory at a deeper level.

f. you need to continue to do diagnostic assessment, conduct mental status, and write treatment plans.

Mike, you have been a very good counselor-in-training. You have provided me samples to review your work and to provide you feedback. You have been an effective counselor, processed your work and self, conducted homework, and supported your peers. I have enjoyed listening to your counseling work, noting your involvement and desire for client and personal growth.

REFERENCES

Allport, G. W. (1942). *The use of personal documents in psychological science* (Bull. 49). Social Science Research Council.

Bernard, J. M., & Goodyear, R. K. (1996). *Fundamentals of clinical supervision* (2nd ed.). Boston: Allyn & Bacon.

Buck, R. (1984). *Communication of emotion.* New York: Guilford.

Carifio, M. S., & Hess, A. K. (1987). Who is the ideal supervisor? *Professional-Research-and-Practice, 18* (3), 244–250.

Efstation, J. F., Patton, M. J., & Kardash, C. M. (1990). Measuring the working alliance in counselor supervision. *Journal of Counseling Psychology, 37,* 322–329.

Friedman, D., & Kaslow, N. J. (1986). The development of professional identity in psychotherapists: Six stages in the supervision process. *The Clinical Supervisor, 4,* 29–49.

Glickauf-Hughes, C. (1994). Characterological resistance in psychotherapy supervision. *Psychotherapy, 31,* 58–65.

Kagan, N. (1980). *Interpersonal process recall: A method of influencing human inter-action.* Houston: Mason Media.

L'Abate, L. (1992). *Programmed writing: A paratherapeutic approach for intervention with individuals, couples, and families.* Pacific Grove, CA: Brooks/Cole.

Nunnally, E., & Lipchick, E. (1989). Some use of writing in solution focused brief therapy. *Journal of Independent Social Work, 4* (2), 5–19.

Pennebaker, J. W. (1990). *Opening up: The healing power of confiding in others.* New York: Avon.

Riordan, R. J. (1996). Scriptotherapy: Therapeutic writing as a counseling adjunct. *Journal of Counseling and Development, 74* (3), 263–269.

Riordan, R., & Soet, W. J. (2000). Scriptotherapy: Therapeutic correspondence for couples and families. In R. E. Watts (Ed.), *Techniques in marriage and family counseling* (Vol.1). Alexandria, VA: American Counseling Association.

Riordan, R., & White, J. (1996). Logs as therapeutic adjuncts in group. *Journal of Specialists in Group Work, 21,* 94–100.

Shanfield, S. B., Matthews, K. L., & Hetherly, V. (1993). What do excellent psychotherapy supervisors do? *American Journal of Psychiatry, 150* (7), 1081–1084.

Smyth, J. M. (1998). Written emotional expression: Effect, sizes, outcome types, and moderating variables. *Journal of Consulting and Clinical Psychology, 66* (1), 174–184.

Watzlawick, P., Beavin, J. H., & Jackson, D. D. (1967). *Pragmatics of human communication: A study of interactional patterns, pathologies and paradoxes.* New York: Norton.

Watzlawick, P., Weakland, J. H., & Fisch, R. (1974). *Change: Principles of problem formation and problem resolution.* New York: Norton.

White, M., & Epston, D. (1990). *Narrative means to therapeutic ends.* New York: Norton.

Wojcik, J. V., & Iverson, E. R. (1989). Therapeutic letters: The power of the printed word. *Journal of Strategic and Systematic Therapies, 8* (2), 77–81.

Worthington, E. L., Jr. (1984). Empirical investigation of supervision of counselors as they gain experience. *Journal of Counseling Psychology, 31,* 63–75.

Worthington, E. L., & Roehlke, H. J. (1979). Effective supervision as perceived by beginning counselors-in-training. *Journal of Counseling Psychology, 26,* 64–73.

Wynne, M. E., Susman, M., Ries, S., Birringer, J., & Katz, L. (1994). A method for assessing therapist recall of in-session events. *Journal of Counseling Psychology, 41* (1), 53–57.

PART V

The Status and Future of Distance Writing and Computer-Assisted Interventions

CHAPTER 12

Distance Writing and Computer-Assisted Interventions in the Delivery of Mental Health Services

Luciano L'Abate

As two recent treatises (Hubble, Duncan, & Miller, 1999; Routh & DeRubeis, 1998), among many others, indicate, DW and CAI are not yet part of the therapeutic mainstream, at least in clinical psychology. There seems to be more interest and less resistance to this approach in the psychiatric profession, if the contributions by Gould in Chapter 6 and De Giacomo and De Nigris in Chapter 7 are any indication. Hence, one needs to question whether this work and works of the same ilk (Gackenbach, 1998) are merely spinning their wheels. Resistance to change is so great and so ingrained in the mental health professions that it will take more than just information to produce it. Change, as most therapists should know, is not an intellectual process, and it takes more than rationality to obtain it.

The purpose of this final chapter is to suggest possibilities about change that go beyond the medium used. All three media, verbal, nonverbal, and writing, are necessary to produce change (L'Abate, 1999a, 1999b) and as long as talk is the only medium of healing, the status quo in mental health services will prevail.

EQUIPOTENTIALITY AND EQUIFINALITY IN PSYCHOLOGICAL INTERVENTIONS

If principles of equipotentiality (one cause can have multiple and different effects) and equifinality or multicausality (multiple or different effects can lead to the same outcome) (L'Abate, 1994) are valid, then both principles are relevant to the process of change in psychological interventions. Recently, Kiesler (1999) suggested how mental disorders are not the result of singular, causal factors, but are caused by a particular combination of biological, psychological, and sociological factors. L'Abate (1998), on the other hand, edited a volume with chapters suggesting that a great deal of psychopathology may be the outcome of disordered and dysfunctional family relationships. It does not matter whether nature or nurture may be primarily or prominently responsible for the production of dysfunctionalities. It does matter that there are many causes leading to the same outcome, either functionality or degrees and types of dysfunctionality. By the same token, given the identical negative outcome, there are as many ways to treat it as there are causes producing it. However, causes and treatments may well be independent of each other.

Taking depression as an example, this condition can be produced from a variety of sources, acting independently or co-existing (e.g., childhood abuse and neglect, faulty modeling from one parent, traumatic experiences in child-hood, adolescence, or even adulthood, that were not shared with anyone, low self-esteem or impaired sense of self-importance) (L'Abate, 1997). Given the same outcome (e.g., depression resulting from different causes), there are just as many different ways to treat it, like medication, psychotherapy in all its multifarious forms (individual, couples, family, experiential, cognitive, psycho-dynamic, etc.), changing the environment, or changing the precipitating source of the depression, if it can be done. Why not add DW/CAI to this list of treatment possibilities?

The outcome, if positive, would be the same, regardless of the type of intervention, that is, the respondent would no longer suffer from the original condition, in this case, depression. L'Abate (1997) has argued that as long as the treatment is positive, novel to the respondent's past experiences, strong and predictable, with a sense of direction or purpose, and with sufficient duration, rate, and frequency to produce positive changes, it really does not matter what kind of treatment is taking place. Those are the common elements in most forms of treatment that produce positive results, not just the therapist's personality, manner, or style or the therapeutic alliance alone.

Positive results will take place regardless of the ideology underlying a particular treatment or the therapist's personality, provided certain conditions, listed above, prevail. If people are distressed enough and want help, they will use whatever positive plan and direction is offered to them. Of course, there are many distressed people who might need help but who do not want it, for what-ever the reason. These people are very difficult and oftentimes impossible to help. The level and type of distress plus wanting help are the two necessary ingredients for successful change, if the treatment is competent and adequate. As De Giacomo and De Nigris have suggested in Chapter 7, workbooks as software for computer-assisted interventions can provide a helpful alternative for those individuals who, for whatever reason, avoid traditional, talk-based therapy.

PASSIVE VERSUS INTERACTIVE INTERVENTIONS

A great deal of talk psychotherapy is passive, in the sense that talking to a therapist, even though a seemingly active pursuit, relies on differences among therapists for how active the process will be. For instance, on one hand, there are therapists who are content to listen, react, and reflect on what they are being told. There are therapists, especially those of a behavioristic bent, on the other hand, who prescribe tasks, administer homework assignments, and expect respondents to assume responsibility for some aspects of the therapeutic process. Hence, the more passive the therapist, the more active the respondent may or may not need to be. By the same token, the more active the therapist, the more active the respondent may or may not need to be. Some activities required of respondents, even though representing homework assignments, may ultimately be rather passive. For instance, bibliotherapy, even though it involves reading a specific book, does not require anything else from respondents. Hence, the activity is ultimately passive and seldom interactive. Personally, we have found this type of activity distracting and not particularly helpful. Can we do better? Can we involve respondents in interactive tasks that increase the change-oriented loops necessary for a successful outcome? Once a respondent is faced by a series of questions or tasks to perform, there is one change loop already established. If in addition to this loop, the respondent was asked to share, compare, and discuss answers with a partner or even with members of the family at a pre-set time, two additional loops are introduced. Finally, when submitting the results of completed homework assignments (either in person or through the Internet), as well as notes of what happened during the discussions with partners or family members, the feedback from the therapist would constitute another change loop. The more change loops are introduced, the greater the chance that a real change may occur. If the only loop in the process is what the therapist says in the office, then the process of change remains limited and, possibly, respondents may be shortchanged.

DW and CAI have open vistas that were undreamed of a generation ago. There is no excuse or reason for mental health professionals not to avail themselves of these new media except for fear of the unknown or ignorance of their potentials and possibilities (Conrad, 1998; Friedman, 1985; Gackenbach, 1998; Jones, 1995; Kobak, Taylor, Dottl, Greist, Jefferson, Burroughs, Katzelnick, & Madell, 1997; Magaletta, Fagan, & Ax, 1998; Nickerson, 1998; Stamm, 1998). Relying only on talk and face-to-face contact limits how many people can be helped at a distance from professionals. Yet, both talk and face-to-face contact are so ingrained in our everyday and professional lives, that to think otherwise is extremely threatening and frightening to many professionals. Admittedly, there are ethical and professional issues that must be considered in making this shift (Kiesler & Kraut, 1999; L'Abate, 1999b; Rierdan, 1999; Shapiro, 1999; Silverman, 1999). However, if we do not try, we will never know whether and how DW and CAI will work.

THE INTERNET AS A VEHICLE AND INSTRUMENT OF CHANGE

Verbally based psychotherapy suffers from a variety of shortcomings, reviewed elsewhere (L'Abate, 1999a). The major shortcoming, however, as Seligman (1998) indicated, lies in its inadequate specificity. Talk is not specific enough as a medium of communication to produce effective change efficiently. L'Abate has argued repeatedly (1994, 1997, 1999b) that DW, and especially focused, expressive, and programmed DW, consisting of workbooks, may be more cost-effective, mass-produced, and specific than talk. Talk may have been thought as being necessary to establish rapport, support, and trust with the therapist (i.e., Rogers' [1957] relationship factors). Are talk and face-to-face contact really necessary to establish a professional relationship? Recent experiences on the Internet (Gackenbach, 1998) suggest otherwise. It seems like many relationships, professional or otherwise, can be established without talk or personal face-to-face contact. If this conclusion is valid, it would challenge and even discount traditionally held values of personal, face-to-face verbal contact, therapeutic alliance, and the personality of the therapist. To paraphrase an old dictum, the message is in the medium and, in the writing medium, there is a method that cannot be matched by the verbal one. Of course, for those who consider psychotherapy as an art or as a religion, the notion of change based on method may appear as anathema.

Talk and face-to-face contact may not be sufficient to structure treatment in a replicable manner that is as practical, clear, direct, and concise as writing (L'Abate, 1997). One could even argue that talk and personal contact are not necessary, since unstructured Internet communications can assume the same functions as talk in establishing a professional relationship (Gackenbach, 1998; Jones, 1995). Hence, what is important is the method of treatment. If psychotherapy is to become a science, it has to give up the qualities of an art and assume the qualities of a science, the major quality being replicability. As long as psychotherapy is conceived as art, and for some, as religion, it will remain what therapists say it is, with few if any criteria to evaluate it. After all, art is what an artist says is art. Has anyone met a therapist who denied that her or his interventions were anything less than helpful? By the same token, has anyone ever met an artist who denied his or her productions being anything less than art? Lack of criteria for evaluation except what therapists affirm about the validity and usefulness of their products would lead to chaos. After all, how many types of therapy have been estimated to exist (Freedheim, 1992)? The number is in the hundreds, producing what has been called a veritable Tower of Babel. Of these, how many have been found to be "therapeutic"?

As long as talk is the major medium of communication, replicability, one of the major criteria of scientific pursuits, even if possible, is very expensive to reproduce. Even if and when manuals are used to ensure replicability in psychotherapy, proving that the process is the same from one therapist to another is a very expensive proposition, left only to a handful of researchers and not available to therapists in independent practice. Thus far, it has not been possible to show such a replicability, since a variety of processes are taking place without one ounce of evidence about the process linking evaluation with a specific intervention. Different case studies, each based on one particular instrument used to evaluate outcome, seem the best that can be done when talk is the sole medium of communication and possible healing (Maruish, 1999). The reason for this inadequacy lies in the nature of the medium itself. Talk is too expensive to replicate and to codify, a process limited strictly to relatively few researchers and, certainly not, to independent practitioners.

Once DW and especially PDW are introduced as additions or alternatives to talk-based psychotherapies, a much greater degree of specificity can be obtained. For instance, going back to depression, at least seven different workbooks are available to treat it, each based on a different theoretical or empirical basis, as shown in Appendix C in Chapter 1. There is a depression workbook based on an interpersonal view of depression (L'Abate, 1986), one on Beck's (1976) view of depression, one on Hamilton's view (Moras, Di Nardo, & Barlow, 1992), two on Blatt's view (Blatt, Quinlan, Chevron, McDonald, & Zuroff, 1982; Blatt & Homann, 1992) of two types of depression, one on the empirical view of depression according to the MMPI-2, and one based on the PAI (Morley, 1999). When three workbooks (Beck, L'Abate, and MMPI-2) were compared with each other in their outcome on a student population, the results showed that there were no differences among the three. The results suggested that all three workbooks were indistinguishable from each other in producing change (L'Abate et al., 1992), just as is the case of comparative evaluation of different psychotherapies (Hubble et al., 1999). Nonetheless, as the meta-analysis of mental health workbooks (Chapter 5) suggests, workbooks may become a relatively inexpensive way to compare different theoretical viewpoints that have been incorporated into each workbook. Given the same clinical condition, there are a variety of workbooks to treat it. Different processes, as long as they are as positive, predictable, clear, concise, and replicable as are workbooks, should produce the same outcome. The method is more important than idiosyncratic personal factors in each therapist. Methods are replicable and correctable, whereas therapists are very difficult if not impossible to change once they have established their unique style.

Does this mean that therapists should be done away with and that workbooks should or could be administered mechanically without any clinical appreciation or evaluation of the referral question? On the contrary, responsible and sensitive professionals must be behind any intervention at a distance from respondents on the Internet or through the mail. Using this medium, at a distance from respondents, professionals are still necessary and responsible for: (1) the evaluation of the referral question, through structured and unstructured approaches, interview and objective tests or questionnaires; (2) establishing a therapeutic contract through a signed informed consent form; (3) assignment of specific workbook(s) to treat the referral question; (4) continuous contact and feedback for each completed written homework assignment; (5) reading above and beyond what has been written, detecting trends and themes that transcend the concrete level; and (6) evaluating the outcome of treatment and deciding whether the condition has been successfully completed or whether additional and alternative courses of action are necessary, including referral somewhere else, medication, and/or hospitalization. The unstructured aspects of treatment that constitute the establishment of a professional relationship, like rapport, trust, support, and continuous availability on the therapist's part, are still ingredients necessary for structuring treatment. However, these ingredients do not need to take place through talk or personal contact. They can take place just as well at a distance from respondents.

In addition to being cost-effective, workbooks put the burden of change squarely on respondents rather than on therapists. By cutting out talk and face-to-face contact from the professional interaction, workbooks are a replicable method of intervention with considerable advantages over traditional therapies based on talk and personal contact. They are reproducible ad infinitum, and, more important, they can be matched with symptoms and referring problems. For instance, most of the WFBL (Appendix C in Chapter 1) can be classified according to either a test profile or a referring question. Given any psychological test, one can match the various dimensions covered by that test with matching, written homework assignments. To date, most common psychological tests for individual children, adults, couples, and families are matched with isomorphic workbooks that are derived from the specific dimensions covered by that particular test. For instance, a widely used test like the MMPI-2 has 15 workbooks that cover all of the 15 content scales derived from that test. By the same token, a couple referred for too much arguing and fighting would be administered a workbook on the very same topic (L'Abate, 1993). Hence, the match between evaluation and intervention is much closer than could be achieved through talk and personal contact. The 80+ WFBL (see Appendix C in Chapter 1) covers not only the most common psychological tests but also the most frequent clinical and nonclinical questions or reasons for mental health referrals.

GIVING UP ON TALK AND PERSONAL CONTACT: HELPING PEOPLE AT A DISTANCE

Giving up on talk and face-to-face contact is tantamount to a paradigm shift in the mental health professions and in the delivery of their services (L'Abate,

1999b). However, the alternative is a status quo that endangers not only the livelihood of mental health professionals but the welfare of countless people who want and can rely on distance learning to improve their lives. There is no question that the threat and dangers of a paradigm shift imply decisions that mental health professionals will need to make if they want to survive and succeed in the twenty-first century. Hence, in spite of these dangers, there are at least four decisions (L'Abate, 1999a) that mental health professionals will need to make (whether these professionals like them or not) in the twenty-first century. Mental health professionals will need to decide whether (1) they want to go forward, that is, change their practices or whether they want to stay the same, that is, keep the status quo; (2) they want to remain in the twentieth century; (3) they wish to limit the impact of psychological, mental health interventions, or enlarge them; and (4) they want to see psychological interventions as an art or a science.

Stay the Same or Move Forward

Whether mental health professionals want to go forward (i.e., change their practices) or whether they want to stay the same (i.e., keep the status quo) depends on giving up shopworn practices and acquiring new, more cost-effective ones. Certainly, one cannot move forward and stay the same. What practices need to be given up or limited in import? Two cherished practices are reliance on talk as the major, if not the sole, medium of communication and healing and reliance on face-to-face contact. Both practices are expensive and not cost-effective. Talk is both cheap and expensive, depending on how it is used. The therapeutic alliance is expensive because it can be used by only a limited number of people. How can these practices continue to exist if they are not replaced or bolstered by the use of additional media, the nonverbal (movement, body awareness, kinesthetic exercises, etc.), and DW and CAI? The former requires face-to-face contact, even though the same results could be achieved through videotapes. The latter can be administered without ever seeing the patient. In addition, there are a host of new treatment procedures that minimize talk and maximize action, like psychoeducational skill training programs, neurobiofeedback, and eye movement desensitization and reprogramming, among others. Even though most of these new treatment approaches are well documented scientifically, they are not yet part of mainstream clinical practices. They all require more action than talk and can be administered by technical or para-professional personnel.

Stay in the Twentieth Century

New technologies, like television, telephones, faxing, e-mail, and the Internet, allow therapists to interact at a distance from patients. Yet, many professionals are loath to give up or at least limit the two most cherished practices that are so much taken for granted by these professions: talk and face-to-face contact. Unless both are limited, it will be difficult for many practitioners to increase their therapeutic armamentarium and move forward in a century where new technologies will become commonplace.

Limit the Impact of Mental Health Interventions or Enlarge It

As long as talk and face-to-face contact are the two most cherished and used media of communication and healing, the status quo will prevail. Furthermore, an enlargement of methods may imply an enlargement in personnel, where a hierarchy of technicians and para-professionals may be able to carry out practices that have been traditionally limited to licensed practitioners. Think about the advances made in intelligence and personality testing. Most of these functions can be carried out by computers and no longer rely on the personal experience of the doctorate-level professional. Why not apply the same functions to interventions? DW and CAI have the potential to reach many populations that could not be reached if talk and face-to-face contact are considered prerequisites for helping. Shut-ins, handicapped individuals, military personnel, Peace Corps volunteers, missionary families in foreign lands, and criminals in jails could be kept in contact and helped through this technology.

Decide Whether Psychotherapy Is an Art or Science

Most psychological interventions as presently practiced are considered by most practitioners as art rather than as science. Indeed among many mental health practitioners runs a very deep anti-empirical stance that looks at research as irrelevant. The mental health professionals (preventers, therapists, and rehabilitators, regardless of discipline) are facing a crucial period in their undoubtedly successful progress achieved in the past century. Change, however, does not take place during periods of serenity and success. It takes place during periods of crisis. It is at a time of crisis that confrontation and reevaluation take place. However, how can one convince a profession that it is in a state of crisis while it is in a state of denial? The issue of change is germane to these professions as it is for the very people they purport to help. People do not change if they do not want to. However, if these professions are not willing to recognize the need for change, how is one going to convince them?

The answers to this question lie in considering what has been happening to the mental health field in the past few years. First of all, there is the pressure and restraints of managed care, limiting access, decreasing number of sessions, demanding accountability, and requiring cost-effectiveness. The criteria demanded by managed care companies have really never been considered by mental health professionals. Self-determination and what is good for the patient and for one's economic survival were the two major motivating factors in one's practice. How can an art like psychotherapy account for itself? How can delicate, difficult, ephemeral interpersonal processes in the face-to-face session be sub-jected to external and objective scrutiny and quantification?

Clearly, demands from managed care have changed the complacent, taken-for-granted view that practitioners were only responsible for themselves and their patients. No external interference was acceptable or required. This position, of course, is no longer tenable because practitioners can no longer claim to live and practice in a safe, self-contained cocoon of "independent" "private" practice. They are no longer independent and their practices are no longer private. They are now open to the scrutiny of peer reviews and intrusions from managed care.

Second, face-to-face personal contact with a professional is so expensive that unless patients have support from managed care companies, more and more practitioners have to lower their fees or find additional sources of income outside the therapy session. Private practice is no longer the sinecure for academic clinicians who reverted to it after failing to achieve tenure. Clinicians who do go directly into private practice, bypassing academic possibilities, can no longer hope to become solvent immediately. Some might have to spend one or two or more years making connections, networking, and spending a great deal of time on public relations and marketing. Even established practitioners can no longer take for granted that their referral sources will continue to send them patients unless a concerted effort is made to keep these sources informed and satisfied. Private practice, therefore, is just as competitive as academia where there are usually over a hundred applicants for every clinical position open.

Third, in spite of their progress and their many successes, talk therapies have had little impact in reducing rates of attrition among patients, recidivism among criminals, and readmissions to psychiatric hospitals. Undeniably these therapies have improved the overall levels of functioning in relatively few cases in com-parison to the staggering mental health problems faced by this and other coun-tries. Face-to-face, talk-based psychological interventions are a drop in the bucket in view of the overall mental health needs of this and other nations. These needs will remain unfulfilled as long as the status quo of face-to-face personal verbal contact is the mainstream accepted and rewarded norm for men-tal health professionals.

Researchers consider most clinical practice as superstitious, random, and id-iosyncratic to individual styles of practitioners. Hence, this gap is real and deep-ening without any rapprochement between the two fields. Whether mental health interventions should remain an art or whether they should progress toward a science will make the difference between becoming irrelevant and limited or enlarging and reaching more people in need than traditional practices could ever achieve. Most mental health practitioners use fads and fashions that they would not allow to be used on their pets when they take them to their veterinarians. Faddism, fashions, and personal idiosyncrasies are still the staple of many men-tal health interventions. Research-based interventions, based on empirical foun-dations, are viewed as being irrelevant or useless in the therapy office. Hence, this chasm is being bridged as managed care companies require cost-accounting and cost-effectiveness in empirically based practices over personal preferences or biases.

CONCLUSION

Change in mental health delivery systems will not come from the inside because no existing system can be self-healing. No malfunctioning system fixes itself. It will need interventions from the outside. These interventions may be mandated from managed care companies that foot the considerable bill that mental health systems require. Unless the mental health professions change by enlarging their practices with new and more cost-effective methods, their impact on people in need of help will be minimal and short-lived.

NOTE

A portion of this chapter originally appeared in L'Abate's (1999a) paper and is reprinted with permission of Sage Publications and the editor of the *The Family Journal*, Jon Carlson.

REFERENCES

Beck, A. (1976). *Cognitive therapy and the emotional disorders*. New York: Meridian Press.

Blatt, S. J., & Homann, E. (1992). Parent-child interaction in the etiology of dependent and self-critical depression. *Clinical Psychology Review, 12*, 47–91.

Blatt, S. J., Quinlan, D. M., Chevron, E. S., McDonald, C., & Zuroff, D. (1982). Dependency and criticism: Psychological dimensions of depression. *Journal of Consulting and Clinical Psychology, 50*, 113–124.

Conrad, K. (1998). Making telehealth a viable component of our national health care system. *Professional Psychology: Research and Practice, 29*, 525–526.

Freedheim, D. K. (Ed.). (1992). *History of psychotherapy: A century of change*. Washington, D.C.: American Psychological Association.

Friedman, P. H. (1985). The use of computers for marital and family therapy. *Journal of Psychotherapy and the Family, 1*, 37–48.

Gackenbach, J. (1998). *Psychology and the Internet: Intrapersonal, interpersonal, and transpersonal implications*. San Diego, CA: Academic.

Hubble, M. A., Duncan, B. L., & Miller, S. D. (1999). *The heart and soul of change: What works in therapy*. Washington, DC: American Psychological Association.

Jones, S. G. (Ed.). (1995). *Cybersociety: Computer-mediated communication and community*. Thousand Oaks, CA: Sage.

Kiesler, D. J. (1999). *Beyond the disease model of mental disorders*. Westport, CT: Greenwood Press.

Kiesler, S., & Kraut, R. (1999). Internet use and ties that bind. *American Psychologist, 54*, 783–784.

Kobak, K. A., Taylor, L. H., Dottl, S. L., Greist, J., Jefferson, J. W., Burroughs, D., Katzennick, D. J., & Mandell, M. (1997). Computerized screening for psychiatric disorders in an outpatient community mental health clinic. *Psychiatric Services, 48*, 1048–1057.

L'Abate, L. (1986). *Systematic family therapy.* New York: Brunner/Mazel.

L'Abate, L. (1992). *Programmed writing: A self-administered approach for interventions with individuals, couples, and families.* Pacific Grove, CA: Brooks/Cole.

L'Abate, L. (1993). An application of programmed writing: Arguing and fighting. In T. S. Nelson & T. S. Trepper (Eds.), *101 Interventions in family therapy* (pp. 350–354). New York: Haworth.

L'Abate, L. (1994). *A theory of personality development.* New York: Wiley.

L'Abate, L. (1997). The paradox of change: Better them than us! In R. S. Sauber (Ed.), *Managed mental health care: Major diagnostic and treatment approaches* (pp. 40–66). Bristol, PA: Brunner/Mazel.

L'Abate, L. (1998). Discovery of the family: From the inside to the outside. *American Journal of Family Therapy, 26*, 265–280.

L'Abate, L. (1999a). Decisions we (mental health professionals) need to make (whether we like them or not): A reply to Cummings and Hoyt. *The Family Journal: Counseling and Therapy with Couples and Families, 7*, 227–230.

L'Abate, L. (1999b). Taking the bull by the horns: Beyond talk in psychological interventions. *The Family Journal: Therapy and Counseling with Couples and Families, 7*, 206–220.

L'Abate, L., Boyce, J., Frazier, L. M., & Russ, D. (1992). Programmed writing: Research in progress. *Comprehensive Mental Health Care, 2*, 45–62.

Magaletta, P. R., Fagan, T. J., & Ax, R. K. (1998). Advancing psychology services through telehealth in the Federal Bureau of Prisons. *Professional Psychology: Research and Practice, 29*, 543–548.

Maruish, M. E. (Ed.). (1999). *The use of psychological testing for treatment planning and outcomes assessment.* Mahwah, NJ: Erlbaum.

Moras, K., Di Nardo, P.A., & Barlow, D. H. (1992). Distinguishing anxiety and depression: Reexaminination of the reconstructed Hamilton scales. *Psychological Assessment, 4*, 224–227.

Morley, L. C. (1999). Personality Assessment Inventory. In M. E. Mariush (Ed.), *The use of psychological testing for treatment planning and outcomes assessment* (pp. 1083–1122). Mahwah, NJ: Erlbaum.

Nickerson, D. W. (1998). Telehealth and the evolving health care system: Strategic opportunities for professional psychology. *Professional Psychology: Research and Practice, 29*, 527–535.

Rierdan, J. (1999). Internet-depression link? *American Psychologist, 54*, 781–782.

Rogers, C. R. (1957). The necessary and sufficient conditions of therapeutic personality change. *Journal of Consulting Psychology, 21*, 95–103.

Routh, D. K., & DeRubeis, R. J. (Eds.). (1998). *The science of clinical psychology Accomplishments and future directions.* Washington, DC: American Psychological Association.

Seligman, M. E. P. (1998, December). Why therapy works. *Psychological Monitor, 29*, 2.

Shapiro, J. S. (1999). Loneliness: Paradox or artifact? *American Psychologist, 54*, 782–783.

Silverman, T. (1999). The Internet and relational theory. *American Psychologist, 54*, 780–781.

Stamm, B. H. (1998). Clinical applications of telehealth in mental health care. *Professional Psychology: Research and Practice, 29*, 536–542.

Index

About the Editor and Contributors

GARY L. ARTHUR is Professor of Counseling and Psychological Services at Georgia State University, Atlanta, Georgia.

JEFFREY ASHBY is Assistant Professor of Counseling and Psychological Services at Georgia State University, Atlanta, Georgia.

PIERO DE GIACOMO is Professor and Head of the Department of Neurology and Psychiatry and Director of the Psychiatric Institute, University of Bari (Italy) School of Medicine.

SABINA DE NIGRIS is Assistant Director of Clinical Services in the Department of Mental Health of Conversano (Italy).

BRIAN A. ESTERLING is Senior Manager at the Merit Behavioral Care Corporation, Morrisville, North Carolina.

ROGER L. GOULD is President of Interactive Health Systems, Santa Monica, California.

KARIN B. JORDAN is Assistant Professor in the Department of Counseling at the University of Nevada at Las Vegas.

LUCIANO L'ABATE is Professor Emeritus in the Department of Psychology, Georgia State University, Atlanta, Georgia.

OLIVER McMAHAN is Director of Counseling Services in the Church of God Theological Seminary and Lee College, Cleveland, Tennessee.

EDWARD J. MURRAY is Professor Emeritus of Psychology at the University of Miami, Miami, Florida.

JAMES W. PENNEBAKER is a Professor in the Psychology Department at the University of Texas, Austin.

RUDY REED is Pastor of the Grayson Church of God, Grayson, Kentucky.

RICHARD J. RIORDAN is Professor Emeritus in the Department of Counseling and Psychological Services, Georgia State University, Atlanta, Georgia.

DANIEL L. SEGAL is Assistant Professor in the Department of Psychology at the University of Colorado at Colorado Springs.

JOSHUA M. SMYTH is Assistant Professor in the Department of Psychology, Syracuse University, Syracuse, New York.

DOUGLAS K. SNYDER is Professor and Director of Clinical Training in the Department of Psychology, Texas A&M University, College Station, Texas.

DATE DUE